(850) #559x 12⁵⁰

D1123786

Marge Schott —— *Unleashed*

Mike Bass

Sagamore Publishing
Champaign, IL

©1993 Mike Bass
All rights reserved.

Production supervision and interior design: Brian J. Moore
Dustjacket and photo insert design: Michelle R. Dressen
Editors: Steve Otto, Russ Lake, Susan M. McKinney
Proofreader: Phyllis L. Bannon

No part of this book may be reproduced, transmitted, or utilized in any form
or by any means, electronic or mechanical, including photocopying, recording,
or by any information storage and retrieval system, without written permission
from the publisher, except in the case of brief quotations embodied in critical
articles or reviews.

Publisher's Cataloging in Publication
  (*Prepared by Quality Books Inc.*)

Bass, Mike, 1959-
    Marge Schott: unleashed / Mike Bass.
    p. cm.
    Preassigned LCCN: 92-84086.
    ISBN 0-915611-73-2

    1. Schott, Marge. 2. Baseball--Ohio--Cincinnati--Biography. 3.
Cincinnati Reds (Baseball team) I. Title.

GV865.S368B37 1993   796.357'092
                               QBI93-973

*For Adam and Danny, who taught me about
love and laughter and life*

— Contents —

— Acknowledgments —

If I thanked all the people who provided me information that directly and indirectly produced the background for *Marge Schott: Unleashed,* I wouldn't have enough room to write the book. My research for this project really began in December 1984, when I started reporting on Marge Schott for *The Cincinnati Post* upon her purchase of the Cincinnati Reds. That translates to hundreds if not thousands of formal interviews and informal conversations with those who knew Marge—and Marge herself—all of which helped lay the foundation for the book.

Then there are those who came forward to offer their insights specifically for this project—I don't look at *Marge Schott: Unleashed* as simply my book, but theirs, as well. Others helped me fill in the blanks, whether with a point of information or a quote or a source, and I am indebted to them, too. I apologize now if I leave someone out, but my thanks go out to:

May Belle Barrett, Howie Bedell, Bill Bergesch, Joe Bick, Roger and Maggie Blaemire, John Borcherding, Ron Borcherding, Jim Bowden, Don Breen, Marty Brennaman, Debbie Browning, Gary Burbank, Cris Collinsworth, Murray Cook, Dave Davis, Brad Del Barba, Mary Jo DiLonardo, John Erardi, Andy Furman, Bill Geoghegan, Frank Gilligan, Brian Goldberg, Ed Goren, Steve Greenberg, Warren Harding III, Greg Hoard, Bob Howsam, Dennis Janson, Tracy Jones, Rick Kennedy, Carl Kroch, Michael Lawhon, Cal Levy, Joe Link, Jay Mariotti, Chet Montgomery, Phil Mushnick, Joe Nuxhall, Michael Paolercio, Dave Parker, Bill Peterson, Tony Perez, Joe Pfaffl, Lou Piniella, John Popovich, Lou Porco, Michael Rapp, Steve Reece, Bill Reik, Howard Richshafer, Branch Rickey III, Tim Sabo, Joe Schott, Steve Schott, Walter Schott, Jr., Larry Schwalbach, Robert Stachler, Keith Stichtenoth, George Strike, Jake Sweeney, Jr., Skip Tate, Ron Taylor, Carlos

Todd, Mary Clair Torbeck, Peter Ueberroth, Frank Watkins, Dick Wenstrup, Dick Whelen, Bill Williams, and Tyrone Yates.

Numerous other sources I've learned to trust over the years agreed to help with the book but didn't want to be quoted, for fear of retribution. I appreciate their assistance and their circumstances.

Thank you to *The Cincinnati Post* for the use of its resources and to sports editor Mark Tomasik for being so flexible and supportive—as always. Thanks also to former *Post* sports editor Barry Forbis for getting me started on the story in 1984 and to former *Post* sportswriter Jerry Crasnick for recommending me to write the book eight years later.

Everyone at Sagamore Publishing deserves mention for his or her hard work. But I would be remiss not to specifically acknowledge Sagamore's Joe Bannon, Jr., and Jude Lancaster, who guided me (if not put up with me) on almost a daily basis; Brian Moore, Susan McKinney, and Michelle Dressen, who turned my manuscript into a book; and Lauren Benson, Lora Coslet, Arwen Domenico, Robin Ortiz, and Cathy Smith, who spent many long hours transcribing my interviews. To my research assistant, P.J. Combs, I can't thank you enough for the time and the effort. And to Don Owen and Michael Clark, thanks for helping me out when I truly needed it.

— Introduction —

On December 21, 1984, Margaret Unnewehr Schott paraded her St. Bernard before the city's microcassettes and minicams to announce her purchase of the Cincinnati Reds. She called it her "Christmas gift to the people of Cincinnati," an act she proclaimed would prevent the national pastime's oldest team from bolting the area. This above all else would endear her to the city.

Too bad it wasn't true.

And so marked the beginning of the strange and tumultuous reign of Marge Schott, certainly one of the most bizarre and controversial regimes in the annals of sport, one that turned to scandal when she was suspended in February 1993 for making racial and ethnic slurs.

As a sportswriter and columnist with *The Cincinnati Post*, I have followed her general partnership since the onset, my first contact with Marge coming two days after the initial press conference. We talked by telephone in what had to be one of the most unusual interviews I had ever attempted. It was like trying to rope a wild steer with a can of Silly String. I would ask a question, and she would answer a previous one. She would bounce from topic to topic with one off-the-wall response after another. As I would come to learn, this was not unusual. This was just Marge.

The interview also marked the first time her mouth made national sports headlines. She blasted New York Yankees owner George Steinbrenner for his irresponsible spending, sparking a stinging retort from Boss George when her words reached the New York media. Later, she tried to make nice with Steinbrenner and even came to rely on him as an adviser. As I came to learn, this also was just Marge. You see, Marge wasn't trying to start a war with Steinbrenner; she simply has no filter between her brain and her mouth.

Over the years, Marge and I have had our ups and downs. I never looked better in her eyes than the day I was interviewing her in her living room, and the irrepressible Schottzie suddenly and affectionately jumped into my lap. "She's never done that to a man with a mustache," exclaimed Marge, who prohibited her players from wearing facial hair. On the down side, Marge once banned me from the Riverfront Stadium dining room to protest some of the columns I'd written about her. She probably did me and my cholesterol level a favor. Many a writer has turned queasy at the sight of Marge sticking her hands in the buffet food for a free sample, proving once again she had to get her hands into everything.

Her obsession to control every aspect of the club was a trademark, even in areas she knew little about. I'll never forget the time I asked her before one season which teams would be the Reds' biggest competition, and she tagged St. Louis, Kansas City, and Pittsburgh before she stumbled on a team in her own division, Los Angeles. Over the years, I heard some of the horror stories about Marge Schott. Some came out in the papers; others were spoken in confidence, for fear of retribution and termination. If ever I doubted her employees' concerns, I understood quickly when I did some part-time work for WLW—the 50,000-watt Cincinnati radio station that owned the rights to broadcast the Reds' games, meaning she owned the rights to its soul. I was told I could not blast Marge Schott on the air. Period. That the lucrative contract that was the foundation of the station could be violated if I did. This was the same woman, mind you, who years later clutched the First Amendment to defend her slurs. Suffice it to say, I didn't last very long at WLW.

Yet the public saw the other side of her, the benevolent owner who would sit behind the dugout and do the wave and sign scores of autographs while schmoozing with the masses. She was one of them, a chainsmoking, trash-talking, dog-walking, blue-collar owner. Say what you want about her, but she always spent the money necessary to keep the team competitive on the field while making sure to keep ticket prices affordable for the fans. Her earthiness ingratiated her to the folks of the world's biggest small town. And even as her reputation crumbled before the nation amid her scandal, her stock in her city remained amazingly strong, as one local poll after another indicated.

Did she make racial and ethnic slurs? Of course she did. I heard one myself. When former Big Red Machinist Ken Griffey, Sr., wanted his status changed from retired to released so he could join his son with the Seattle Mariners—and Schott was bellowing behind closed doors, "What's in it for me?"—she told me she couldn't understand why he'd want to go to Seattle, anyway. "The Japs own everything there," she said. But it wasn't a total shock. In 1987, in the aftermath of Los Angeles Dodgers vice-president Al Campanis questioning whether blacks had the "necessities" for certain baseball management jobs, I asked Marge about baseball dedicating the season to the 40th anniversary of Jackie Robinson breaking the color barrier.

"Well, that's because Jackie Robinson's been a great player," she said, "I don't think so much because he was black."

"That tells me some things," home-run king Hank Aaron said when told of her remark. "This goes a little bit further than Al Campanis. It goes to the top."

But nothing happened to her. From a tumultuous marriage to Charles Schott, to a battle with General Motors over her late husband's car dealership, to a scandal that threatened to rid her of her beloved franchise, Marge Schott would persevere. Sometimes in spite of the odds.

Sometimes in spite of herself.

— Chapter One —

The Furor and the Fuehrer

The feuding partners of the Cincinnati Reds were assembling in a private room in Cincinnati's haughty Queen City Club for a rare meeting, the first since the general partner had become the nation's poster child for racism in the 1990s. Two months earlier, on February 3, 1993, Major League Baseball had suspended Marge Schott for one year—eight months, if she behaved herself—for hurling such slurs as "million-dollar niggers" and "sneaky Jew bastards" and "Japs"—embarrassing herself, her team, and her game. Some of her partners were now ready to explore whether she had been stripped of enough power to be dethroned from the monarchy she had established. The rest of the partners were just happy to get an update, any update, of the team she considered not just hers alone but an extension of herself. Robert Kheel, the National League counsel who had served as the point man in baseball's investigation of Marge, was sent to oversee the proceedings and make certain she did not overstep her limited authority. But the meeting was closed to the public and the press, and security was posted to ensure it, including Tim O'Connell, the Reds' director of stadium operations. Right before the meeting, O'Connell was standing in the doorway next to a lone reporter when Marge walked by. She looked past the media member and addressed O'Connell.

"Hi, Hitler," Marge Schott said.

Then she repeated it.

"Hi, Hitler."

It was as though the scandal and the ridicule she had just endured were r.eaningless to her, as though it wasn't important that she now watch her words, if not rethink her attitude. But Marge said it as easily as most people say, "Good morning." Then she asked O'Connell, "Hon, come on in and have a doughnut. Can I get you a cup of coffee?"

She obviously did not mean to insult O'Connell with her nickname, but she just as obviously did not consider the impropriety of it, especially considering the circumstances.

"It's an ongoing thing," O'Connell said of the nickname. "I can't recall when it started, but Mrs. Schott has referred to me that way for a number of years. From my belief, it stems from her believing I'm too strict with stadium policies and procedures and I worry too much. She at times even feels some of the security issues regarding herself are a little bit too much. I've always taken it as a joke, never as an insult."

But nobody was laughing shortly thereafter, inside the meeting room, when the topic turned to the Reds' minority hiring and Marge was asked whether the Rev. Jesse Jackson was still following the team's exploits.

"Jesse Jackson never had a job except when he was a waiter and spit in the white people's soup," said Marge Schott.

Granted, the civil-rights leader had claimed such an act— although he later admitted he hadn't spit and was just boasting in his youth—but that didn't excuse the insensitivity of Marge's comment. If Marge wasn't violating the terms of her suspension, she was certainly testing their limits, especially with Bob Kheel sitting right there. Point 1 of her sanctions says, "Mrs. Schott is reprimanded and censured in the strongest terms for use of racially and ethnically insensitive language and sternly warned not to engage in such conduct in the future." Nobody who knew Marge Schott thought this stipulation would change her; they just hoped it would change her actions.

Those who *really* knew Marge realized that would be hopeless, too.

But here she was, still part of Major League Baseball despite the initial outcry to run her out of the game. As the process had unfolded, baseball had attempted to ignore and then diplomatically avert the minefield of her scandal by formulating a penalty that all sides could tolerate—Marge, baseball, the public, the

United States Congress, and the Rev. Jesse Jackson. Lean too far toward stringency, and baseball faced what could be an eternity in litigation, not to mention the possibility that each of the eight owners on the 10-member Executive Council then ruling baseball could be looking face-to-skull at any skeletons they had hidden themselves. Lean too far toward leniency, and baseball faced possible race riots and revocation of its exalted antitrust exemption—and a public-relations nightmare that would last as long as Marge's tenure with professional baseball's oldest franchise.

The result was a suspension gutted of substance, plus a $25,000 fine, plus multicultural training. The limited partners, who were hoping to seize power if Marge were stripped of any, were stunned when baseball not only maintained her status as general partner during her exile but allowed her to name new general manager Jim Bowden to run the day-to-day operations in her absence. The potential for another coup attempt appeared vanquished—or so it seemed. Her most avid opponents in the partnership, Cincinnati businessman George Strike and Chicago bookstore owner Carl Kroch, consulted the legal profession to see if baseball had missed something they could use to overthrow her this time. They had watched what she had done to the team and the terror she had caused so many within the organization, while portraying such a compassionate (if eccentric) image to those on the outside. They had witnessed a number of good people inexplicably fired or understandably fleeing, and they had seen a great deal of money made in spite of Marge, who turned away millions more. Yet over the years they were helpless to do anything except try to push her publicly, privately, and legally in an effort to become true limited partners and not just silent ones. And they never quit. Kroch seemed to be on a personal quest not to let Marge believe she had defeated him, while Strike was determined not to let one general partner ruin the entire experience.

Kroch calls Marge "an embarrassment." And he, Strike, and fellow limited partner Louise Nippert released a statement during baseball's investigation saying that if the allegations of racial and ethnic slurs were true, Marge should be removed from baseball. But that didn't do any good. To make matters worse, Kroch and Strike became worried that Marge was going to stick the partnership with attorney bills for baseball's investigation. They sent her a certified letter to get the details and learned that the club had been charged for the first bill ($63,000) and that Marge was going to pay the rest personally (roughly half a million dollars). Kroch and Strike wanted to know if she planned to reimburse the club for the initial charge, and they wanted to explore whether baseball had minimized her authority enough to violate the terms of the partnership, so they pushed her into calling a partnership meeting. And she did. Unfortunately, she called it on a day when Strike was out of town on business and Kroch was in town but committed to another business meeting. The two sent attorney Anthony Covatta in their place. Without Strike and Kroch, anticipation of a power struggle proved unwarranted, and Covatta ended up performing only some exploratory surgery in their place. Marge, who the night before had told *The Cincinnati Post* she was paying the entire legal bill, informed the partners that she was not going to pay the $63,000, that she *was* still in charge, and that her hold on the general partnership was unchanged—and when she debased Jesse Jackson, they knew she hadn't changed, either.

Marge survived this meeting, and Strike and Kroch decided not to challenge Marge in court this time. Her general partnership was again safe for the moment, and the club was out the $63,000, which she insisted was a legitimate partnership expense, claiming it went to such areas as formulating an Equal Employment Opportunity Program for the Reds. But there will be other incidents that could provoke legal action—there always are with Marge Schott. That's been evident since the day she announced her purchase of the Cincinnati Reds, on December 21, 1984—the day she unleashed the chaos.

— Chapter Two —

Buying a Team, Selling a Myth

To understand the essence of the team whose owner was suspended in 1993, you need to transport back 124 years—back to when a jeweler named Harry Wright, from over the Ohio River in Newport, Kentucky, organized a club then known as the Cincinnati Red Stockings. Like so many names in this country, "Red Stockings" may have been shortened over the years, but the tradition has carried on through the generations, with the Reds forever boasting its claim as the national pastime's first professional team.

Tradition. It is paramount to the Reds, almost to the point of absurdity, with the club still banning its players from wearing beards or mustaches and the city council for years chastising other cities for denying Cincinnati its inalienable right to throw out the season's opening pitch. Fortunately the council's grandstanding has ceased, because it only fed a misconception; the city is only ensured of opening the season at home every year. But that is more than enough on which to base the team's most honored tradition. Opening Day is the Queen City's unofficial holiday—this conservative town's G-rated equivalent to Mardi Gras in New Orleans. Children and adults are semi-excused from school and work, the town gets decked out in red, and there's a parade through the streets of downtown, where someone named Mr. Spoons displays his unique musical talents. It all may sound a bit Capra-esque, but to deny such traditions would be tantamount to forgetting historical firsts such as Cincinnati being the site of the initial night game in major-league history, and being the team that employed the youngest player of modern times in 15-year-old Joe Nuxhall.

The Reds might have won the World Series as early as 1919, as the beneficiaries of the infamous Black Sox Scandal, and as recently as 1990, in a landmark wire-to-wire performance; but no team in the city's annals has evoked as much awe and reverence as the 1975 and 1976 championship clubs, arguably the premier professional sports team of its era. As parity and mediocrity began to spread through the ranks of major-league athletics, this team featured a starting eight unparalleled in depth and destruction: Pete Rose . . . Ken Griffey . . . Joe Morgan . . . Johnny Bench . . . Tony Perez . . . George Foster . . . Davey Concepcion . . . Cesar Geronimo.

Or, more concisely and more famously, The Big Red Machine.

The man behind the Machine was one of the most respected architects in baseball, Bob Howsam. To get Morgan, Geronimo, Jack Billingham, Denis Menke, and Ed Armbrister from Houston, Howsam dealt Tommy Helms, Lee May, and Jimmy Stewart— a heavily criticized deal that turned out to be one of the franchise's most successful. To steal Foster from San Francisco, Howsam dealt Frank Duffy and Vern Geishert. The rest, essentially, were there. The rest, in fact, was history. The Big Red Machine won back-to-back world championships and sent Morgan and Bench to the Hall of Fame, with Perez and Concepcion strong possibilities and Rose a given if he hadn't gambled away his first-ballot induction. If general managers were more readily recognized for their contributions, a certain wall in Cooperstown could carry the likeness of Bob Howsam, too.

The ownership? Who outside Cincinnati even remembers the ownership? The Big Red Machine was owned by Louis Nippert, a man of class and grace who felt that the best way to run the team was to leave it to Howsam. Oh, sure, he'd meet with Howsam to be updated, but if Howsam was on the phone when Nippert entered the office, Howsam would have to motion Nippert to come on in and not to leave. "No one," said Howsam, "could have ever had a better owner or boss than he was."

Suffering from severe back problems and wanting to spend more time out West, Howsam decided to retire into consultancy in 1978, leaving his assistant and hand-picked successor, Dick Wagner, to run the club. But it wasn't the same, and Wagner became a villain in Cincinnati. During his tenure, popular manager and potential Hall of Famer himself Sparky Anderson was fired, and a number of top players left via trade or free agency. Despite winning a division title in 1979 and finishing with baseball's best overall record in 1981 (albeit out of the makeshift playoffs in the strike-shortened season), the team belly-flopped to 101 losses and last place in 1982.

Nippert sold the team in late 1980 to two of the Reds' minority owners, brothers Jim and Bill Williams, who formed a limited partnership that included Nippert and his wife, Louise, as limited partners. In looking for other limited partners, the name Marge Schott was mentioned. They had known Marge for years—and they knew she was interested in sports. When they asked her if she'd be willing to purchase a share, Marge said yes.

In time, she became the most outspoken of partners—without even opening her mouth. The Williamses were similar to Louis Nippert, overseeing the club and not seizing it, quietly letting Dick Wagner operate. Not so Marge, who was known in Cincinnati for appearing with animals in commercials for her car dealerships. She chose another visual medium to air her feelings about the team. She often flew banners over Riverfront Stadium to promote her dealerships, and she wasn't above using them to provoke opinion. In 1983, for instance, when the struggling Reds were playing a Philadelphia Phillies club that featured three of the Reds' most noted former Machinists, Perez, Rose, and Morgan, Marge's banner read, "Tony, Pete, Joe. Help—Love, Marge."

"It showed me a woman with balls," said Reds' broadcaster Marty Brennaman. "I thought it was very impressive. I think she did then what a lot of people were thinking, but probably didn't have the guts to say or display in the manner in which she did."

The banner may have been a hit with the fans, but it wasn't quite so popular with the Williams brothers, and they relayed their displeasure their way—not with an aerial banner but with a private word. "I thought it was in bad taste," said Bill Williams. "Sometimes she does or says something on the spur of the moment that she regrets later."

Even if her chutzpah seemed admirable, her display lost its credibility because she never voiced her concerns in the proper mode first, when it could have made a difference. After all, she was a limited partner of the team, with the ability to speak up at the Reds' ownership meetings, and she never did. "She never in any meetings said anything like that—complain or anything else," said Bill Williams. "In fact, she didn't attend many meetings. She wasn't too interested."

She didn't attend some of the more laid-back affairs, either. While the Williamses held controlling interest in the Reds, they welcomed the partners to join in the fun and not just the finances. They went to Florida to meet the team during spring training and took some road trips during the season. Bill Williams figured it was a way to let the partners get some joy out of their investments. But even when Marge accompanied the partners, she didn't always fit in. Carl Kroch, a limited partner then and now, says Marge was somewhat of a loner during the Williamses' administration and seemed to get along only with Kroch's wife. Kroch remembers one time when the partners went on a road trip with the Reds and some of the other partners were making fun of Marge at dinner. Marge called Kroch's room at about midnight looking for his wife, who was sleeping. So Marge told Kroch, "I'm fed up with the rest of the partners. I'm leaving." And she did, going home ahead of the team plane.

Eventually, the Williams brothers agreed with Marge on one matter—the ballclub needed help. Attendance was sliding, the ballclub was floundering, and it was time for a change. And in July 1983, they decided to fire Wagner and exercised their option to recall Howsam to active duty. His contract read that if the Reds got rid of their general manager, Howsam was to either (a) help them find a new one or (b) if they so desired, run the club until a new one was found. Actually, they wanted Howsam to run the club, period—to return as president and chief executive officer. Howsam, whose consulting duties up until this point had consisted primarily of checking out some of the minor leaguers, says he didn't really want the position again, but he accepted the Williamses' request. He agreed to stay for three years but said he hoped he could leave after two. That made the Williamses happy—and the front office ecstatic.

"It was like somebody picked up the shade and the sun came through," said former chief financial officer Lou Porco.

"It was like he was the cavalry coming back to save you," said former ticket-office worker Keith Stichtenoth.

Those who knew Howsam knew he not only would revive the team, but would resuscitate the business operation and restore morale. In the front office, he was "Mr. Howsam," a term spoken with appreciation and respect for the way he treated the staff during his two stints in the position. There was always a smile, a hello, a thank-you for a job well done. On Secretary's Day, each secretary received a rose. On Thanksgiving, everyone received a certificate for a free turkey. At least once a season, members of the front-office staff would dine with him in the general manager's box at Riverfront Stadium, and he'd often invite them to the same box for a Bengals football game, as well. At Christmas, he'd advance the paychecks a couple of weeks so the staff could use the money for holiday shopping. And for the scouts, the foundation of the organization, Howsam made sure that their three-year contracts were extended one year annually, that they had a good benefits program, and that their cars, equipment, and incidentals were always taken care of. He would call them regularly to get their input and to make them feel wanted.

Everything Howsam did seemed to be with people in mind. Most of the costs were minimal, but they were investments in the people, who returned the favor by forming one of the most respected organizations in the game.

"I haven't heard anybody that was working with the Reds ever complain about anything that he did," said former Reds scout Chet Montgomery. "You just don't hear that, especially today."

Wagner certainly didn't elicit that type of response. At best, he was respected and accepted. At worst, he was reviled. And it certainly didn't help when he declared that all doors inside the office were to stay closed, although he eventually gave in on that one. He continued some of the same policies Howsam had instituted, but he lacked the same people skills, the same warmth, the same ability to make everybody feel like a part of the organization.

"If he [Wagner] was joking about something, it was a joke you inevitably wouldn't get," said Stichtenoth. "He probably felt like he made the effort, but it was like a suit that didn't fit. With Mr. Howsam, it didn't matter what he did, he was beloved."

Howsam certainly didn't hurt his status by coming in and raising front-office salaries. Wagner had downsized the scouts' cars, and Howsam upgraded them again so they would be big enough to hold baseball equipment easily and would include cruise control to ease the strain of the long jaunts across America's highways. He also made sure each car had an emergency repair kit for a flat tire. "It makes you realize how little it takes to make people happy," Howsam said, "but how important it is."

On the field, Howsam spent the rest of 1983 assessing the team. He decided after the season to replace manager Russ Nixon with Vern Rapp, whom Howsam considered "the best finisher of prospects at the Triple-A level I'd ever had." But it didn't take long before Rapp was finished, lasting all of 121 games, 71 of which were losses.

Howsam had another idea. Peter Edward Rose, the greatest name in the city's sporting archives, was wasting away as a sometimes player with the Montreal Expos. Well aware of Rose's knowledge of the game, Howsam thought he would be just the man and manager to help enliven the outlook at Riverfront Stadium. Rose wanted the job, but he wanted more. Though his playing career was waning, Rose was within reach of Ty Cobb's celebrated record for all-time hits, and Rose wasn't ready to stop trying. Rose said he'd manage, but only if he could play, too. Howsam wasn't thrilled with the idea, but acquiesced, figuring, if nothing else, that Rose on the field would be a box-office spark for a team in dire need of one. So the deal was done, Montreal getting utility infielder Tom Lawless in return for Rose, who helped the Reds to a respectable 19-22 finish for the year.

Actually, prospects for the once-proud franchise were starting to brighten. Bill Williams, criticized for not spending the money to keep the top players in Cincinnati or to acquire new ones, had approved the signing of free-agent outfielder Dave Parker, a former National League Most Valuable Player, before the 1984 season. And by the end of 1984, top prospect Eric Davis had reached the parent club and a number of others laden with potential were not far behind. If the Reds weren't expected to contend in 1985, they at least were destined to be competitive, and that was one hell of an improvement. Expectations were almost as hopeful as dispositions around the riverfront. With Howsam in charge and Rose back, the smiles were contagious.

In the fall of 1984, Howsam came to the Williamses and asked if his contract could be restructured to let him go early. Howsam felt the club was properly directed now, and he wanted to go back to being a consultant for the third year of his contract, beginning in July of 1985. By then, he planned to have a general manager in place, poised to replace him. The Williams brothers agreed, and in November Howsam brought in Bill Bergesch from the New York Yankees as his general manager and heir apparent. Meanwhile, the Williamses were considering leaving, too—and had been for a year or so. Jim Williams was ill, and Bill Williams figured he'd had a part of the Reds since 1966 and it was time to get out. First, the Williamses offered it to the limited partners. According to George Strike, one of the limited partners, local business tycoon Carl Lindner appeared ready to take it. Lindner, a private man, figured to run the Reds as they had been for years—quietly, unobtrusively. But talks between Lindner and the Williamses snagged, and Lindner pulled out.

Outsiders had expressed interest, as well. Former baseball commissioner and ex-Kentucky governor Happy Chandler and Louisville Cardinals owner A. Ray Smith made a bid on the team, and their intentions became public knowledge. Meanwhile, Bill DeWitt, Jr., whose father used to own the Reds, and Bill Reik (who would later become a limited partner), a Northern Kentucky native and a New York investment adviser, combined to make a bid of $21 million, only this was done privately. Bill Williams told them the price was not enough, that out-of-towners had bid $25 million. Reik and DeWitt huddled for a couple of hours and decided to match the price. "It's yours," they were told, with one possible obstacle. There was this one limited partner who was trying to scrounge up the money necessary to buy the team—one Margaret Unnewehr Schott.

She had called Bill Williams to tell him she was interested, too, but was noticeably unsure and concerned. She asked him if he thought she could handle it—being in charge of the team, putting together the necessary cash. He told her he couldn't answer that. "Jim Williams told me up to the last minute he didn't think she would be able to raise the funds," said Kroch. In the end, she did. She was able to secure enough money to buy the Reds, and she did it by borrowing money from a local bank. "My understanding," said George Strike, "was that Fifth-Third Bank loaned her in excess of $10 million to do the transaction."

As a limited partner, Marge already owned one of the 15 shares. And at $1.6 million per share, she had to put up more than

$22 million for the purchase of the rest of the shares, in case all the other limited partners left with the Williams brothers. The more partners she could convince to stay with the team, the less money she would have to spend on shares; and if half or more of the 15 shares were sold in a 12-month period, the partnership agreement would be dissolved and have to be rewritten, which would prove costly in taxes for all the partners. As it turned out, she had to purchase seven new units—including the all-important two general partner shares from the Williamses, the ones that provided complete decision-making power over the franchise. At $1.6 million per share, that came to $11.2 million, but she soon cut that back, selling one to Frisch's Restaurants, Inc., and one to Reik the following June, although she later purchased another half-share from Priscilla Gamble. Essentially, Marge Schott bought the Reds for less than $9 million.

"She very aggressively did a selling job for me to stay in," said Strike. "She assured me she would have no active role in the management of the Reds, that she would be involved even less than the Williamses because she didn't know as much as them, didn't have the background, because the Williamses had been part of the previous ownership group. She said that Bob Howsam would continue as the president and the head of operations."

Bill Williams remembers at least twice talking to Marge about how much she should get involved with the team, which was essentially not at all. He had two pieces of advice: (1) keep your mouth shut, and (2) let your general manager run the Reds. At the time, she agreed. Bill Williams felt the club would be safe in her hands, little knowing the bomb she was about to drop.

On December 21, 1984, Marge Schott announced to the world that she had purchased the Cincinnati Reds. She showed up at the press conference with her venerable St. Bernard, Schottzie, and proclaimed this her "Christmas present to the city." She said she felt it was her civic duty to step forward, purchase the team, and prevent it from leaving Cincinnati. To a frightened city that had heard the stories about Happy Chandler and A. Ray Smith and feared losing its single most cherished resource, this seemed wondrous news. And Marge was the Wonder Woman who had made it so. The people of Cincinnati never forgot what she did for them—and she never let them—the city not realizing that the rescue was all in Marge's mind. The Reds, in fact, were never in danger of leaving Cincinnati.

"Never," said Bill Williams. "I have no idea where she gets this impression. As you go along and own a ballclub, you usually get a letter every two or three months that somebody wants to buy it. The only person who had any real, hard interest was Happy Chandler. He called and came up, and we had lunch, and he said he'd like to buy the ballclub. I said, 'Happy, if we sell the ballclub, we want to keep it Cincinnati ownership.' He said, 'Oh, well, hell, we're just across the river. We're practically Cincinnati.' I said, 'You're too far down the river. No, we're going to keep this in Cincinnati.'"

To jump from Chandler and Smith attempting to buy the team to assuming the Reds were on the verge of leaving Cincinnati is absurd. Smith even said at the time, "I couldn't legally do it with the lease they have." Even if he had tried, anybody who wanted to move a team faced an almost impermeable force field in Major League Baseball, which used its exemption from antitrust laws as a seemingly unbeatable tool of enforcement. And there was no way baseball was going to allow the relocation of the Reds, whose drop in attendance was obviously a result of a drop in the standings and not a decrease in the city's passion. Every year from 1973 to 1980, more than two million fans filed into the antiseptic stadium on the riverfront to watch a high caliber of baseball. Even during the dregs of 1982-84, the turnstiles never failed to turn at least a million times. The Reds leave the birthplace of professional baseball? Preposterous.

"That," said Carl Kroch, "was an absolute lie."

It wasn't like Marge was reacting to some inside information discussed within the partnership. According to George Strike, there was never any indication or fear that the Reds might be leaving Cincinnati, and the Chandler-Smith bid "would never have been considered seriously." Bill Williams told Bob Howsam at the time he would have no qualms about keeping the team if he couldn't find a reasonable offer, but it never reached that point. It never got past the limited partners. If it had, Reik and DeWitt were ready to purchase the team, and they certainly didn't want to move it. To give Marge every benefit of the doubt, perhaps she didn't know about Reik and DeWitt. Perhaps Marge just panicked when the news of Chandler's and Smith's interest hit the media. Perhaps she just didn't understand baseball's permanent niche in the city. Then again, perhaps she never bothered to learn the truth.

Or maybe she just ignored it to make herself look good.

"It bothered me a little bit," said Bill Williams. "We didn't have to sell the team, but we decided we'd like to sell it. She didn't save the team for Cincinnati. She probably believes it now. But that wasn't a bit true. The team wasn't going to leave Cincinnati, if we could help it."

"When she made that statement, I knew it was a falsehood, and I didn't like it, because it reflected on the Williamses, one of the outstanding families of Cincinnati," said Howsam. "They didn't deserve to get a rap for someone to make PR. A lot of people believe that now. She's lived on that type of thing."

Nine years after the fact, Marge still claims to have saved the Cincinnati Reds from leaving the city. Maybe Bill Williams was right. Maybe she actually came to believe it after saying it for so long. It became her legacy to Cincinnati, the *"Yeah, but . . ."* the locals used to defend her whenever she was accused of something outlandish. It would be easy to write off as one mistake on her part if it didn't become such a pattern. Before long, she also was claiming to have brought Pete Rose back to Cincinnati. But she had nothing to do with that.

"Absolutely nothing," said Williams.

"Again, that was a falsehood," said Howsam.

Marge's misstatement about the team leaving Cincinnati was not the only point of concern for Howsam from her initial press conference. It was the matter of bringing the dog. Howsam was out of town at the time and unable to make the proceedings, but Marge said, "When I told [Howsam] I was bringing the dog, he got the giggles." His reaction shortly thereafter was somewhat short of amused. "I just think there are certain things in the sports field which we are in that you probably don't do," he said at the time. In retrospect, he says it was downright unprofessional; and though he has no problem with pets, he doesn't like the way Marge has paraded hers around from Day 1. "I think it's been verified it is not in the best interests of the organization," said Howsam.

As for Bill Williams? He was at the press conference, and he says about her bringing the St. Bernard to the proceedings, "I just wondered a little." He wasn't alone, really. If you were part of the organization or just a follower, you had to wonder what was next. But it wasn't all bad. While Howsam saw the dog as detracting, others found it rather refreshing. Keith Stichtenoth saw the dog, the enthusiasm, the banners, the outspokenness, and he thought, hey, this could be fun.

"The idea that someone like her could come in following the Williams brothers' ownership, which was just invisible, I think struck us all as a positive, that this could be interesting, this could be exciting, we're not going to be some boring team," he said. "We certainly thought it would be worth sticking around and watching."

Bill Bergesch, the general manager who was supposed to succeed Howsam as head of the team's baseball operation, was knocked a bit off balance by that opening press conference, too. When he called to congratulate Marge on her acquisition of the team, he was put right through to the new owner.

"She picked up the phone, and I didn't realize the press conference was still going on," said Bergesch. "I told her, 'This is Bill Bergesch. I just called to congratulate you and assure you that I'll do anything I can to work with you and make the thing a success.' So she thanked me and said that was very nice and so forth, and that was all. Somebody asked her who it was that called, and she said, 'That was our general manager, Whatchamadoodle.'"

Bergesch says it didn't bother him. He claims it wasn't the easiest name in the world to pronounce (BURR-gish) and says "I've been called a lot worse"—no doubt a lot worse by Marge herself over the next few years. Her era as general partner was one of such turbulence and controversy that Bill Williams regretted selling her the team, even if he has problems saying it in so many words publicly. But what he does say certainly implies as much.

"You're asking me a tough question," he said. "You're asking me a very, very tough question. I'd rather not answer that. I never dreamed that it would go this way."

In fact, Williams offered to buy the team back from Marge a few years later, but she declined. This was her team, operated her way, the way she'd always operated. Bill Williams thought he knew her somewhat, being friends with her late husband and even developing a shopping center for her. Had he *really* known her, he could have predicted the way she would operate the Reds, based on the history of Marge Schott.

Chapter Three

A Woman in a Man's World

B orn August 18, 1928, Margaret Unnewehr, a sixth-generation Cincinnatian, was the second of five daughters to Edward and Charlotte Unnewehr. As was typical of her generation, her mother raised the family and her father raised the funds to do it, through the family business, the Cincinnati Veneer Co. "We were the largest wooden cigar box manufacturers in the world," Marge said. "Then we went to plywood and veneer, because they started bringing in paper boxes from Japan."

If Marge knew anything, she knew her father's business. Now that *wasn't* quite so typical of the females of her generation, but Marge hardly matched the stereotype of the day. Her personality and her father helped see to that. Because Ed Unnewehr had no sons, and because Marge showed an interest and an affinity for the business world, her father turned her into the son he never had, even nicknaming her "Butch," as she became his favorite.

"He told me one day that she should have been a boy because of how she'd take over," said Joe Link, who knew the Unnewehr family from the time Marge was little, when he worked on a fruit-and-vegetable delivery truck. He later became Marge's friend and then her stepfather-in-law. "She was sort of dominant. Her father took her under his wing, and she took to that. Margie was always the toast of her father."

The other daughters did not share her love for business. Marge's older sister, Lottie, was more like her mother in her affection for the arts and in her appearance, according to Mary Clair Leis Torbeck, Marge's friend since the first grade (and whose brother Simon would later become Cincinnati's pornography-busting sheriff). Torbeck won't go so far as to call Marge a tomboy, although she can understand such a description if Marge were compared to Lottie. She describes Marge as "fun-loving" and eager to get out in the neighborhood and play with the boys. "We played in the streets, you know," said Torbeck. "You can't do that today."

The Unnewehrs were not wealthy, certainly not compared to the riches Marge would later come to know, but they did well and lived well in an upper-middle-class section of the city's Clifton area, the community best known as the home of the University of Cincinnati. The Unnewehrs sent Marge to Sacred Heart Academy, which Marge has described as "white gloves, 12 years of French and curtsy." Still, there was room for Marge to try to be Marge. She channeled some of her seemingly endless energy into sports, playing field hockey for the school. And even in as disciplined an environment as Sacred Heart, Marge's independent nature could not help but come out.

"One time, Marge decided she wasn't going to bother carrying her French book home every day, so she just started tearing one page out every day," said Torbeck. "All of a sudden, the nun noticed it was thinner. I can still see her walking up to Marge and taking this book and the eyes she was giving her. I thought it was hysterical."

After her graduation from Sacred Heart, Marge's father promised her a Packard Clipper if she stayed at home and went to school instead of going away to college, so she worked for him while attending the University of Cincinnati. Although Marge said she lasted at UC for about a year, UC records show she actually attended the university for three years. In any case, she dropped out to work for her father full time. She spent roughly the next three years working for her father in a job she has described as, "Heir apparent, manufacturing. I was in the office, and he told everybody I knew how to run every machine. My mother thought I'd lose my hands. It was factory and office. In those days, you were with your help 100 percent, and they were part of your family. I did everything Daddy wanted me to do."

Here she continued her education as the lone student in the Edward Unnewehr Unofficial School of Business, where she learned her father's values not only in business but in everyday life. He stressed hard work, hands-on management, and looking at the employees as sort of an extended family. Joe Link says that if one of the employees had a baby, the Unnewehrs would buy gifts for the child and carry on as if the newborn were a relative. Being a former chairman of the Department of Business Administration and Economics at Xavier University, Link naturally focuses on the economic aspects of Marge's father. At the risk of sounding stereotypical, Link says Marge's parents reflected the old German money ethic that was common in the old German town of Cincinnati.

"They were very solid Germans," he said. "They were very frugal. Very economical. Real conservative. They would never waste anything. If a hamburger could take the place of a T-bone steak, you got a hamburger. They were frugal in their food, their clothes, and their cars. Education wasn't as important as hard work, saving your nickels, investing wisely. And don't flaunt it. Play it down, always play it down—then you'll get a better deal. The German heritage does that for you. If you let people think you have a lot of money, they'll try to take it away from you."

Granted, it's unfair to categorize a person according to her heritage and disregard the possibility of individual differences, but Marge herself has described her family as "Achtung! German," and she has talked about her father's bent for fiscal restraint. Later, as owner of the Reds, she became noted for low-budget outerwear that often consisted of sweaters or pullover sports shirts, polyester slacks, and loafers. "It drives people nuts," she has said. "I never shop anymore. If somebody sends me something that fits, I'll wear it. . . . My daddy preached Depression. The lucky people are those who never had anything. When they get it, boy, they enjoy spending it. I'm not that way at all."

Something else Marge either inherited or learned from her father was her disposition. Joe Link says Ed Unnewehr was "a very domineering father. He felt that you've got to fight for everything in this world, that nobody gives you anything, that you've got to be tough." And Link saw the same attributes in Marge, along with her father's stubbornness and bluntness.

People who have known Marge, either as an Unnewehr or a Schott, describe a woman who speaks what she thinks, like it or not. Personally, Link claims he prefers her straightforwardness to the hypocrites who think one way and speak another, but he knows Marge's personality has caused her trouble. "That," he said, "might be her downfall."

Marge worked for her father until she married Charles Schott, a member of one of the city's wealthiest and most influential families. Charlie's dad, Walter Schott, Sr., had built a fortune on some shrewd financial dealings when so much of America was impoverished. Joe Schott, Walter's nephew, considers himself somewhat of the family historian and says Walter Schott, Sr., built a fortune in the '20s by buying car companies that were going under and by selling the inventories.

"He would buy the cars for a couple hundred dollars, drive them to Texas, and sell them for four or five hundred," says John Borcherding, who worked for Walter and later for Charlie. "This," said Borcherding, "is where Marge got the idea of liquidating companies."

But that came later. The son Marge married looked at his father not only as a role model, but a hero. Charlie's friend, Frank Gilligan, calls it a "father complex" and says Charlie used to refer to "Daddy" all the time and believe Daddy could do everything. It got to the point where his buddies would kid him and say, "What would Daddy think about that?" Bill Geoghegan, Charlie's friend since first grade, says Charlie admired everything his father did, and his father seemed to take to Charlie, too, to the point where he may have overindulged Charlie a bit. "Charlie kind of hero-worshipped his dad," said Geoghegan. "And because he did, as he grew older, he wanted to emulate his father in every way that he could."

Unlike his father, however, Charlie never had to worry about money. Frank Gilligan remembers one time when it really sank in how well off Charlie was. Charlie saw a shoe-repair store with a sign advertising shoes being resoled, and Charlie was taken by this, saying, "That's a good idea." Indeed, he had never heard of resoling shoes. "In the '30s," said Gilligan, "everybody did."

Charlie's personality translated into popularity. He loved to have fun and hated to sit still, and he had a touch of "bad boy" in him, according to Geoghegan. Charlie didn't take to the business world right away (although he would later), his younger days being spent in the pursuit of enjoyment. "I wouldn't call him an academic type," said Geoghegan. "The intellectual side of life wasn't necessarily of great interest to him. Maybe Marge was a bit more intellectual. She might have read more. I don't think reading was one of Charlie's ideas of how to spend time, unless it was the sports section."

The term "playboy" comes up a lot in describing Charlie Schott. "He did date a lot," said Gilligan. "There's no doubt he liked the ladies, and it was rather reciprocal. He never seemed to be at a loss for a date." But Charlie was not the only one in his crowd to date Marge. John Kauffman dated her. And so did Geoghegan. "And sometimes all three of us were out with her," said Geoghegan. "A couple of times, one of us would have the date and the other two would come along."

It wasn't as though there were three males trying to hit on one female at the same time—although her looks were certainly noticed. Marge's appearance was much softer back then, before the years and the turmoil of the next four decades chiseled the features into her face. It was Marge's personality that made her fit in as one of the gang. At the risk of making another generalization, Geoghegan said, "She always had a touch of masculinity about her. She had sort of a strong voice, and when she was out with three guys like Charlie, John, and me, she seemed to enjoy the whole evening. She liked being in male company. She didn't mind if she was the only woman." They found Marge great company—personable and energetic, fun and funny. And one thing was for certain. The conversation never dragged with Marge around. "She liked to talk," said Geoghegan. "There's not a lot of dead mike time with Marge."

But it was Charlie who eventually became Marge's beau. Charlie would escort Marge to dances at Xavier University, where he was taking classes after World War II—and where Joe Link was his professor—and Marge attended Charlie's graduation. That night, Walter Schott, Sr., threw a party for Charlie at the Vernon Manor, and Link remembers sitting at the bar with the family patriarch and discussing his son. "Charlie was the first one in the family to get a degree, and Walter Schott, Sr., was so proud of him," said Link. "He said, 'What do you think of my son?' I said, 'Walter, you've got a son who's very sharp. He's like you. He's a workaholic.'"

At Xavier, Link and Charlie became friends. According to Link, Marge and Charlie would sometimes go out together on Saturday nights to a black Dixieland jazz club. The three of them might be the only whites in the place, but Link says they didn't mind, and neither did the rest of the patrons. Other times, the three of them got together for a drive-in movie and some White Castles. Even after Marge and Charlie married, they traveled with Link to Florida on occasion and invited him to stay overnight at their house back in Cincinnati. When Marge and Charlie married in 1952, Joe Link played the wedding march on the organ. Edward Unnewehr "pouted during the wedding," Marge has said, "because he lost his heir apparent."

The marriage would have some happy moments. They purchased a 70-acre estate in the posh community of Indian Hill and resided in the house Marge still occupies. Every Christmas, they invited friends and family over for a storybook celebration, complete with Santa Claus and decked halls and Marge at her very best playing "Aunt Marge" to relatives and friends alike. Sadly, these were snapshots of joy in what was an album of misery for Marge and Charles Schott. Some of the chapters she described privately a quarter-century later, after she became the supposedly unflappable if not tyrannical owner of a major-league baseball club. They were moments when the vulnerability surfaced and provided a rare glimpse of her humanity, evoking genuine empathy from those who wanted to care about Marge if she would only allow it.

"The best moments for me with Marge were when the two of us were together, one to one, and she didn't have to play the Tough Marge role, and she'd talk about her life with Charlie," said Don Breen, Marge's former vice-president of business and marketing with the Reds. "She told me all about when they got married. You felt sorry for her at times. She told me that on her wedding night, her husband left her for a while and went to play cards with the guys, and that he used to go out all the time playing cards, and she'd be at home crying. She figured she'd get even taking up little hobbies around the house and try to drive him crazy with her hobbies. It's easy to say, oh, that's BS, and she's trying to draw on sympathy. But several times, she'd cry. She'd be upset and thinking about something, or something bad would happen that would trigger a bunch of bad memories, and she'd come in and she would talk and you'd see that she was really upset."

But cards were not the problem. In fact, cards were more than likely a euphemism for alcohol, because Charlie Schott had a drinking problem, and he knew it. He tried quitting. He tried Alcoholics Anonymous. He tried going to church every day. But nothing lasted. Although his brother tries to downplay, if not deny, the severity of Charlie's alcohol problem, Walter Jr. says the drinking seemed to pick up after their father, and Charlie's idol, died in 1956. And it appeared to intensify a few years later when their mother married Joe Link. It was hard enough for Charlie to endure the death of his father, but the idea of someone now taking his place probably had something to do with Charlie's increased drinking, says Walter Jr. It went even deeper, though.

"He thought Joe Link was kind of a mooch," said Walter Jr. "I think the rest of the family felt the same way. I wouldn't say Joe was accepted that well. It divided the family. After my mother married Joe Link, I don't think Charlie had much respect for him and they didn't get together all that much."

Charlie's drinking was so bad, he would disappear on binges for days at a time. With Charlie's responsibilities on the business end intensifying after his father's death, taking off like that could have been hazardous not only to his marriage but to his business holdings, but Charlie's hands-off approach and his reliance on his right-hand man, John Borcherding, protected him in the workplace. Borcherding, who had worked as a salesman for Charlie's father at one time, came to Charlie one day at his dealership (then called Schott-Lippert Buick), and asked for a job. Borcherding told Charlie to name the position and the salary, but Borcherding had one prediction: "I will wind up sitting in that chair you're sitting in"—in other words, running the dealership. He was hired.

"Charlie went over to the used-car lot and immediately fired his manager and announced, 'Boys, this is your new boss,'" said Borcherding. "In less than two years, I was running the place. The sales manager had quit, and Charlie wasn't available at the time. He'd get lost for a week or two at a time because he had this problem with alcohol, so I went over to run the new-car store, and I hired a used-car manager. I more or less made myself the sales manager. Later, I started getting involved in other things for

Charlie, so I hired a new sales manager. Charlie said, 'What does that make you?' I said, 'General manager.'

"You had to be strong to work for Charlie. He was eccentric. And with this alcohol problem, when he'd get wound up, he could be a bear. One time when Charlie was drunk, I had to carry him over my shoulder and told the porter working in the shop to take him home. Charlie was screaming, 'You're fired! You're fired!' But he wouldn't remember it."

Link says that Borcherding was close to Charlie—perhaps too close. He says Borcherding was a nice man, a good man, but he protected Charlie, running his businesses when Charlie was off drunk somewhere. Borcherding didn't mind taking over. Like Charlie, Borcherding was driven to be successful and didn't mind working around the clock or flying to some of Charlie's other businesses in other locales to manage them, too.

"Charlie would be apt to call at three in the morning, seven days a week," said Borcherding. "We never took a day off. Never. It's just the way we were. Driven. I think he was trying to prove himself in business. I think maybe he was trying to convince Harold he could be a big mogul like his dad."

Harold was Harold Schott, Charlie's uncle. Borcherding says Walter Sr. and Harold were big drinkers, too. "Charlie was like his Uncle Harold," said Link. "They worked hard, and they played hard. Drinking was an outlet."

Joe Schott recalls one story about Harold and Charlie when they were more than likely drunk—or at least a good way there. It happened in the mid-'60s. "They made a couple of good deals in Palm Beach, and they were celebrating, and they went to the Rolls Royce dealer and took a Rolls Royce for a demo ride—only they never came back," said Joe Schott. "They sent the man a check, and that's the car that Margie's got today."

Other stories were far more tragic, particularly the stories of how Charlie's drinking affected Marge. Walter Jr. says that many times he'd pick up Charlie at a bar and drive him home because he was hammered. Marge, worried, would call Walter Jr., asking him to go get Charlie either on his own or with her. It was a scenario John Borcherding knew too well.

"I felt sorry for her," said Borcherding. "Charlie gave her a hard time—I mean *really* gave her a hard time. He'd get drunker than a monkey, and he'd say anything. He'd get nasty and mouthy. She'd just want to get away from him when he was like that. There were different times when she'd try to get me to get him sobered up."

Charlie didn't think much of Marge's business acumen and would tell her so, beating her down in front of Borcherding. He'd tell her, "Keep your damn mouth shut" or "Get out of here" or "You don't know what you're talking about." And numerous times, Charlie would tell Borcherding, "Don't ever let Marge wind up with everything if something happens to me. Be sure she sells everything, or she will destroy it."

"One time when we wanted to change the front of the building at Schott Buick, Charlie said, 'Marge always wants to do something, why don't we let her handle that?'" said Borcherding. "She drove the guy we hired to do the work insane. You would have to be around her to realize the things that she would nitpick about that would absolutely drive you crazy. The guy would come to me and say, 'I'm going to have a heart attack because of her.'"

Charlie couldn't imagine Marge with her abrasiveness and her cheapness being in a position of authority with his businesses, and he could already see that such traits weren't doing much for intrafamily relations. Marge and the Schotts may have shared a name, but not always the same values. Link remembers a time when he and Charlie and Marge were at Sacred Heart for a festival, and she won two hams but could use only one. Link suggested she give the other to the nuns. Instead, she told Link she'd pick him up the next day and take the ham to Findlay Market to trade for a roast beef. And she did.

"That was Margie," said Link. "She was more of an Unnewehr. The Schotts were real generous. Margie didn't relate to that."

"The Schotts went first-class," said Borcherding. "If they went to a restaurant, it was always the best. Marge couldn't stand this."

Still, Marge seemed to get along pretty well with Charlie's father, the liquidator. Mary Clair Torbeck calls them "the best of pals," and Link says Walter Sr. found Marge "a sharp little businesswoman." Link and Borcherding disagree as to whether Marge got along with Charlie's mother—Link says yes, Borcherding no—but they agree on one matter: Marge and Charlie regularly feuded, and it wasn't just Charlie belittling Marge; Marge did her share of berating Charlie, too.

"I think it was a two-way street," Link said. "I've been in their company long enough to know. They both would fight and argue tooth-and-nail. Even at their home, it would be very touchy. It would have been wonderful if they had a bunch of kids. Margie would have had a family around her. Charlie would have had a family around him. They would have other interests in their lives. But not having any children, they were on their own. It was two strong-willed people, really."

Marge has long contended that one of the great tragedies in her life was never having children. Torbeck says Marge and Charlie tried, but to no avail. "I don't know what the problem was, and I don't think the doctors knew, because she was never told that she could not have children," said Torbeck. Joe Link says his wife, Charlie's mother, would attempt to arrange adoptions for her son and daughter-in-law, but Marge and Charlie refused to go that route.

"My wife was very upset about that," said Link. "She had a couple of children lined up, but they wouldn't do it. My wife said they didn't want to do it because they didn't know the background. In those days, they didn't take too many tests. You might be getting a mentally deranged child."

Without children, and with a husband who wasn't always there, Marge found other ways to occupy her time, such as volunteer work, and other outlets to channel her love, most notably her St. Bernards. The issue of children was stressful, but perhaps it was for the best that there were none; bringing a child into this turbulent marriage could have been a mistake.

"Charlie would tell the story that he got on a binge and they went to Indiana and got married, but he was too drunk to remember and woke up the next morning and said, 'Who are you?' and she said, 'I'm your wife,'" said Borcherding. "Charlie might have been bullshitting."

And Marge would tell Borcherding she still harbored knight-in-shining-armor dreams, saying, "I wish someone would come along and take me out of all this." Link says he heard that Marge and Charlie had separated once or twice, but that his wife would always write it off as a "lovers' squabble." Borcherding says it was hard to categorize their living situation.

"Charlie and Marge weren't exactly living together, but it wasn't a complete separation," said Borcherding. "A lot of times, when he was on one of his binges, she wouldn't even let him in the house. Sometimes when he was drunk, he'd have somebody driving him home, and she wouldn't let him get out of the car. He'd end up staying downtown at the Barn."

That was one of Charlie's favorite drinking spots, and there was a bed upstairs if he needed it, says Borcherding. But when Charlie wasn't there, he might be with other women. Borcherding says he knew of two of them. The last one, he says, was named Lois Kenning, who worked for Charlie.

"She was a very attractive blonde and a really sweet gal," said Borcherding. "He had furnished an apartment for her with about $40,000 worth of furniture. She was the one I thought Charlie was going to marry."

Indeed, the marriage of Marge and Charles Schott often appeared to be coming to an end. But it never did.

"They were on the verge of getting a divorce," said Borcherding, "when Charlie died."

On February 19, 1968, Charles J. Schott died of a heart attack at the age of 42. For the next quarter-century, the location and circumstances of his death would make for some of the most popular pieces of gossip inside Cincinnati, with all sorts of variations and guesses as to the truth. Walter Schott, Jr., says he believes Charlie died at the Barn and that Charlie's physician, Dr. Charles Barrett, went there to get him—the same Dr. Charles Barrett who signed the death certificate, which does not list where Charlie suffered the heart attack, only that he ended up at Bethesda Hospital. But Barrett's widow, May Belle Barrett, says her husband went to an East Walnut Hills apartment complex to get Charlie, who had died of a heart attack "in the bathtub."

Borcherding says Charlie did indeed die at that apartment complex—in the apartment that Charlie had furnished for Lois Kenning. "Lois called the life squad," said Borcherding, "but Charlie was dead already."

Even if Marge hadn't known about Charlie and Lois Kenning, she certainly found out after his death, when she got the bill for the $40,000 worth of furniture Charlie had purchased on account for Lois's apartment. "Marge wanted me to see if we could get them to take the furniture back," said Borcherding. "I told her I didn't want to get involved with that, I had other things to do."

Borcherding still had Charlie's businesses to run and was more than willing and capable of continuing. Marge later claimed that she was forced into the business world, using the term "by necessity" in her biography in the Reds' media guide, but that's not true. Actually, Charlie's uncle tried to buy Marge out of her inheritance of Charlie's holdings.

"When I started with Charlie, we figured he had $6 million worth of assets and $6 million of debts," said Borcherding. "When Charlie died, we figured we had just about turned it around where he had no debts. Harold Schott offered her about two or two and a half million dollars for all her interests in Schott enterprises. That's what he estimated the land and buildings were worth. He was probably on the low side. Charlie's assets were probably worth four to five million."

It didn't matter. Marge wanted to run the businesses herself.

Borcherding believes Marge wanted to prove that she could do it, especially after the way Charlie had degraded her and her business sense. After all, Marge considered herself pretty astute in that area, considering all of the hands-on training from her father. Had there been children, Torbeck said, "she never could have taken over Charlie's businesses." Marge would have buried herself in her kids instead of in her work. Torbeck says none of the women in her group worked when their children were little, a reflection of the times.

Marge has said she decided to take over Charlie's businesses when some managers of his out-of-town companies came to his funeral and tried to bill her for their expenses. "I thought all of the guys would come forward and carry me," she told the *Cincinnati Business Courier* in 1992. "But they had a plan of their own—how to bury Mrs. Schott and get rid of her. I was so proud of all the people that worked for Charlie that showed up at the funeral from all over. The worst disappointment I had was all the wonderful people who came in to honor him and had these big expense accounts and tried to write off the trip. I fired them all on the phone that day."

It's a revealing story for one reason.

According to John Borcherding, it never happened.

"I don't know where she got that one," he said. "Maybe it's something she dreamed up. No one was discharged at that particular time. I can't remember her saying anything about the people who came to that funeral and putting it on their expense accounts."

Borcherding would know, because he and Marge ran the businesses in tandem for roughly a year after Charlie's death. But it became quickly and painfully clear to Borcherding that life with Marge was not going to be the same as life with Charlie. For one thing, as driven or eccentric as Charlie could be, Borcherding could ignore his antics and run the companies on his own if need be. But not with Marge. She wanted her hands on everything, and she wanted to slash whatever expenses she could.

"Her method was bleeding companies, taking all of the expense out," said Borcherding. "I remember one fellow we had at the Alton Brick Company, he was making $30,000 a year. That's pretty good money in the '60s. And Charlie might give him a 10-grand bonus at the end of the year if he did a good job. When Marge came in, she said, 'Hell, we don't need him.' She hired a young fellow at about six or seven thousand a year and said, 'Besides, I like his baby blue eyes.'"

Borcherding found Marge pretty friendly toward him that first year, but her business decisions were getting to him, this obsessing over pennies and disregard for her employees. When Charlie was sober, he enjoyed people and treated his employees well. About the only thing Marge and Charlie had in common seemed to be a certain term Borcherding heard each of them say that used to take him off-guard. "*I'm one of the blessed.*" "Charlie always said he was blessed by the Creator, and other people don't deserve things," said Borcherding. '*I'm one of the blessed.*' This was a new one on me. But I heard both of them use it. I guess that made me one of the peons."

Charlie's actions, at least, didn't seem to follow those words. Marge, on the other hand, appeared to mean it. She may have adopted some of the methods of her father-in-law, but she adapted them to her way of thinking. She may have followed the lead of her own father, but this was a much different era and a far different scale than she had known.

The more Marge became familiar with the way Charlie's companies were run, the more she wanted to put her touches on them with her heavy hand. Cutting expenses was one thing, and

Borcherding could understand that—to a degree. But Marge was taking it beyond common sense. For instance, she was checking the phone bills and worrying about relative pennies.

She didn't like it when Borcherding would fly out to some of the Schott holdings to oversee the operations and help them with problems; she wanted him to take a train or drive. When he explained that a car trip to the Galesburg (Illinois) Brick Co. would take two or three days, not to mention his valuable time, she'd say, "Why don't they run their own goddamned businesses?" Borcherding didn't know what to say. It was like telling the boss he couldn't be the boss anymore and expecting the employees to automatically know what to do. But Borcherding agreed to try it, and the head of the Galesburg plant ended up calling him every day—until Marge found out.

"Marge checked the phone bills and said, 'I don't want the expense,' and told him to quit calling," said Borcherding. "Instead, he went out to a pay-phone station and would call me without her knowing it."

Borcherding grew weary of this. He felt he had spent years helping, molding, educating, and encouraging people, and Marge seemed bent on disregarding if not eliminating people. He told Marge he was willing to oversee her operations, but he wanted to be the dealer at the Buick store. He owned 10 percent of it, anyway, and he had invested years of effort into building it. He didn't think it was fair that she got the dealership simply because her husband died. On the other hand, it was her husband's dealership, and she didn't necessarily believe she should have to turn over her rights to it just because Borcherding wanted it.

Meanwhile, Borcherding was approached about purchasing the option on another dealership, Metropolitan Buick. He said yes, because he wasn't certain he would end up with anything in his dealings with Marge, and he wanted a Plan B in case he didn't get Schott Buick. A deal with Marge seemed imminent, however. Marge was supposed to meet with Borcherding on a Sunday at the American Building and bring the papers that would allow Borcherding to buy Schott Buick. But when Borcherding got there, the parking attendant told him Marge had left and would be back in a couple hours. When he came back, he met with Marge, who told him she had learned his secret about Metropolitan. The two got into such a hot argument over it, Borcherding told her what she could do with the dealership.

"Stick it," said Borcherding.

"If you walk out the door, don't come back," said Marge.

"That's great," replied Borcherding.

With that, Borcherding "damn near tore the door off the hinges" and stormed out, thus ending his association with Marge. Borcherding sold his stock for "several thousand," purchased Metropolitan Buick, and established himself as a successful dealer. Marge spent years clinging to the story that she fired her general manager. Borcherding maintains that he quit.

"It's not that big a deal with me," said Borcherding. "I don't care what Marge does or thinks. Buick had understood I had the Schott Buick dealership. She and her attorney, Bob Martin, flew to Detroit to insist upon her having the Buick dealership. The regional manager she had an appointment with had to leave, so she got the assistant. Now the regional manager had told me there was no way she was going to get it, that there were no women dealers and I had run the place for 10 years. But Marge got a hold of the assistant regional manager, who didn't know the decision had been made that I was going to be the dealer, and he said he didn't see any reason why a woman couldn't have a dealership. But she had a hell of a time ever getting it."

Indeed, it took Marge roughly two and a half years before she finally was awarded the dealership, making her the first woman in the United States to own a GM dealership in a major metropolitan area. Perhaps, then, Marge deserves some acclaim as a pioneer. She renamed the umbrella company over Charlie's holdings as Schottco, and she made Schott Buick the most identifiable of her holdings until the Reds came along. Borcherding rightly says that Charlie Schott was wrong about Marge. She didn't run the business into the ground. "People, yes," Borcherding said, but not the business.

"Underneath it all, I think she is a real feminist," said Bill Geoghegan. "She's a very conservative feminist. Her political views and everything are very conservative, but I think that she is a real feminist in the sense that she wants to succeed in a man's world and was determined that she would. She was one of the first to stand up to General Motors in a situation where all these other widows always had to sell the agency. She told them she was ready to go to court with them right then if they weren't going to let her continue on. Most of the heroines of today probably don't look upon Marge as a role model, but they should, because she paved the way for a lot of things."

Ron Borcherding, who worked for Marge and Charlie at Schott Buick and later left to join his father at Metropolitan Buick, says that Buick wasn't picking on Marge—it was just the standard procedure of the day. "It just didn't happen that an owner's wife who had never been in the business wanted to keep it if her husband died," he said. "But with women in the workforce today, that's changed."

A woman in a man's world. She would use that phrase throughout her quarter-century in the automobile industry and during the years that intersected her purchase of controlling interest in the Cincinnati Reds. There is no question she has invaded domains where few females dared, and that it has forced her to fight sometimes. "She's been on the defensive since Charlie died," said Joe Schott. But sometimes this *woman in a man's world* has been more aptly a *woman in her own world,* seemingly losing track of the facts and even losing touch with reality.

John Borcherding says this whole idea that Marge was kept from owning Schott Buick out of pure sexism was overstated. He acknowledges that it was a different time, and Marge's gender certainly didn't help her claim to the dealership back then, but a woman running Schott Buick was a minor issue, if one at all. It was *this* woman that was the problem.

"She had no experience whatsoever," said Borcherding. "Why would you put someone in a dealership who had absolutely no experience?"

Marge Schott and General Motors have been fighting each other ever since Charlie died. In 1987, for instance, GM challenged her right to continue operating Schott Buick, claiming that sales had declined since 1980, with the slide accelerating after 1983; that consumer reports were poor; and that the dealership had not had a true dealer-operator on the premises for several years. Robert Stachler, who later met up again with Marge when he defended Pete Rose during Rose's gambling scandal, was the attorney representing GM in litigation, and he remembers the case because of its unusual compromise. Instead of a settlement and dismissal, the agreement approved by the court provided that Marge make certain changes and improvements or she would lose the dealership. And she made them, but not without using her standard defense before it was through: she suffered the burden of a woman in a man's world.

"That's exactly her theme—every time she would not do something, her defense would be, 'Everybody picks on me because I'm a woman,'" said Stachler. "That was her theme from the time her husband died, and there was some question about whether she would succeed at the dealership. She announced to the world she was battling General Motors because she was a female. From the very outset, General Motors welcomed her as a minority, as a female, to take over the dealership, but like any other franchise, wanted to make sure she understood her obligations and she would satisfy them. Whenever she didn't, she would put up her shield, 'I'm a woman, and they're picking on me.'

"It's nonsense. Utter nonsense. I had the files. I read every document that was involved. To show the good faith of General Motors, after she acquired the Buick franchise, they later awarded her a Chevy franchise. General Motors, then as now, was interested in getting a qualified dealer-operator, one who had financial backing and know-how. If they questioned her know-how, it wasn't because she was a widow, it wasn't because she was a female, it's just because she didn't have experience."

Yes, Marge also got the Chevy dealership. She got it when none other than John Borcherding was in the midst of negotiating to buy that dealership himself, a deal he had put together with Bob Martin. Borcherding can't help but wonder if this was another nose-thumbing at him, but he has no proof. Besides, it's just as well he didn't get it. "It's never been a good dealership," Borcherding said.

The automobile dealerships became Marge Schott's life, her family, her identity. Two years after her landmark receipt of Schott Buick, she became the first woman named to the board of trustees of the Cincinnati Chamber of Commerce. Indeed, the dealerships became a steppingstone into the spotlight. She had some fun with it, placing the new Buick Opel in her living room as a promotional gimmick, appearing on television commercials with different animals as a vehicle to hawk her vehicles. There were men in her life, but she did not marry again, even though Torbeck claims at least two of her male companions were interested. "She was so tied up with her businesses that she just didn't do it," Torbeck said, realizing that Marge had become married to her workplaces. "The thought of changing her lifestyle and all that probably just wasn't appealing to her."

Then again, there were those employees who wish she had left. Whatever her reason.

Take Larry Schwalbach. A one-time employee of Charlie's, he returned to Schott Buick in 1975. He claimed that Marge promised him $100 per week in salary (plus commissions), two weeks of paid vacation, and any new Buick he wanted to drive, and she broke all of them. He said that within two months, his salary was lowered to $50 per week.

"I had to quit twice because she wouldn't give me a decent car to drive," said Schwalbach. "Her manager had me come back to work again, and they'd give me the car back again. It was a continuous fight with her."

Although Schwalbach says he was one of her top salesmen, bringing in $300,000 to $400,000 per year in sales, he never forgot how he was treated when he had an accident at the dealership. Schwalbach says he was in the service department when he slipped on some transmission fluid, fell, and injured his back. The doctor told him to stay off of his feet for two to three weeks.

"Within three days, Marge sent me a letter stating that if I didn't come back to work within 24 hours, she would replace me," said Schwalbach. "And then I didn't have a job. I went to Workers' Compensation, and she fought me there and lost, and I won the claim. I was off then for four or five years with the back injury."

But the painful memories of Marge predated the accident. He remembers the way she treated the salesmen, screaming and yelling and, even worse, interfering and ruining their sales.

"I'd be on a deal, trying to sell a car, and she'd butt in," he said. "I would already have the customers sold on a particular car and then I'd lose the deal 'cause she'd come running in saying, 'Oh, you need electric windows and an electric seat on that car,' and the car I was trying to sell the people didn't have them on there.

She did that on several occasions. We tried to keep the customers away from her. You never knew what she was going to say. You'd spend five hours on a customer selling them on something, and she'd come over and unsell them in five minutes. One of the managers made the remark that it would be better to give her a hundred thousand a year to keep her away from the place."

Dick Whelen, another former Schott Buick salesman, remembers a winter evening when the sky was dark and business was light, and some of Marge's friends drove by and saw her in the showroom. They stopped in to say hello, and after a good five or 10 minutes of conversing with Marge, they told her how pretty the LeSabre in the showroom looked. Marge proceeded to try to sell them the car. "They'd made it very clear to Marge that they weren't in the market, but Marge insisted she could give them the deal of the century," said Whelen. Meanwhile, one of the salesmen was in an adjacent sales office taking a credit application and closing the deal with a customer who had put down a deposit and agreed to buy that same car some 45 minutes earlier. The salesman came out to the car and placed a "Sold" ticket on the hood, which angered Marge.

MARGE: What are you doing?

SALESMAN: I've sold the car, Mrs. Schott. The customer is here in my office, and we have a deposit on it.

MARGE: I don't care what your customer's doing, I'm gonna sell to my friends here.

MARGE'S FRIEND: No, we're not buying this car. We'll come back in the spring when we are ready.

Marge's friends left the showroom, and the salesman's customer, indignant at Marge for trying to take the car away from him, stood up and demanded the money back and left, too. That, said Whelen, was "her way of doing business." No matter how much money Marge made, she could have made more if she'd been more appreciative or at least respectful of her employees. She would scream at them, berate them, refuse to give them enough leeway to do their jobs. "She is not a very good businessperson," said Whelen. "She has very little common sense when it comes to business savvy or conducting business personally."

Whelen remembers the morning a woman in a bright red coat was sitting in the service area, waiting on repairs for her car, and she stood up to stretch her legs and wandered into the showroom. Marge was in her upstairs, glass-fronted office overlooking the showroom and saw the woman all alone. Using what Whelen terms a "loud, rough voice," Marge got on the loudspeaker that could be heard dealershipwide and bellowed, "SALESMAN TO THE SHOWROOM! SALESMAN TO THE SHOWROOM!" Whelen knew the woman was just biding her time while waiting for her car. He signaled to Marge that the woman was being taken care of in service, and he went back into his office. Undaunted, Marge again took to the loudspeaker and boomed, "SALESMAN TO THE SHOWROOM! WHO'S TAKING CARE OF THE WOMAN WITH THE RED COAT?!"

"Now the woman with the red coat looked around, got very red in the face, kind of pulled her collar up, walked back into service, and was never seen again," said Whelen. "She got her car and left. She was so embarrassed that when she left, she never came back."

To work with Marge was to witness and experience a never-ending string of tales and anecdotes. Around 1977, Ron Taylor worked for her as a salesman at Schott Buick. Overall, he says, she treated him pretty well. She liked his father, another car man, and had hoped that he, too, would come to work for her. But Ron Taylor didn't last very long. One morning, he says, he got pulled over for a speeding ticket. When his name was run through the computer, there was a record of an old problem that actually involved a case of mistaken identity, and the police arrested him at the dealership showroom.

"I was in the showroom," said Whelen, "and Ron came in, and said, 'Dick, Dick, they're arresting me. Get a hold of my dad.' His dad was Milt Taylor, who was working at Columbia Olds, and I did call him right away. It took about a day to get his son out, to get the misidentification squared away. The funny part is, someone in the Schott organization drew a Thompson submachine gun on the piece of cardboard with the wording, 'Here sits Machine-Gun Ron Taylor' and put it up on the wall over his desk in the showroom. When Marge Schott came back from lunch, she glanced past the big grandfather clock and saw this paper hanging on the wall. She didn't really understand what it meant, walked about halfway up the stairs, and came back down and looked at the paper a second time, then went into [manager] John Moulliet's office and asked, 'John, what the hell's going on here?' She brought John out of his office, showed him what was on the wall, and it was taken down, and nothing more was said about it."

Except that when Marge learned what had happened to Ron Taylor, he was fired. "It cost me my job, even though she was sent letters by the police chief and the judge," said Taylor. "She did apologize later. She told my dad she was real sorry, and if I wanted to come back to work, I could. But I didn't because I got another job."

Sometimes worse than the tribulations with Marge were the trials. Dick Whelen ended up getting fired by her—three times, for the same reason. Sometimes he lent his demonstrator car to customers whose cars were being serviced—always reluctantly, because that left him without a car, but a manager would always approve it. His third and final firing came when Marge asked him for the keys to his demo car so that she could run some errands, and Whelen told her the car was out. Marge came back about 20 minutes later and said, "You're out of here. You're done." The other times, a manager would settle Marge down and call Whelen to tell him he was reinstated. When the call came this time, Whelen refused to go back. By the time Marge had told Whelen he was fired, his demo had been returned, so he took the keys and drove away. Whelen says he still had authority to drive the car, but one of the managers convinced him after a couple of weeks to bring it back, which should have ended his relationship with Marge right there. If only it were that easy. "She never paid me some of the commissions," said Whelen, "so I had to take her to court."

Whelen claimed he was owed commissions on about 20 deals and that Marge had changed the pay plan under which he'd been hired, altering the point where his commissions kicked in and affecting about 300 cars he had sold. In all, he asked for about $35,000. Whelen won the judgment, but only for about $300 and legal fees. "But it was a judgment," he said. "That, in itself, is significant. It was the principle."

Plus, he was away from her, and that, too, was significant. If it wasn't her domineering way it was her cheap manner, even on the little things. Those who worked with Marge at her dealerships said she couldn't stand to see a light or a radio or television turned on when nobody was in the room that second, a savings of virtual pennies. But she went beyond that—far beyond that. Dave Davis, a salesman at Schott Buick in the late '80s and early '90s, says Marge also would turn off the showroom floodlights that accentuated the gleam on the new cars and helped attract customers. And when she'd enter the dealership, she'd turn down the heat in the winter and turn off the air conditioning in the summer. It might have saved a few dollars in the short term, but it could translate into thousands lost from customers who'd rather not shop in 80- or 90-degree temperatures during the summer.

"We'd beat her to the punch," said Davis. "If we saw her pulling up, we'd turn the air off. That way, she didn't have the satisfaction of turning it off. Same with the heat. It was so funny. She'd stand there and look at it, acting like, 'It's cold in here—how could it be cold if this is off?'"

It didn't take long for Davis to understand that working with Marge would be, well, different. He'd been at the dealership about two days when he first met her, and he was warned not to speak to her. He was told that she had a reputation of either (a) not speaking to you, if you were lucky, or (b) saying something nasty to you. And when she came in, he watched most of the employees get nervous. But Davis ignored the advice and spoke to her, anyway, and he claims they've had a good relationship ever since. Not that he was enamored with her management style. He wasn't. Especially when it came to the way she treated some of her salesmen.

"There was an instance where a guy had sold a car, and he thought that he was doing the right thing—he went to Mrs. Schott and said, 'Oh, boy, look, I made you this much money,'" said Davis. "He had sold the car for the sticker price, which is what he's supposed to do. She didn't say another word to him. She went and got the paperwork, called the customer and told the customer, 'We owe you a refund.' And she took the salesman's commission. If you made money on a customer, she didn't want to know."

Now looking out for the customer has a certain charm to it, but Marge didn't seem to grasp that this was the way the business worked, the way it made money, the way her salesmen made a living. Davis remembers a time when the salesman had a "good rapport" with a customer until Marge came along and said, "I don't want you dealing with a salesman, because he's low on the totem pole. I want you to deal with John Moulliet, who's my vice-president"—and who worked on straight salary and not on a commission. The customer walked out. The salesman almost did, too.

Dave Davis also saw the other side of Marge. He genuinely liked her—and she, him—and she pleaded with him to come back after her general manager and brother-in-law, George Verkamp, fired him. Davis is also an African American, and although he doesn't doubt she has slurred blacks, he says he never heard it—the only questionable term being when she would go on about how people should buy American and not "Jap" cars. In fact, Davis found Marge to have a good relationship with blacks. She attended his wedding and sat next to Richard Walker, another African American and a long-time mechanic at Schott Buick, who absolutely swears by Marge. Walker says she attended his son's wedding even though it meant missing part of a Reds game, and Marge helped his relative overcome a problem securing a home mortgage loan. And when Walker attended a party at Marge's home and he told Marge it was his wife's birthday, she became upset that he hadn't told her earlier. "She then bent down on one knee in front of Anna and led everyone present at the party in singing, 'Happy Birthday,'" Walker said. "We are long-time friends, and there is more than a mere employee-employer relationship between us."

Indeed, there were times when Marge looked upon her employees as family, especially when it came to their families.

"She's a fascinating lady," Davis said. "I witnessed a gentleman come into the dealership who had lost his job, and he asked her for a job. He told her he was Catholic and told her he had a lot of children. She gave him a job and helped him back on his feet. She does a lot of good, but she doesn't ask or take credit for it. I've seen people come in from United Way saying that Marge had given a sizable contribution the year before, and they wanted to set up a meeting with her to get another contribution, and I helped set up the meeting. And with the customer, she can be grace in action. She'll say, 'Honey, if you don't think you've got enough money to buy this car, maybe you ought to start thinking about something else.' I think she's really concerned about the people."

From the moment Marge would enter the dealership, previous activity would pretty much cease and Marge would start working the room, honing in on the customers. She would pepper the prospective buyers with question after question about how they were being treated and insisted they let her know if the salesmen didn't do right by them. And if the customer complained, the customer was always right—even if the customer was wrong. "Unfortunately, she feels the people who work for her are deceiving the customer, that you're doing something wrong and you're the bad guy and the customer is the good person," Davis said. "In a lot of cases, the customer has gotten things that they normally would not have gotten because she believes the customer."

As a salesman, Davis had to learn how to use Marge correctly. He knew her name alone was a great lure for customers, that Schott Buick attracted independent women who thought of Marge as one of them, as well as baseball fans who wanted to deal with the owner of the Reds. He realized that her presence—not to mention her presents—could help clinch a deal. If the customer had children, Marge often would go out to her car and bring back Reds paraphernalia. "I knew that if she came in, nine times out of 10 I was going to close the customer," he said. "I would actually try to delay the customer until her arrival."

Her dogs were another matter. As popular as they might be, especially with children, her St. Bernards had a tendency to urinate in the showroom and Siegie would snap, all of which was embarrassing, if not dangerous. Fortunately, Marge brought them in during the day, when the showrooms were less crowded and devoid of kids.

Davis also knew Marge could be a problem even without the dogs, that she could screw up a deal if she stayed too long with a customer. "When she comes up to you and you're with a customer, you want her to hurry up and say whatever she's got to say and get her out of there, because she will say the wrong thing," said Davis. Other salesmen would just as soon Marge stayed away from their customers—and them. "She'd drive up in front of the place," said Larry Schwalbach, "and everybody would run the other way."

Usually, they had warning. As she made her daily rounds from business to business, someone from each of her stops would call the next destination and warn of her impending arrival.

At 100 Riverfront Stadium, to be certain, that would be greatly appreciated.

— Chapter Four —

Marge in Charge

Although Marge Schott announced her purchase of the Reds in December, baseball waited approximately seven weeks to approve the sale. Commissioner Peter Ueberroth said it was the first change of ownership in his tenure—that the owners were going to approve her quickly and almost matter-of-factly, and he found that unwise. His objections, he claims, were with the process and not with the candidate. "I felt that ownership should take their time and contemplate carefully who the new owner of every team was going to be," he said. "It was brought to me as a fait accompli."

Meanwhile, Reds president Bob Howsam was growing impatient. Even though his contract dictated that he would run the baseball operations for the Reds until July 1, and even though he received no indication that baseball had any problem with Marge Schott, he didn't like for the club to be put in limbo. While at a baseball meeting in New York, he approached Ueberroth about speeding up the process, and he pleaded his case for expediency to National League president Chub Feeney.

"Chub, this is a tough way to operate," Howsam said. "We don't have ownership. Why don't you go and approve her? I know nothing wrong with her. I've been at social events and a few things with her. It would seem to me we need approval to know where we stand."

Not long afterward, Marge Schott received approval. Howsam looks back at his push for her acceptance as owner, and he cringes.

"It was the worst mistake I ever made in baseball," he said. "She has made Cincinnati the laughingstock of baseball."

On February 7, 1985, Marge received word that baseball had approved her ownership of the Reds. That evening, when contacted by a reporter to get her reaction, she claimed that her dog, Schottzie, had become the topic of much of the conversation between Marge and Ueberroth when he congratulated her on the decision. "I told him he could have her first offspring," Marge said. "Now it's up to her to see how sexy she is." Marge also said she had not broken the news yet to her prized canine. "She just had dinner," the new owner of the Reds said, "and I didn't want her to throw up."

It didn't take long for Marge Schott and Bob Howsam to clash. Already, Howsam wasn't too thrilled about Marge's dog-and-phony show at her initial press conference, although he insists he was looking forward to working with her. But he knew he was in trouble just before Opening Day, when he went over the guest list with her for a Reds' party, which usually included such dignitaries as the mayor and the limited partners.

"I hit Johnny Bench's name, and she said no," said Howsam, referring to the celebrated catcher from the Big Red Machine. "I said, 'Marge, goodness gracious, here's a guy who's going to be in the Hall of Fame, he's done such a great job for Cincinnati, he lives in Cincinnati, that doesn't make sense.' At first, I thought she might be kidding. But she wasn't. She was vehement about that. Then came the Williamses, who she bought the club from, and she didn't want to have them, either. I was just shocked. So we didn't have Johnny Bench, but the Williamses I went and invited myself, anyway. She just treated them terribly after she got control of the club—as she did so many people."

Soon, Howsam became more and more offended by her taking credit for accomplishments actually made by others. There was the return of Pete Rose. The agreement on a new scoreboard. Even the lounge for the players' wives, which was the project of Howsam's wife. "We found a room not too far from the players' dressing room," he said. "Mrs. Janet Howsam got permission from the city to paint it and put furniture in it and did it up real nice so the children could play and the wives could sit and enjoy TV after a game. Marge told the wives she had done that. Again, another falsehood. She's taken so much credit for things she didn't do, it was unbelievable."

Marge took her turns at Howsam, however. He received a few late-night calls, the kind that became infamous in Reds annals, and Howsam recalled one that pretty much doomed their relationship some two months before he left.

"She was very irate because we had a very positive article in the paper about our promotions coming up for the season," Howsam said. "She called me up and said she didn't want articles like that in the paper anymore. I said, 'This is great. We're so pleased we can talk about the wonderful events and promotions coming up.' She said, 'I don't want any more of those kinds of articles. I want the people to think I need the money.'"

There it was, one of the great themes and greater cons of Marge Schott's tenure as owner of the Reds. Here she was, trying to apply the Depression-era tenets and teachings of her father to the Cincinnati Reds baseball team. Hardly a minute or a microphone would pass during her administration when Marge didn't cry poverty and insist the Reds could not pay competitive salaries or compete with the major markets—even as she continued to pay the millions and the team continued to profit on the field and off. *I want the people to think I need the money.* Howsam wouldn't buy this shell-game mentality.

"I said, 'Marge, I don't sell baseball on that premise. I sell it because it's fun, it's reasonable entertainment, and we have a good ballclub, and I am not about to change,'" said Howsam. "I slammed the phone down, and I don't think she spoke to me three or four times after that, unless she had to. But she might not have even remembered it the next day.She was a little tipsy. When she called you late in the evening, she always was. I read where Pete Rose said that's why you shouldn't talk to her after 10 p.m."

Marge's drinking and her use of ethnic and racial slurs were the two most obvious personal flaws effectively hidden from the public. Sure, there were rumors and hints and behind-closed-doors anecdotes. But unless you were around her, you didn't know for sure. Bob Howsam only had to deal with her for a few months, and because he was president and chief executive officer she wasn't around that much back then. Still, he experienced her drinking and he heard her use a slur. "I heard her make one remark about Jews that wasn't very complimentary," Howsam said. "I warned her, 'You don't say those kind of things.' I didn't realize it was a big problem with her. But I wasn't there very long."

Howsam lasted longer than Jerry Sullivan, the 72-year-old employee who used to run the press-room snack bar. In June, Marge got rid of him—and the snack bar. Too expensive. Marge said she wanted to run the Reds as efficiently as her other businesses. "I can't stand waste, and we've got to watch expenses," she said, "especially in a franchise like this." Jerry Sullivan's last day also marked the first game since 1983 that there were no fireworks for a Reds home run at Riverfront Stadium, although Marge preserved the display for home victories. "I think it was stupid that you couldn't tell the difference between a home run and a win," Marge said. "People in Kentucky didn't know if we had won a game or hit a home run. Besides that, the cost has escalated beyond belief."

Two weeks after that, and two weeks before he found sanctuary in a consultant's role, Bob Howsam and Marge Schott took their feud public for the first time in what might have been their most heated disagreement yet. Howsam hit Marge in her most vulnerable areas. He attacked her lies and her poverty with one verbal punch. Marge was claiming that she took over a financially distraught team that lost $4.5 million before taxes in 1984, but Howsam said the Reds actually ended up *making* $51,000. Howsam said the new figure came after the amortization of players, after signing bonuses were spread out over the length of players' contracts, and after settlements and interest were taken into account. Marge countered that the actual loss was more than $2.6 million and that Howsam was wrong. "That comes as a great surprise to me," she said. "If he wants to be a hero, fine. But it's just not true. This makes us look like lying fools."

Howsam insists that Chris Krabbe, the assistant for chief financial officer Lou Porco, told him about the profit, and Howsam even went back to Krabbe to double-check it before announcing it to the public. Krabbe told him that, yes, the team made $51,000. Porco was in New York at the time. "When I came back from New York, Chris was telling me about it and checking it out," said Porco, "and I said, 'You guys are right.'" Indeed, Marge's supposed loss was only on paper; Howsam's alleged gain was in cash—and in reality.

Although Howsam was accused of trying to show up his owner, he says he was trying to protect the management of the team and of Major League Baseball. Baseball was in the midst of labor negotiations, and he says he didn't want the union to use the Reds as an example of teams' trying to be deceptive by advertising huge losses when they actually made money. Once again, Howsam says, this fell into the category of Marge wanting people to think she needed money, and he didn't want any part of that. He says he wasn't trying to make her look bad, just tell the truth.

"If the truth hurts," said Howsam, "it'll have to hurt."

On July 1, Howsam left, and it probably wasn't soon enough for either the outgoing president or the disgruntled owner. But they weren't finished feuding. When Howsam was gone and in Arizona, he received a letter from Marge's attorney, Bob Martin, blasting him for extending the contracts on all of the Reds' scouts by another year before he left. Howsam claims it happened every spring—he rewarded the scouts by extending their three-year deals an extra year to ensure their security and the team's future—and he simply continued that tradition in the spring of '85.

"I wrote her back a letter saying that she would find out it was the best thing that had been done over the years to keep an organization sound," Howsam said, "and that I resented the fact that she was trying to make such a to-do about it."

Not that Marge had a great grasp of the importance of scouts. Even though she was publicly talking about relying heavily on the farm system, she didn't seem to comprehend that the scouts were the ones who located and evaluated the talent that would be drafted and signed, and she didn't appear to understand that cutting them down to one-year deals, as she would have preferred, could force them to look elsewhere for security. Bill Bergesch, the general manager and Howsam's heir apparent, remembers a comment that proves how little she really understood about the matter.

"What do we need all of these scouts for?" Marge asked Bergesch. "All they do is sit around and watch ballgames."

In retrospect, Bergesch said, "Sometimes you feel so sorry for her because she's like a duck out of water in so many ways."

Still, when Howsam left, Marge decided to get more involved, to annex Howsam's office at Riverfront and his titles of president and chief executive officer. She added the vice-presidency to Bergesch's general managerial title. Bergesch was not offended. In fact, he says he suggested she take Howsam's labels if she wanted to be active.

"I can't be more active than I am," Marge said when the changes were announced. "It's just the title 'president.' It's usually been held by most of the majority owners. Most titles will get you a loaf of bread."

Shortly thereafter, the other major loaf of bread went to Roger Blaemire, who became vice-president of business operations and marketing. At first, he simply was supposed to replace director of broadcasting Jim Winters, who had left just before Howsam did to join what would become a popular escape for former Reds employees, the San Diego Padres. Blaemire left his job as vice-president of marketing and broadcasting for the NBA's Indiana Pacers to take the job with the Reds and pursue a career in baseball, his first love, and the field of dreams of his father, former major leaguer Rae Blaemire. So Roger and his wife drove to Cincinnati to interview with Marge at Riverfront Stadium.

"She was nervous," said Blaemire. "She was chain-smoking, and she said she felt she was a woman in a man's world and that people were taking advantage of her and she needed someone who could help in the business portion of the team and protect her interests in baseball."

The interview lasted 10 or 15 minutes, basically ending when Marge asked if he was married, and he told her his wife was in the lunchroom. Suddenly, Marge was out the door, leaving Blaemire and Bergesch to make small talk for about a half-hour while Marge "flew into the room" and startled his wife, according to Maggie Blaemire, who grew admittedly nervous while Marge talked "a mile a minute."

MARGE: You're Roger Blaemire's wife.

MAGGIE: Yes.

MARGE: We really need him. Boy, we need him to help us turn things around. Boy, this is just terrible. We're losing money. We can't do this. We've gotta have him.

MAGGIE: He's the right person. If anybody can help, Roger definitely can.

MARGE: Well, come with me. I want to show you some of this.

Whereupon, Marge led her around to . . . the refrigerators.

MARGE: Look at all this food in here. Look
                at this waste of food. It would be
                better if I could just take it home
                and give it to the dogs. Don't you
                think so?

MAGGIE: Oh . . . well . . . yes, ma'am.

They were employees' lunches, but Marge didn't care, and Maggie didn't quite know what to make of it. When Marge wasn't rummaging through the refrigerators, she was showing Maggie Blaemire other points of interest. "She was upset because the coffee pot was left on and was wasting electricity," said Maggie. "She was, like, hyperventilating."

Roger would learn later that if someone left a lunch in there and Marge found it, odds were it was headed home for Marge's dogs. "You did not leave your lunch around there," said Blaemire. "If Marge got into the lunchroom, it was history." But when Marge was through touring the appliances with Maggie Blaemire on this day, she told Maggie that the job was between Roger and one other guy, but "I really like you." The phrase would come to haunt Maggie, because later on Marge would admit to anyone who asked that the reason she hired Roger Blaemire, the man who headed her business operations, was because she liked his wife.

It was a strange start to an unusual relationship between Marge Schott and the Blaemires. Not only did Marge quickly make Roger the head of her business side, she saw Roger and Maggie socially with a few others who would regularly get together. Marge could be a lot of fun and very funny, but the things that went into her mouth (alcohol) and came out (slurs and diatribes) often overshadowed all of that.

One night, Blaemire secured tickets for a Neil Diamond concert from a business connection who knew the singer's road manager, so Roger invited Marge's close friends Bonnie and Larry Paul and Marge to join them. The only request made by Roger's connection was that he get Diamond a Reds jacket. Roger bought two and had the names of the singer and the manager sewn onto their respective jackets. Now Roger knew that Marge being Marge, she would never cover such an expense—and that she would fume if the jackets weren't purchased at *her* gift shop, meaning the Reds' gift shop. One of Marge's favorite phrases, in fact, was "I am the Reds."

"When we got into the arena, I had to explain to Marge who Neil Diamond was," said Blaemire. "She had never heard of him. She wanted to make sure he wasn't 'one of those druggie groups.' The manager came over, and I gave him the two jackets. Marge wanted to know where I got the jackets, and fortunately I had the receipt."

The manager came back and gave them dozens of T-shirts, programs, pictures—probably $1,000 worth of merchandise. Blaemire said Marge never got into any of this, didn't seem to enjoy the choice seats, the souvenirs, the concert, or much of anything about the event—with one exception. "The only thing that excited her was when she saw two Reds jackets and worried if I had paid for them," said Blaemire.

Later, they all went back to the Blaemires' house in the upscale community of Mt. Adams, site of some of the city's better nightspots, and Marge questioned their choice of home sights. "Why do you live up here with all the whores and the pimps and the queers?" she asked. By this time, the Blaemires were used to this type of language from her.

"Over the course of the evening, she threw in a couple of other ones," Roger said. "The term 'nigger' was used. But it got to the point where it wasn't surprising anymore because it was done all the time. When you work with her all the time, that's the accepted way she talks."

Blaemire says she also has an alcohol problem. He knew because he used to fill up her glass for her. Over the course of an evening, she'd have a good half-dozen water tumblers filled half with vodka and half with soda.

"If there was vodka produced in this country, and Marge liked that certain label of vodka, I would definitely invest in stock in that company," said Blaemire. "That is the seed of her problem right there. She's a .400 hitter when it comes to drinking. But that doesn't put her in an elite class in baseball, either."

At Marge's Christmas party at her home, she asked her vice-president to act as bartender. She had one bartender but needed another, and, well, an employee was an employee. Marge also had Blaemire bring in the logs from outside and load them onto the fireplace, to keep the fire going. Blaemire remembers meeting a couple of former baseball greats, U.S. Rep. Jim Bunning and Ted Kluszewski, and one of them asked:

"Roger, what do you do?"

"I feed the fireplace."

"No, what do you really do?"

"I'm vice-president of the ballclub, but tonight I'm the bartender and I keep the fire going."

The next day, Bonnie Paul called Maggie and asked her if she would help take some of the prized decorations off the Christmas tree at Marge's house, some cherished heirlooms, and Maggie agreed. She thought it would be fun, kind of an informal get-together. Instead, when she got there, she was handed a vacuum cleaner and told to get started on the downstairs. Marge wasn't even there. And Bonnie was on the phone, taking care of things for Marge. So Bonnie and another friend of Marge's, Sally Sumerel, were left to do the bulk of the work so that Marge wouldn't have to pay a cleaning service.

If she wasn't going to pay that expense she certainly wasn't going to replace the old coal-burning furnace. When she had a problem, she had the same solution: Call the Blaemires. One night, she called Roger at 11 p.m. to come over and take care of it. "Her stoker on her furnace had clinkers in it again," said Roger. "We used to go out there and take all the clinkers out of her furnace and get the stoker working again."

Actually, it wasn't unusual for Marge to call right around the time the Blaemires would be sitting down to watch the nightly news. "She and Jerry Springer would appear at the same time," said Roger, referring to the local news anchor who later became a national talk-show host. And when she'd call, she was most likely drunk.

"She was most of the time that I ever saw her," said Maggie.

"She was drunk almost all of the time," said Roger. "She'd be three sheets to the wind on some afternoons, too. How did I know? Every time she lit a cigarette, she looked like Ollie the Dragon—she'd blow a flame across the room. You could smell it on her breath. She'd have personality changes. Depending on the situations, she'd flare quicker than she normally flared. And she flared all the time."

If Marge wasn't dialing up Blaemire for one of her late-night calls, she might have been targeting Bergesch. He got his share, but one in particular stood out.

"We talked for a half-hour, and she had gone over and over different things—*over and over*," said Bergesch. "I'd say, 'Yeah, Marge . . . Yes . . . Yes . . .' We hung up, and 15 minutes later, she calls me again and starts talking. I said, 'Marge, we just talked about that.' It didn't faze her one bit. We went through the whole thing again. Obviously, she didn't remember one bit about just talking to me 15 minutes before that for a half-hour."

Was she drunk?

"Well, I have to assume that," said Bergesch. "Those are the kind of things that make me feel sorry for her. I can just envision her sitting in that big house of hers, of which she only uses about one room, all by herself, pouring them down, and I feel sorry for her. I think, one by one, everybody that has ever been close to her has dropped her."

The Blaemires tried to get close to her and continued to see her socially. Often, that was because they had become friends with Marge's friends at the time, the Pauls and the Sumerels, and that meant Marge would be involved, too. Like Bergesch, the Blaemires felt sorry for Marge and found her to be a lonely woman who lived alone in a huge, cold house. She might let others in her door but not into her life, not for very long. She had a difficult time giving of herself and perhaps an even more difficult time giving *to* herself. On Thanksgiving morning, Roger Blaemire got into his car and drove out to her house, where she was sitting home alone, and he spent a couple of hours with her. Another time, Blaemire was over at her house one night and asked her where her television was because he wanted to watch the news. She steered him into the den.

"I go in there, and she has maybe the original color set manufactured in 1954," he said. "It couldn't even get a decent picture in black and white. It had rabbit ears. This was before UHF. It had 12 channels on it and a round color tube and the picture is *horrible.* I said, 'Marge, we've got to buy you a television set.' She said, 'Nope, don't spend the money.' I said, 'I've got one in my office.' So I took the 19- or 17-inch Sony out of my office and got one of the ballpark maintenance guys to take it out there, and I went out and hooked it up, got the rabbit ears, so she had a television set she could watch."

No matter how much money she had, no matter how little money she wanted her employees to spend, she probably spent less on herself than anyone or anything. Marge didn't know how to enjoy money. Her good friend Mary Clair Torbeck says that Marge finally broke down and got rid of the coal-burning furnace some years later. But she says Marge got rid of her place in Florida and wouldn't take any vacations, wouldn't take any time to get away from it all. "She deserves it," said Torbeck. "I wish she'd take time to go on a trip, relax a little bit. It's probably her biggest fault."

Blaemire remembers a time when he was with her in Florida, and he saw a side of Marge she often kept hidden. "I saw her cry when she looked at the apartments that she and Charlie used to own, " he said. "I was quite touched. That was a part of her life that was gone. She was very moved by that."

Then again, he also saw the more familiar side of Marge in Florida. They were checking out possible spring training locales, and Bergesch and the Pauls were there, too. After being entertained and courted by the Chamber of Commerce, the hotel bill came to $450, probably a fraction of what it should have been, and Blaemire put it on his credit card. A few days later, Bob Martin told him he had no authority to pay it, that the hotel should have given them the rooms at no cost, and that Marge was not going to reimburse him. Blaemire went to Lou Porco and got reimbursed, anyway.

Indeed, working with Marge became insufferable for Blaemire. The Reds had an organ player who would be hydraulically lifted above the field and play "Take Me Out to the Ballgame" during the seventh-inning stretch. Marge told Blaemire, "Let's get rid of the son of a bitch. He costs me $25 a ballgame." Blaemire said OK, the Reds could play tapes instead, and Marge went along with that. "She announces that over the winter and says it was my idea," said Blaemire, who became the target of fan anger. "Holy mackerel—the roof fell in on me. Suddenly, I was this cheapskate, cutting the prices. To make a long story short, we reinstated the organ player real quick."

When something played badly in the press or the public, it was always someone else's doing. When something went well, it was her idea. And if somebody else inside the organization got too much publicity, that meant trouble with the owner. "The joke inside the Reds was, if you want to lose your job, get between Marge and a camera," said Blaemire. In fact, Blaemire contends that when the Jumbotron scoreboard went in with its high-tech video screen, Marge ordered that she be put on camera at least once a game.

Honestly, that wasn't a bad idea. Marge was becoming a popular and familiar sight, anyway, and people would line up all game long to see her. She was an original—a Cincinnati original. Who ever heard of an owner doing what she did, signing auto-graphs throughout the games in her familiar seat alongside the Reds dugout, schmoozing with the fans, cussing and smoking and doing the wave and becoming as much a part of the atmo-sphere as the seventh-inning stretch? This was her glory. The fans loved her, and she loved the adulation. To Cincinnati, Marge was a local hero. She was everything the Williamses weren't, and even if that translated into chaos behind the scenes, it equated to charisma in the public eye. But she was also a national story. Owners just didn't do what she did. And so, she became one of baseball's most recognizable owners, right up there with the Yankees' George Steinbrenner and the Braves' Ted Turner—only different.

"I think more people can relate to Marge Schott than to George Steinbrenner or Ted Turner," said Reds broadcaster Marty Brennaman. "I mean their lifestyles are a thousand times more grandiose than hers is. While she may be, as they are, a very wealthy person, she doesn't portray that image. If there's such a thing as a blue-collar owner, I think Marge would fall into that category."

And even if she dressed in a Kmart wardrobe in the stands, she showed quickly that she was willing to let Bergesch and Rose go specialty shopping for high-priced merchandise. After a few years of lean budgets and leaner ballclubs under Wagner and the Williamses, the Cincinnati fans couldn't have been more appre-ciative of their new benefactor, even if she was a little quirky. In separate deals, Bergesch acquired third baseman Buddy Bell and catcher Bo Diaz, both with Marge's blessing. Added to the power supply provided by Dave Parker and blossoming young talent from the organization such as Eric Davis and Tom Browning, the Reds were able to make a mild run at the division title and finish in second place. With more prospects about to make the leap from the minors, Howsam and the scouts had the Reds well-stocked for the rest of the decade. "I don't think there's an owner in the history of sports who could have timed their purchase of a team as well as she timed the purchase of this one," said Brennaman.

The team rose in the standings and climbed more than half a million fans in attendance, surpassing the 1.8 million mark for 1985. Still, Marge took credit for reviving the franchise—Marge and Schottzie. She gave Pete Rose some credit, as well, while claiming she was the one who brought Pete back to Cincinnati. Actually, Rose had a lot to do with the renewed interest in Reds baseball, because he spent most of the 1985 season chasing one of baseball's most hallowed records, Ty Cobb's mark for most hits in a career. The pursuit of No. 4,192 engulfed the city in great box office and drama. The suspense was agonizing when, during the last game of a road trip, Rose had two hits in Chicago to tie Cobb and had two more opportunities to break the mark before the day was over. Blaemire made the mistake of calling Marge at her home after Rose hit No. 4,191. Marge, Blaemire said, was going "nuts."

"If that son of a bitch gets that base hit, I'm gonna kill him," Marge said. "If he gets that base hit in Chicago, he doesn't even need to come back to Cincinnati."

Actually, the Blaemires and all of Cincinnati felt the same way—at least about not wanting Rose to break the record outside of Riverfront Stadium. Rose did not end up breaking the record in Chicago, and when the Reds came back home for the next series against San Diego, the city was ready to celebrate his next base hit. The traveling media sideshow that had been following his exploits was now a full-fledged circus. Tickets to see the hometown hero's quest for immortality were hot, and the requests were numerous. Blaemire said one of Marge's relatives on the Schott side asked for four tickets. "Don't sell it to them," said Marge. "I don't want them in the ballpark." The limited partners were coming to the park, too, and they already had tickets. But if they wanted any more? "Don't sell them any," she told Blaemire.

"She wanted to be the center of attention with Pete," said Blaemire.

Commissioner Ueberroth and National League president Feeney also came for the festivities. Blaemire said he and Reds vice-president for marketing Bob Howsam, Jr.—the son of Marge's arch-enemy—traded tickets for the use of a limousine. When Marge found out about the limousine, she forced the commissioner and his wife and the league president to use a Schott Buick after the game. Meanwhile, Marge refused to serve the commissioner anything more than peanuts and pretzels in the owners' box. "Not even sandwiches?" Blaemire inquired. No.

"Marge, we've got the commissioner," Blaemire said.

"I don't give a damn," Marge said.

And if that wasn't bad enough, Reds limited partner Bill Reik and a number of others who were in the private box insist they witnessed Schottzie urinate on the commissioner's shoe. Ueberroth himself won't admit it, saying the dog was 10 feet away from him at the time. But he added, "I'm told that it was not an unusual performance for the dog. It was not a great dog."

Blaemire says Ueberroth was forced to give up the limo and ride in a Buick after the game—during which, by the way, Rose failed to break the record. Blaemire happened to meet up with the commissioner in the parking garage afterward. It was 45 minutes after the game when Blaemire walked out of the Reds' executive offices and into the virtually empty parking structure. He saw, two spaces down from his car, a certain Schott Buick. Inside, the commissioner was behind the wheel, the commissioner's wife was sitting next to him, and the league president was planted in the back seat. Why they were still there, he had no idea.

"Can I help you, Mr. Commissioner?" said Blaemire.

"Well, I don't know how to get out of the parking lot."

"No problem."

"Then I don't know how to get to the hotel."

"Just follow me. "

Ueberroth was not able to stay for the next game—the one that became so historical when Pete Rose broke the record and so hysterical when Marge Schott gave him a Corvette as a token of her esteem. Unfortunately, it was a token of somebody else's esteem.

"She led the public to believe that she donated the Corvette," said Blaemire. "I was there. I know the deal. It came from the plant in Bowling Green, Kentucky, where they build Corvettes—courtesy of General Motors."

Marge seemed so benevolent toward the players in public, hugging them and mugging with them and acting so maternal. Yet behind the scenes, she could be vicious. Take the case of Dave Parker. That first season was the year Parker, the team's Most

Valuable Player, was among the players implicated in one of baseball's ugliest incidents—the cocaine trials in Pittsburgh. Bergesch was working with Parker's agent, Tom Reich, on a way to keep Parker from missing time with the ballclub during the trial.

"We're paying this guy a lot of money," Bergesch told Reich. "I know he's got to go there, but we've got to reduce the time we lose him."

"Look," Reich told Bergesch. "we'll fly him back and forth if you let him go, and we'll pay for it."

So Parker agreed to pay to charter a plane going back and forth to Pittsburgh for the few days he was needed there. When Bergesch tried to explain the agreement to Marge, she didn't get it. For one thing, she didn't seem to grasp that this would be at Parker's expense, not the club's. Marge didn't want to go for it at first, saying she didn't want to do it for Parker.

"I guess that was one of those times when she referred to him as a 'million-dollar nigger,'" said Bergesch. "She called him a 'million-dollar nigger' not only then but on several other occasions."

"I was standing there when she said it," said Blaemire. "She would refer to him that way commonly. When she talked about the 'million-dollar nigger,' she was referring to Dave Parker. And she always referred to Eric Davis as the 'trouble-making nigger.'"

"That's accurate," said Bergesch.

Marge could not refer to Davis as a "million-dollar nigger" because he wasn't making a million dollars then. That slur would come later. Blaemire said the "trouble-making" designation stemmed from Davis successfully pushing the Reds to switch from black shoes to red shoes.

"That was the way she felt about it," said Bergesch. "But let's face it. If you have a Parker and a Davis and a Kal Daniels, and they all come to you in a body, you've got to listen. They thought it would brighten things up. They thought the black shoes were drab, not in keeping with our red and white uniforms. And I have to admit, the shoe man brought out some samples, and I thought they looked attractive with our color scheme. Pete liked it, too. So we went to Marge with it. She went along with it, but she felt these guys were rabble-rousers about it and they were stirring up things."

Bergesch says he can't remember if that was one of the times Marge referred to Davis as a "trouble-making nigger." But it might have been.

"She used it on several occasions," he said. "She talked so much like that, that I never really paid much attention to it. I heard her do it so many times. I don't think she said those things with any vengeance, I think it was just the way she talked. She didn't know how to say good things about people, so she'd just say bad things about them. Everybody was a 'Jew bastard' or a 'trouble-making nigger' or a 'Jap' or something."

One of Marge's ethnic slurs would begin the end for Roger Blaemire. It is a story to which he later swore in a legal deposition:

"We were putting a deal together that involved TicketMaster coming into the Cincinnati market. TicketMaster was going to come in from the Indianapolis office. I had been vice-president of the Indiana Pacers in the NBA prior to joining the Reds. The owners of the Pacers are Herb and Mel Simon, who are big shopping-center developers around the United States. They also held an interest in TicketMaster. The manager of the Indianapolis office wanted to expand to Cincinnati and asked me if he could come and visit with us and talk about doing some type of a deal. I said, yes, we certainly will if it's in our benefit. We were able to structure a deal that brought TicketMaster in as a ticket seller at various locations for the Cincinnati Reds and for other venues around Cincinnati. The Reds, in turn, for dealing with TicketMaster, would receive a percentage of every ticket sold in the Cincinnati marketplace, be it Riverbend [an outdoor concert site] or wherever the tickets were purchased for.

"I was walking Mrs. Schott through this deal—and the deal could probably result in hundreds of thousands of dollars over a period of time—and she said, 'Why are you doing this?' I said, 'Marge, it is going to make you and the Reds a lot of money,' and I tried to explain to her how the deal worked. She got mad, and she said, 'I don't want to be dealing with those guys you work for, those Jew bastards.' I said, 'Mrs. Schott, don't ever refer to the Simons that way again. Those are good people. You have no reason to talk like that or say that about them. The only thing they are guilty of is putting us into a business deal where you are going to make more money.' She didn't understand anything. And that's how she referred to Jewish people, either as 'Jew bastards' or 'dirty Jews,' and she didn't want any part of them."

Big Red Machine second baseman Joe Morgan, who was doing analysis on television for the Reds at the time and later was elected into baseball's Hall of Fame, was another target of Marge's slurs behind his back—which is her modus operandi. To Marge, the diminutive Morgan was "the little nigger."

"She always wanted to know, 'Is the little nigger in town?'" Blaemire said. "Anybody that drew any attention away from her concerning the ballclub, she took personal offense to. She felt, as the general partner of the Reds, she should get the attention, not ex-ballplayers. She really disliked Johnny Bench and the attention he got. She canceled the Johnny Bench scholarship set up by the Reds when Bench retired. In the fall of 1985, when it was time to contribute to that scholarship in Bench's name, I asked her about it, and she said, 'We're not going to contribute to that.' She did not like Bench at all. She didn't like him around the ballpark, and he was around the ballpark all the time."

Still, Marge targeted just about everybody at some time or another.

Pete Rose? They had a strange relationship, two public figures on the opposite end of the baseball knowledge meter, one deriving popularity from years of success, the other trying to feed off of it for her own celebrity while establishing herself as top dog.

"She didn't like him," said Blaemire. "She'd say, 'Why did they have to name a damn street after Pete Rose?' She never had a good word to say about Pete Rose behind his back. Never. She'd say he costs too much money. And she wasn't sure how much he knew about baseball—now that's a great statement. And, without saying it, she was always threatened by him because she knew he was more popular than her."

Joe Nuxhall? The radio broadcaster and former Reds pitcher known affectionately as the "Ol' Lefthander" was as cuddly a figure as you'd find in Cincinnati, but she didn't like the attention he could command. "She didn't like him pitching batting practice because she thought he had no business being in the clubhouse," said Blaemire.

Tom Browning? The first-year pitcher became the first rookie in the major leagues to win 20 games since Bob Grim with the New York Yankees in 1954. And though he was succeeding rather quietly amidst the glare of some of the other players and the new owner, he was offered the use of a pickup truck for a year in exchange for doing commercials for a local Chevrolet dealer in

Florence, Kentucky. Nothing unusual about that, except that the dealer was not Marge Schott. Blaemire walked in Bergesch's office one day and heard the general manager trying to reason with her on the phone, then later that day witnessed Marge continue the harangue when she arrived.

MARGE:	If he does a commercial for another dealer, you trade him.
BERGESCH:	Why don't you have Tom do that for you?
MARGE:	Why? I do the commercials.

In the end, Blaemire says Browning canceled the arrangement with the Chevrolet dealer, but not before the incident became public. In fact, a series of Marge's foul-ups, bleeps, and blunders met the press right about the same time. She was accused of threatening to release catcher Dave Van Gorder if he won his salary-arbitration case. ("Someone made that quote up," she said. "I don't even know how to spell arbitration.") She also said Rose lacked class. ("Oh, that was just some Kentucky writer. You know how they are.") And she told a group in Indianapolis, a city craving a major-league team but part of the Reds' fan base, that Indy would get a franchise "over my dead body." ("I was just kidding.")

The latter was one of Marge's favorite outs. She covered up her slips of tongue by saying that her humor was misunderstood. Roger Blaemire was there. He claims she was not joking about her comment to the Indianapolis group, and an embarrassed Blaemire left the room after she said that. Actually, going back to Indiana was always a little awkward for Blaemire. To those who didn't know what it was like working for Marge, it was a little difficult explaining how the job was going. To those who did, it could be even more uncomfortable. Months before Marge's "over my dead body" proclamation, she asked Blaemire to approach Indianapolis businessman Arthur Angotti, who was looking into bringing Major League Baseball to Indianapolis, about buying a share of the Reds. Blaemire knew him and called him, and Angotti replied, "I wouldn't let Marge Schott handle five cents of my money, let alone a million dollars. I know Marge Schott."

Blaemire understood. The more he was around Marge at the office, the more he saw an owner who had little business sense and maybe less common sense. He calculated that he made her in excess of $2 million in new revenue during his time there, and he estimates that if somebody "competent" replaced her, the Reds could gross another $5 million more annually. If the Reds became lucrative under Marge, it was more a combination of the staggering riches accorded baseball by the national television contracts, an increase at the gate because of improvement by the team, and some good people working under Marge than anything Marge ever did.

For one thing, Marge refused to allow any automobile dealer other than herself to be involved with the Reds. That meant no more trading Reds tickets to dealerships for the use of their automobiles—the company cars had to be Schott cars. And if other dealerships wanted to advertise with the team, good luck. "I was told not to accept any kind of advertising from any automobile dealer in the Cincinnati area, other than herself," said Blaemire. "Eighty-five was the last time any other dealer got in there with cars."

Other times, Blaemire tried to explain prospective business deals to Marge, and she couldn't follow them. She reacted quickly, emotionally, without ever understanding what he was trying to do for her or the money she would be earning. For instance, Marge never seemed to grasp that the deal between her and TicketMaster would not only provide Marge with revenue on Reds tickets but on other events in the city, as well. All she could comprehend was that the deal was through the Simons.

"After about 30 seconds of explaining a deal, normally she'd say, 'I don't like this, I don't want to do it, I don't care what it is' and explode," said Blaemire. "She has absolutely no attention span."

And her memory wasn't much better. Whether out of convenience or reality, Marge would lose track of deals and promises, and if people were hurt in the process, then that was their problem. Employees were expenses, and expenses could always be cut. She would often refer to them as "the help" or "the bodies," even right to their faces, as though they weren't human. "We were like pod people, sort of," said Keith Stichtenoth.

And she never let them forget it.

—— Chapter Five ——

Dollars to Doughnuts

M aybe it wasn't fair that Dick Wagner had to follow
Bob Howsam as the head of day-to-day operations when Howsam semi-retired into consultancy
the first time, just as it wasn't fair that Marge Schott had to follow
him the second time. Certainly someone new could be an effective manager and still cut some of the Howsam extras in the name
of fiscal conservatism. Anyone replacing "Santa Claus," as ticket-
office worker Keith Stichtenoth likened him, was bound to look
a little like Scrooge because of the way Howsam spoiled those
who worked for him. So maybe it would be wrong to compare
Marge to Scrooge.

"She makes Scrooge look like a piker," said Roger Blaemire.
Marge took the morale inside the Reds' offices, which had
been so inflated by the return of Howsam and the revival of the
ballclub, and she effectively stuck a pin in it. Where Howsam
provided the little things that made them feel appreciated, Marge
took those away and didn't stop until their dignity followed.
Remember, these were not the millionaires in uniform before the
public eye; these were folks who worked upwards of 16 hours a
day for wages far below those in the real world. They stayed
because they loved the glamour of being in baseball, and they
deserved at least a little stroking in return. Howsam realized that.
Even if it was just providing some facial tissues as a courtesy to
the employees, it meant something to them. It wasn't necessarily
interpreted as a pat on the back when the extras were there, but

it was considered a slap in the face when they were suddenly canceled.

"Believe me, these were not Kleenex—this was the bad stuff," said Stichtenoth. "They're the cheapest that money can buy, and the company used to supply them. We had a couple boxes of those in each department until she stopped stocking those."

Granted, that might not sound like much. Neither might raising the price of the pop machines . . . Or discontinuing the exchange of Reds tickets for Kings Island amusement park passes for Reds employees . . . Or firing the part-timer with the aluminum walker who checked credentials at the stadium for minimum wage to supplement his Social Security . . . Or talking about running the front office with volunteers from the Rosie Reds boosters ("We've got all these women, why don't we put them to work," Marge told Blaemire.) . . . Or looking into putting the grounds crew on standby . . . Or turning down the heat in the winter or the air conditioning in the summer in the front office . . . Or scrutinizing the postage meter ("She wanted to know who the hell was running private mail through the postage meter," said Blaemire.) . . . Or keeping autographed baseballs locked up and forcing the staff to charge business associates for them ("If I wanted to give a sponsor a dozen autographed baseballs, and the sponsor is spending $300,000 a year, I have to charge $4.50 a baseball," said Blaemire.) . . . Or rummaging through the wastebaskets to check for, uh, waste ("She'd come in and check the wastebaskets to see if people were using both sides of the scratchpads," said Blaemire.) . . . Or taking the doughnuts left over from the annual opening day of group sales and trying to sell them to the front office at about 35 cents apiece ("I don't know that the best way to make money and endear yourself to the people who need to work for you is to take the leftover doughnuts and sell them to the staff," said Stichtenoth. "I can't quite imagine Bob Howsam doing that.") . . . Or freezing salaries . . . Or questioning the complimentary tickets ("She cut back on the passes to employees, and she cut back on the passes to sponsors," said Blaemire.) . . . Or questioning if not denying so many expenditures that it became counterproductive ("If you start scrutinizing every damn item, you'll never get anything done," said Lou Porco. "You've got to trust people.").

Put all of that together, and it showed a general disregard and distrust of the people who worked for the Reds behind the scenes. This was nothing like what they had experienced under Bob Howsam. And she would scream at them, belittle them, and even throw things at them.

"I don't know somebody's coming my way until they're in my office doorway," said Stichtenoth. "One day, she came in unannounced—she always comes in unannounced—she didn't say anything to me, and she picked up a pencil and threw it at me from three or four feet away and hit me in the chest. Then she just turned around and walked out without any acknowledgment. A little snapshot of life with the Reds."

Was she joking?

"No."

Angry?

"No."

Then why did she do it?

"It was like I wasn't there, or I wasn't a person, or I wasn't worth acknowledging."

Usually it was just words that came flying at her employees like an endless stream of projectiles. And though her racial and ethnic slurs would capture the headlines years later, they paled in comparison to the everyday abuse she launched at those inside the Reds.

"You weren't just a worker, I felt like you were a damn slave," said Porco. "There are people who crap in their pants when she walks by. I'm not that way because I'd just pounce on her."

Still, Porco wasn't going to put up with this. After a quarter-century with the Reds, through all the changes in ownership and the turnover in personnel, this man who had turned down a request to interview with the new Disney World in the mid-'70s decided it was time to get out in 1986. Seven years later, as he was about to turn a young 70, he admitted he still would have been there if Marge had not.

Some of the things Porco saw he felt just weren't right. Take the time Bob Howsam, Jr., submitted a business expense that Marge denied.

MARGE: You tell him that we're not paying that bill. He has to pay it out of his own check.

PORCO: You can't do this. This is business.
                In business, you pay it and you tell
                the guy you don't do it again. I'm
                not going to take it out of his
                paycheck. I'll tell him what you
                said, but I'm not taking it out of his
                paycheck. That's not ethical.

The fact that it was Bob Howsam, Jr., probably didn't help matters. She was not big on anything with the Howsam name, for all intents and purposes closing up the owners' box better known as the "Howsam Box" and congratulating herself for sitting among the common folks. And here she was saddled with Bob Howsam, Jr.—or "R.J." as he was better known—whom Bob Sr. had brought in to help revitalize the marketing end when the old man returned for his second stint running the team. R.J. "brought us into the '80s" in season-ticket sales, said Stichtenoth, by recognizing the team's regional attraction and instituting partial season-ticket plans that involved weekends.

"He was an outstanding young man who didn't deserve the kind of treatment that he was receiving there," Bergesch said. "I don't think she wanted him to have any freedom at all, to spend any money on promotions. And he'd be downtown at lunch with somebody trying to work a promotion or sell a ticket deal, and she would wonder why he wasn't in his office. 'He's supposed to be in his office from 9 to 5.' It was almost inevitable that he wasn't going to last very much longer, mainly because his name was Howsam and she wanted to have some of her own people that she picked."

Howsam. It was a name that made Marge seethe and a memory that left Reds employees that much more disgusted with Marge's management style.

"Given Mr. Howsam and his reputation in the game and what we now know to be the case about Mrs. Schott," said Stichtenoth, "I doubt that you could possibly come up with a greater bounce on the class meter. The needle went 180 degrees."

Reds broadcaster Marty Brennaman says that when Marge and Howsam clashed, it put Marge in a no-win situation considering how beloved he was, and employees were bound to line up on his side. Even Stichtenoth, who had so looked forward to the arrival of Marge as a possible refreshing change, became disgusted with what he was seeing. He says the mood with Marge that started with, "This is going to be great," became "Oh, this doesn't look so great," fell to "Oh, my God, what have we gotten ourselves into?" and landed at "This is how life is." It was a process that went from delight to disgust, from dehumanized to desensitized.

It was the only way to survive.

Even the positive side of Marge became a negative for her staff. Her emphasis on the fans, so genuinely appreciated in the stands of Riverfront Stadium, became an obsession that could be taken out on a moment's notice on the workers inside the Reds' offices. Just as she would berate her automobile salesmen in public and always side with the customers, Marge would do the same with the patrons at Riverfront at the expense of her own people.

"The customer is always right, business preaches," said Stichtenoth. "But where tickets are concerned, there's lots of room for all kinds of things to happen. We're pretty good at what we do, so often times if there's a disagreement, the customer's not right, but you still take care of him. But anytime something like that would happen, and the customer was in the wrong, it didn't make any difference. When she was confronted with a fan, she would bow down and put on the charm act for them, which is fine, but she would also insult the employee who was involved."

The missing link here was diplomacy.

When it came to her front office, she had none.

"She is almost Jekyll and Hyde in personalities," said Blaemire. "I've seen her sit there and sign autographs and smile and pat little kids on the head then walk into the business office and rip some unsuspecting employee who might have left a Coke can someplace or whose hair was too long or who didn't have the right answer for her."

Marge was not big on long hair. Dave Davis, her former salesman at Schott Buick, remembers one male employee at the dealership who sported hair down his back. She told him, "It's time to get a haircut." When he said no, he was fired. The guy gave in, but he was told it was too late.

About the only one with long hair that Marge tolerated was the one whose leash was real instead of in her mind—Schottzie. The dog could relieve herself on the field, in the elevator, in the office, and Marge wouldn't mind. To Marge, Schottzie was every bit as big a part of the Reds as the players were. Maybe more. And certainly more glamorized. While so many expenses were cut back and so many pennies hoarded, Marge turned downright generous when it came to doling out money to promote the dog.

"She came to me and said, 'I want to do something with Schottzie; I'd like to have a calendar,'" said Blaemire. "I called a printer I'd worked with when I was with the Pacers, and he laid out a 12-month Schottzie calendar that she wanted to sell at the gift shop and the ballpark. We got the proofs, and after we changed the pictures two or three times, we got them. He printed them and delivered them. She didn't like them—and wouldn't pay him. I don't know if he ever got paid. We also ordered Schottzie hats, with the big flaps on the sides like ears. I was a God-damned shill—a court jester playing to a dog."

If not Schottzie hats and Schottzie calendars, then Schottzie pencils. And if the sales brochure didn't have enough Marge and Schottzie to go along with the pictures of Pete Rose, changes had to be made. While nobody denied that the dog could be a good promotional gimmick and was a favorite with the kids, to a front office that had to be wondering when the pay toilets would be installed, this open checkbook for the dog was not exactly helping employee relations.

But the front office was not the only area to face the owner's cost-slashing tactics. The scouts, so coddled and cared for during Howsam's regime that they spurned overtures for higher positions from other clubs, suddenly were treated as expense accounts. Marge put them into smaller cars, instructed them not to make phone calls from hotel rooms because of the service charge, and refused to reimburse them for laundry, even for scouting trips that lasted weeks on end. More than that, they went from being consulted and feeling appreciated under Howsam to sensing they were being ignored by the new owner, who insisted on getting her hands on departments for which she had no feel.

"She was just ignorant as far as baseball was concerned," said former Reds scout Chet Montgomery. "She wanted to get involved, and it was typical of a lot of ownership at that time, in that they have large egos and want to satisfy that more than help the organization. From Day 1, most everything from her was negative and concerned with upping her own image. Had she put baseball people in charge and stayed out of the decision making, she might have had a chance to learn it, step by step. Instead she went full-force right into it, and every time she said something or did something, she would put her foot in her mouth. So it went from bad to worse.

"The majority of people who took a lot of pride in what had happened there through the years now were just slapped in the face and told, in so many words, 'You work, and we'll make the decisions. We don't want your input.' So people eventually started looking. It wasn't too hard to find. I don't know of anybody during that time that left and didn't get a better job."

Montgomery, who had been with the Reds since 1968 and worked his way up to a position as one of the team's three national cross-checkers, left to become scouting director with Cleveland in 1988. Other big names in the scouting field left about that time, too, including Chuck LaMar, George Zuraw, Mickey White, and Don Mitchell. But nobody should have been surprised that they bolted, after the most surprising of defections occurred the previous year, when Larry Doughty, the Reds' scouting director, announced in September that he would quit at the end of November. The cuts in the scouts' expenses bothered him, but the potential cuts in the number of scouts drove him away. The scouts were under contract through the end of 1988, but he was unable to get their contracts extended another year, and he hoped that someone else could. Normally a quiet company man, he hoped his parting words would have an impact on the owner. "I'm not concerned about educating the public," Doughty said. "I'm concerned about educating management."

Doughty became assistant general manager and eventually general manager with Pittsburgh. Even six years after announcing he was finished with the Reds organization, he was not one to look back at what happened to him—at least not publicly. "From the day I left the Reds," he said, "I made a vow to myself never to talk about the owner of the Cincinnati Reds again."

For Bergesch, life with Marge was an unusual experience, too, but at least he was used to dealing with somewhat off-center ownership. He had worked under Charles Finley with the then-Kansas City Athletics and under George Steinbrenner with the New York Yankees before toiling under Marge with Cincinnati, which is baseball's equivalent to switching physicians from Dr.

Howard to Dr. Fine to Dr. Howard. But Bergesch says they had one thing in common: People might have said they were crazy or mean, but they all had the ability to charm you, and they all were brilliant in their own ways. Marge, he says, was not dumb, although she might act that way at times with "that little-girl, innocent face." Don't let that fool you, he warns. Give her a financial statement, and she can decipher it quite adeptly and impressively. The problems came in areas she didn't understand—such as baseball.

Take travel, for instance. Once, after the Reds played a night game in Cincinnati, the team left after the game for Pittsburgh, where the Reds would play the Pirates the following evening. The next morning, Marge called Bergesch wanting to know what in the world they were doing in Pittsburgh. The game wasn't until that evening, and she didn't need to be spending money putting them up for the night if everybody could fly in the day of the game. Bergesch tried to reason with her. He told her that this protected against the possibility of bad weather, of the hotel rooms not being ready when the players checked in, and of forcing everyone to mill about or rush around when they should be settled in and relaxed before heading to the ballpark.

"She couldn't understand that," Bergesch said. "She wanted us to give some thought to leaving on the morning of the game in the future, and we said we would. Pete and I talked about it and decided we didn't want to do that. In fact, further proof of the very thing we're talking about happened with Joe Nuxhall and Marty Brennaman because they didn't come in until the day of the game—I'm talking about this very same episode. They flew in the next morning, and when they got there, sure enough, their rooms weren't ready. They got in about 11 in the morning and had to sit there and twiddle their thumbs until 2. I asked her, 'What if we were going to have a whole lobby full of players who can't get in their rooms?' So we talked about it and decided we were going to keep traveling that way."

That time, Bergesch won out. But explaining baseball to her was as difficult as trying to teach her that sometimes you had to spend a few dollars to make a lot of money. It came as no surprise therefore, that when she met the granddaughter of Reds Hall of Famer Edd Roush during the spring of 1986, she hadn't heard of the player who had been named the greatest Red of the team's first century. But two springs later, after three years as an active owners of the Reds, she didn't even know the teams in her division, the National League West.

QUESTION: Who's your main competition this year?

MARGE: Well, I hope it's St. Louis. Because that would be a fun match. We're so much alike, we really are. Except you won't be able to tell us from our uniforms. We'll all get mixed up.

QUESTION: I mean in the division race.

MARGE: Let me see. I don't know. Maybe the Kansas City Royals.

QUESTION: No, I mean within *your own* division.

MARGE: Within our own? Well, Pittsburgh's got some young ones coming. And Los Angeles is going to come back. It's just hard to say, because I think we could have a lot of surprises this year.

Again, it is excusable that the first time Marge met new Reds farm director Branch Rickey III, grandson of the legendary Brooklyn Dodgers executive who brought in Jackie Robinson to break the color barrier, she told him, "Your grandfather was a great player." But what about the time she and Bergesch were standing in her office, and she looked out at the field and saw "Davis" on the back of a visiting player and thought it was Eric Davis?

MARGE: What's Davis doing in that Pittsburgh uniform?

BERGESCH: Marge, we're playing the Giants, and that's not *our* Davis, it's *Chili* Davis.

The trick for Bergesch and Rose was to keep Marge informed of what they were doing and make her feel involved while keeping control at least of the matters on the field. In 1986, Bergesch continued to make the type of moves that earned him The Sporting News' prestigious designation as 1985 National

League Executive of the Year, solidifying the pitching staff by acquiring high-priced John Denny and Bill Gullickson. Suddenly, Marge's guarantee near the end of the 1985 season that the Reds would reach the World Series in 1986 looked profound. But the team got off to a miserable start, and Marge couldn't stop being Marge. Twenty minutes before her team's 20th game, with the Reds an inexplicable 4-15, Marge called Rose in the clubhouse. She had a priest with her, and she wanted him to lead the Reds in prayer. The Reds lost anyway, 7-2 to the New York Mets, Cincinnati's 12th loss in 13 games.

"Geez, if I had someone who could turn us around, doesn't she think I'd have him in here right away?" Rose said afterward, reflecting on her pregame antics. Rose then paused and muttered, "Marge, Marge."

By then, Roger Blaemire was muttering that and much worse. The day before Opening Day, he was given the word the way it usually came down, from Marge's attorney, Bob Martin. He was fired. Blaemire had figured his tenure wouldn't be long after the fight over her slurring the Simons, and he was so certain he wouldn't last that he had put his house up for sale in January— the one he had occupied since September. Blaemire, who worked on commission as well as salary, said he was owed more than $100,000.

BLAEMIRE: Bob, why don't you pay me half of what I'm owed at this point, according to your numbers, and half after the season's over. That way, I'll have some money, because I'll probably have to move to get another job.

MARTIN: We're not gonna pay you anything.

BLAEMIRE: You're gonna pay me now, or you're gonna pay me later, but you're gonna pay me. I earned it, and you owe it.

The case ended up in court. Marge accused Blaemire of making deals without authorization. Blaemire was not only outraged by her actions but amazed by her reaction to a local TV deal he worked out that also allowed radio voices Marty Brennaman and Joe Nuxhall to do some TV work.

"I make her a quarter of a million dollars off of a redone television deal, and I give Marty and Joe a $15,000 raise each," said Blaemire. "So she comes out of it netting $225,000 to $230,000, and in my lawsuit she countersues me for their raises. She countersued me saying I had stolen money from her."

Blaemire ended up winning the first round in court, and Marge appealed. The case dragged on and on until they ended up settling out of court some five *years* after Blaemire first lost his job. By then, Blaemire was long since forgotten, another former face where so many more had followed. Meanwhile, it was five years for the legend of Marge to grow, five years for Marge to establish herself as an institution. In the high-profile world of baseball, front-office types such as Blaemire were a few lines of type when they came and a few more lines when they left, but Marge was a headline and a photo opportunity wherever she went, whenever she spoke. A month after Blaemire was gone, he was as memorable as a dot on a test pattern, while Marge was being seen on full screen with the hippest TV personality of the time, David Letterman.

Marge flew to New York to do the show, "Late Night with David Letterman," but it was left to Bonnie Paul to drive Schottzie from Cincinnati for the appearance. Bonnie was Marge's friend who had volunteered to help from the time Marge first bought the team. Bonnie would answer her mail, walk the dog, travel with her, go to games with her, go to dinner with her, attend meetings with her, you name it. "Rarely did you see one without the other," said Blaemire. What began as an act of friendship, Marge turned into an excuse for servitude. Even though Bonnie wasn't getting paid until just before she decided she'd had enough of Marge, Marge talked to her as she talked to any of her employees.

"With disdain," said Blaemire.

"One by one, she has lost her good friends," said Bergesch. "One by one, they would just disappear because, sooner or later, she would just hurt them to the point that they wouldn't want to be friends with her anymore."

For Bonnie Paul, it took a few years before she left. Being around Marge had meant so much to her. Indeed, if the Reds became Marge's identity in the city, then Marge became Bonnie's. And Bonnie felt as though she was helping Marge, even protecting her when so many were just waiting to take advantage of the rich widow living alone in a huge house.

"I love her," Bonnie said just before Marge's first season. "She is so stimulating. She knows so much and so many people. Her energy is boundless. From morning to night, she's all business. I wish sometimes she'd stop and smell the roses. But there are doers, and there are those who sit around and gripe. She's a doer."

So Bonnie would be a doer for Marge, even if it meant doing half a country in a car with Schottzie to get the dog to New York for Letterman. But they made it, and Marge and the dog produced one of the classic highlights in Letterman lore. For 12 minutes, it was vintage Marge, a straight line in waiting if ever there was one for the sarcastic comedian. The most memorable moment, though, came when she started to explain how you could tell if a dog was pregnant.

MARGE: They say if their nipples get large . . .
LETTERMAN: Marge!
MARGE: This is a dog.
LETTERMAN: I know, I know. And I don't want to
            hear any more about your damn
            dog. I'm sorry I brought up the dog.

It was a humorous moment and an entertaining segment seen by the nation; it was also a news story back in Cincinnati. The *Post* sent Jay Mariotti, who in only a year in town in his first job as a columnist had already established himself as the most controversial and fearless voice in the city. He flew to New York to cover Marge's appearance, and he wanted to get her reaction about it afterward. She had to attend an owners' dinner after taping the show, but she agreed to talk to him later—later turning out to be shortly after midnight and about 20 minutes before the tape of the show would hit the airwaves. That was fine, considering *The Post* was an afternoon newspaper. But when she finally called Mariotti, she was enraged.

"She was very upset and emotional on the phone," Mariotti said. "She proceeded to criticize Letterman in every way possible. She was trashing Letterman to shreds. The things she was saying were almost nonsensical at times. I don't know if I can say she was drunk. I do know I was having a hard time talking to her on the phone."

She was all over the place, ripping Letterman for asking too many "tough" questions and not enough "human" questions, for dwelling too much on the team's poor start and too little on her role in reviving the team. She also blasted the producer for being rude in ignoring her picture of Schottzie and President Ronald Reagan, and she chastised the band for breaking its vow not to perform while Schottzie was on the set.

Marge Schott also took off on "the Jew director."

Mariotti warned her about what she was saying and advised her to rethink her words. Marge told him she wanted to see the show, and they decided to talk again after she had. They did, and it was a kinder and gentler Marge Schott this time.

"That wasn't bad at all, was it?" she said. "I guess I was maybe nervous because I knew the owners were watching, the team was watching, people at home were watching, everybody was watching. But I'm satisfied. I'm glad I did it now. Write it that way, will you please? And forget all that other stuff I said."

Mariotti wrote some of the things she said in their initial conversation, but decided to leave out her ethnic slur. "I more or less did her a favor," he said. "I bailed her out." In retrospect, he wishes he'd had more time to think about it, to consult with his sports editor, instead of having to make a snap judgment. He realized his assignment was to write a column about Marge Schott appearing on the Letterman show, and that this was not simply a comment he could insert within the context of that type of piece. Mariotti also questioned whether the newspaper would have been too scared to print it, for fear the city would rip *The Post* and him instead of her.

"I wonder how it would have shaken out in Cincinnati, how it would have affected my career," said Mariotti. "Today, being a veteran columnist, knowing what I know now, I wish I would have run it. I would have been the first to suggest Marge Schott was a racist."

Meanwhile, Marge was on the verge of facing another problem, one that threatened her authority as general partner of the Reds. Privately, Marge had decided to sell one of her 6.5 shares back to the team for $1.6 million, and she decided to give herself a $133,000 "incentive payment" equaling the cash given to Pete Rose as part of an attendance clause in his contract. Both transactions appeared to violate the terms of the Reds' partnership agreement. Blaemire says he was with the Reds when she took the money, and when he found out about it, he confronted her. As for the sale of the share, she told him, "I can do anything I want." As for the incentive bonus to match Rose's, she told him, "I was worth as much in attendance as he was."

Blaemire says he didn't push the matter any further until after he was fired, when he talked to Michael Paolercio of the *Cincinnati Enquirer*. But Blaemire would only allow Paolercio to use his name if someone else would go on the record also to confirm it. No one would, and the *Enquirer* dropped it. "At that time, we weren't using unnamed sources," said Paolercio. "And even though I had everything verified by two or three different sources, they wouldn't let me run any of it."

But Blaemire had another outlet. He called Reds limited partner George Strike, who didn't know about the share and the bonus, because Marge rarely reported anything to the partners. "He hit the ceiling," said Blaemire. The deposed head of the Reds' business side also told another limited partner, but this meeting was more by happenstance. As Blaemire was leaving his lawyer's office, he saw a man driving a Stutz into the garage next door, the garage used by Carl Lindner, and Blaemire realized that it was him. Blaemire had never met Lindner, but decided to follow him into the garage.

"A couple of security guys grabbed me, and I said I just want to say hello to him and told them who I was," said Blaemire. "Carl Lindner spent a half-hour listening to me, then took me upstairs and introduced me to one of his corporate lawyers and said, 'Tell him the story.' I spent a couple hours with him. That was the first time anything surfaced that she'd taken the money."

Yes, Blaemire admits, his bitterness toward Marge for firing him and refusing to pay him had something to do with revealing her transactions. For all the loyalty Marge demanded from her employees, she did nothing to earn it and much to repel it. The limited partners were not particularly thrilled with her by this point, either, as Marge progressively distanced them from any participation or information about the club, and they were concerned about the front-office turmoil and turnover resulting from her hands-on management style and her unwillingness to spend any money.

Details of the share and bonus surfaced in the media in late May—Marge initially lied about taking the bonus and the share but eventually admitted it—thanks to an investigation by Rick Kennedy of *The Post*. Kennedy revealed that several of the limited partners were so fed up with Marge that they were considering steps to unseat her. "The solution to the problem is for Mrs. Schott to sell her shares as general managing partner," said Carl Kroch. Kennedy also revealed that National League president Chub Feeney was monitoring the situation and considering stepping in—for a second time. Feeney first stepped in when Marge had refused to pay Howsam his consultant's salary after he left as president and CEO. "It merely amounted to a telephone call to clear up the matter," Feeney said.

Commissioner Peter Ueberroth ended up calling in National League attorney Lou Hoynes to meet with the warring partners in what was becoming known as "Margegate," and Hoynes was there for the June 18 partnership meeting called by Marge and convened at her home—a showdown that was dubbed "The Battle of Indian Hill." There, Marge gave in on the two disputed financial issues. Because the general partner could not take a salary, Marge gave back the $133,000 bonus, although she was encouraged to submit any expenses she might incur. Marge also agreed to buy back the share she had sold to the club, a move the limited partners later regretted as shortsighted. After all, each share of the Reds was worth more if the team was divided 14 ways instead of 15, and the value of the team increased into the nine-digit category during her tenure.

"We shouldn't have forced her to buy back the share," said Strike.

"I wish we hadn't," said Kroch.

Marge also told the limited partners she would hold regular meetings and update them on the financial dealings of the team. More importantly, Marge said she would take more of a hands-off approach to the Reds, leaving the baseball end of the team to general manager Bill Bergesch and the business end to Blaemire's successor, newly hired Don Breen, while she continued to establish good public relations by interacting with the fans in the stands during games.

Short of overthrowing Marge as general partner, which the partners conceded was almost impossible considering the makeup of partnership laws, this appeared a viable and acceptable alternative. And it would have been, had Marge gone along with it. It wasn't long before she began to break the terms of the agreement—a matter of, oh, seconds. Marge and the partners decided to release a statement to the media, but not to comment about the substance of the meeting. So when the meeting was finished, Marge approached the media and proclaimed, "I'm still running the Reds."

And she was, too.

Nothing would change.

Except to magnify.

— Chapter Six —

"A Churlish-Curmudgeon Rip Van Winkle"

T he World Series that Marge Schott guaranteed for 1986 never happened. Neither did the division title that so many had predicted. Instead, the Reds mimicked their second-place finish of 1985. Compared to what had happened earlier in the decade, even two years before, it was a successful season; but compared to 1985, it was a disappointment.

"We finished playing over our heads in '85," said Bergesch. "We probably were lucky to be second in the division. Then in '86, we added some players and made a few trades. We had improved quite a bit, and we made a good run, but the fact is that we finished second again."

But 1986 was a new beginning for a lot of people. It was Marge's first full year as president and chief executive officer, and it was Don Breen's introduction to working for the Reds. Actually, Breen had first met Marge the previous year, when he was the chief operating officer for Coca-Cola Bottling Co. of Cincinnati. At a night for the sponsors at Riverfront Stadium, she started telling him her life story, about how she had always wanted to own part of the Reds, and Breen thought it was a little peculiar that she was so open with him this quickly. Breen found her "flaky but interesting." Breen had been at a similar outing with the previous ownership, and Marge made a big deal about how her spread was different.

"The grand old men of baseball used to have steaks and all this stuff," Marge told Breen, "but not me. I have beans and franks. It's wholesome food. It's Cincinnati food. It's good German food. You'll like it."

By the time the 1986 season came along, Breen had left Coca-Cola and Marge had fired Blaemire, and a friend of Breen's recommended that he go and talk to her about filling the opening. So Breen ended up sitting with Marge at a Reds game, listening to her talk about what a bum Blaemire was and how she got suckered into hiring him because as soon as she met his wife, she figured Blaemire had to be OK, too. "I should have been tipped off that there was something different here," said Breen.

Instead, Breen ended up getting hired as head of the Reds' business operation on June 14, 1986, right in the middle of Marge's flap with the limited partners. Breen even went to the showdown meeting of the partnership four days later. The partners expressed their discomfort about Howsam being gone and about Blaemire coming and going so quickly. General manager Bill Bergesch told them he would take care of the baseball end. Breen assured them he would safeguard their interests on the business end. For Breen, that commitment became difficult at times—he describes it as walking a tightrope between loyalty to the general partner and to the limiteds. Carl Kroch might come to town and want to sit in the owners' box, and Marge might fight it because she considered herself the only owner—part of her "I am the Reds" mentality, as Breen put it. "Throughout my tenure at the Reds," Breen said of this loyalty tug-of-war, "it caused me significant aggravation."

Marge's insistence on hogging the credit and the celebrity left Breen not only in the middle, but directly in her line of fire. Breen negotiated the Reds' agreement to build a spring-training complex at Plant City, Florida, making several trips to the Sunshine State to secure the deal and several more to make certain it was ready on time. When it came time for the facility to open, Marge told Breen he wasn't invited.

"We only want the important people," she told him.

Yes, Breen says, that hurt his feelings, but Breen considers himself "the ultimate capitalist" and concedes that the owner of a company has a right to run the business as she chooses, and any employee who doesn't like it can quit. Still, Breen used to teach a class in principles of management, and one of his tenets was that happy employees made for more productive employees;

therefore it was in a boss's best financial interests to keep the staff motivated and enthusiastic. Marge Schott could never grasp that.

"Marge Schott is Rip Van Winkle—a churlish-curmudgeon Rip Van Winkle," said Breen. "She fell asleep in the '50s and woke up in the '80s. All of her values, her lifestyle, everything she thinks of, is a '40s and '50s lifestyle and a '40s and '50s mentality. It's the good old German 'watch your pennies.' It's her diet—she couldn't care less what she ate; if a sausage product tasted good, it didn't matter if it had fat in it, that's good food for you. And it's her viewpoints on the working man—that the working man is lucky to have a job. She always talks about when her dad walked through the plant, everybody would just cower. That's the way she expected things to be. The times have changed, and she hasn't. She couldn't understand why people didn't thank their lucky stars that they were working at the Reds."

Some people did. That's why they stayed and put up with it. There is something magical about working for a baseball team, especially the Reds in Cincinnati. You can tell your friends you work for the Bengals football team, and they'd think that was nice, and that would be that. But the Reds are Cincinnati's greatest natural resource. If people on the outside know Cincinnati more for being the home of fictional radio station WKRP, people on the inside know it as the home of Proctor & Gamble's headquarters, chili-spaghetti combinations, and, above all else, baseball's first franchise.

Although it will never be confused with the religion of basketball worshipped across the border in Kentucky, Reds baseball has a following throughout the Greater Cincinnati area that even Breen didn't grasp until he went to work there. People were constantly wanting to pick his mind about why the Reds were doing what on the field. He would mow the lawn in front of his house, and neighbors would stop their cars and walk alongside him asking, "Why the hell did they take Browning out?"

"People would make total fools out of themselves to get some piece of memorabilia or to get their tickets upgraded," Breen said. "I remember a guy who was in the hospital, dying. People were calling because he had season tickets on the dugout—and I'm talking about key business people of Cincinnati calling and saying, 'I've used a lot of his tickets, and I want those tickets when something happens to him.' They were calling and calling and calling, sending checks for the tickets. His wife tells us, 'All these people are vying for so-and-so's tickets. Can you imagine, they're trying to take them away? Of course, they're rightfully mine.' She writes this emotional letter about how they're hanging out at his hospital bed, asking him to sign over the rights to the tickets, and she sends a copy to Marge. So Marge finally gets involved in this thing and said, 'My God, who are these people? Who are these vipers?'"

Actually, Marge knew the names and was outraged that they would try to take the tickets away from this woman and that they continued to try after she became a widow. Breen happened to call a friend of his who knew the deceased ticket-holder and told him the story, and Breen's friend informed him that the woman was divorced from the guy for seven years, it was a rocky divorce, and she didn't even go to Reds games.

"There's nothing sacred," said Breen. "This poor guy is lying dead, six feet under, with everybody worrying about the six or eight seats he's got on the dugout. So Marge gets involved. And being Marge, she said, 'I'll solve it. *I'll* keep the tickets.'"

Marge had this thing about tickets. She couldn't stand the idea of giving them away and would hoard them, even if it meant breaking signed contracts to do it. Advertisers of the Reds would normally get a certain amount of tickets at Riverfront Stadium as an incentive to spend money on the team, and even though Marge signed the deals, she sometimes tried to get Breen to renege on the passes.

MARGE: I didn't know they were getting this. I never said this. I don't want to give them the tickets in the box.

BREEN: Marge, it's in their contract.

MARGE: Fine, find me the name of the president of the company. I'll call the president of the company, and I'll tell him that all his people want to do is just come up and freeload at the ballgames. I'll see if that's the kind of company he really wants to run and if he really wants to partici-pate in the advertising of the Reds.

And Marge would do it, too.

And pull it off.

"One thing that absolutely amazed me," said Breen, "is how many mature, intelligent business people or so-called community leaders absolutely rolled over when she called them up."

Marge wasn't big on outsiders being on the field before a game, either, unless they were part of the activities. Blaemire says she didn't want to share the stage with anyone who wasn't necessary, particularly front-office employees. Breen would try to work around Marge whenever he could. If someone wanted a picture taken at Riverfront, it would be done in the morning before she arrived. Or if a business associate wanted to go on the field during a game, he'd plot to get on Marge's good side. Take the time this one sponsor was coming to the game, and one of his employees wanted to take him on the field. Breen went to work on Marge.

"Marge," Breen told the Reds' owner, "we've got this sponsor, and he wants to come on the field, and he *has* to meet the dog. You've *gotta* take him down and see the dog."

And it worked. There was no better way to get to Marge than through Schottzie. One former Reds employee says he used that tactic himself, maybe half a dozen times, because he was getting frustrated dealing with her in the normal, direct manner. So at about 5:30 or 6:00 p.m., when most of the business of the day was done and the office was quiet, he would knock on her office door, armed with an 8 x 10 glossy of Marge and Schottzie and slightly varying versions of the same story.

MARGE: Yeah, what do you want?

EMPLOYEE: Mrs. Schott, I just wonder if you can
            do a favor for me. My niece really
            thinks you're great. Is there any way
            you can give her an autograph?

MARGE: Oh, sure, hon. Come on in. What's
            your niece's name?

EMPLOYEE: Mary.

MARGE: OK. And I'll put "Woofs and
            Licks—Marge." Do you want
            Schottzie's autograph on there, too?

EMPLOYEE: Oh, could you?

MARGE: Sure, honey, anytime. Anything else
              on your mind?

And that's when this enterprising employee addressed Marge with the real business, only then he had a captive audience instead of a hostile one. The thing was, this picture never ended up going to his niece—the guy didn't even have a niece.

"I'd take the picture and put it in the urinal," said the employee, "and we'd all take target practice on it."

Such was the mode of survival inside the baseball offices of Riverfront Stadium. It was a way to get through the rough exterior and into the soft spots of Marge Schott—the dog and families.

The best of Marge often came out when she dealt with the families of her employees, even those she abused when the relatives weren't around. The transformation was astounding. Don Breen remembers the time his parents came to town and he got seats for them at the game, and Marge became upset with him when she found out about it. "Your mommy and your daddy are here, and you didn't tell me?" she said. "Go get them."

So he did. Marge had them sit next to her in the front row, took them up to the owners' box later for drinks, took them to the office, and gave them assorted Reds' trinkets. His father thought Marge was great, and he enjoyed the conversation. And Breen's mother told him, "This is this wild woman you're talking about? I could see the potential, but she was very cordial—a character, but cordial." The next day, when Breen met Marge, she asked him about his parents.

MARGE: So, are your mommy and daddy
              here tonight?
BREEN: No.
MARGE: WELL, LET ME TELL YOU SOME-
              THING! LAST NIGHT, I HEARD
              MARTY BRENNAMAN SAY THIS-
              THIS-AND-THIS ABOUT THE
              DOG ON THE RADIO . . . !

Breen was convinced that if his parents had been there, it would have been another pleasant night with The Good Marge. He typically saw that side of her personality whenever it came to familial matters. If his wife or two young sons came to the park,

Marge would basically let the boys have the run of the stadium. Or if he needed time to be with them, then by all means, go.

"If I told her I wanted to go out with the boys or something like that and have a beer, she couldn't care less," said Breen. "But if I told her I was gonna go home to do something with Michelle and the kids, she would say, 'That's important. You've got to spend time with your family.'"

Marge was especially kind to the players' families. Granted, there were times she might tick off a wife here or there by making some snide comment in the elevator about the players after a loss, but Marge was generally in "Aunt Marge" mode around the Reds' wives and kids. "I think she's a real neat lady, real interesting to talk to," said Debbie Browning, wife of pitcher Tom Browning. "Her first love is animals, and second is children. She really does care about the wives and the kids, although some people think that's for show. It's good, because if you have a player who's unhappy at home, he's not going to be happy on the field. Marge helped Jose and Rosie Rijo get back together. They went in and talked to her, together and separately. During their separation, when Rosie wasn't in town, she kept in contact with her on the phone."

When Cal Levy joined the Reds as marketing director in 1986, he saw the same warm treatment for his family. When he brought them to the park, she was the same kind and compassionate woman the fans got to see on a game-by-game basis—Levy refers to it as Marge's "game face." Sadly, it was a side she wouldn't show inside the front office, and there were those who believed it was a front, that she put on the game face only because she thought it would get her more celebrity and because she thought she could attract more people to the games and therefore make more money. There were times when Marge would rant and rave about all these damn kids coming down to see her and how much she hated having to go through all this. Breen's theory was that Marge did it out of a sense of loyalty, that she didn't particularly enjoy being the interactive owner with the fans all the time but worried that if she wasn't there, people would think something was wrong. And all of that was no doubt true. Yet, there was a certain energy Marge seemed to derive from being around the fans, particularly the young and the aged, one of the few times she would accept adoration and give it back. The fans were thrilled to see someone this famous up close and personal with them, and she talked to them as though they really mattered.

"That is a real side of her," said Levy. "She loves kids. All the stories you'd hear about elderly people calling up and complaining about this or that, they got through to her often because she wanted to know about this kind of thing. She was much more open and tolerant and friendly toward the public than she was toward the staff—or *the help*, as she used to call it. That's different with the people that work for her, because I really think she has a plantation mentality. If you worked for her, she felt she owned you."

It was different with the players. She was their owner, but she doted on them, hugging them and kissing them. And she paid them. No matter how much she bitched and whined about their salaries and about having to contend with the bigger media markets, she continued to pay the big money. Of course, the alternative would be to risk the love of the fans that she so craved, so she was especially generous to the more important players.

For all of the slurs Marge threw at Eric Davis, she sometimes went out of her way to please him. She was always running in at the last minute to sign him to the contract he wanted, and she even kowtowed to the threats of his agent, Eric Goldschmidt, when Davis wanted a car from her. According to Breen, Goldschmidt told Marge that his client had agreed to a deal with a competing automobile dealer, Jake Sweeney, Jr., for use of a car—similar to Browning's nixed deal—and that unless Marge gave Davis a Corvette, he was going to go through with it. Breen called over to that dealership and was told that Goldschmidt had approached the dealer, but Sweeney was already using Cincinnati Bengals quarterback Boomer Esiason and wide receiver Chris Collinsworth as spokesmen. Sweeney told Goldschmidt he wouldn't do anything without the Reds' permission. And indeed when Sweeney talked to Breen, it was clear the Reds wouldn't approve it. A month later, Kal Daniels approached Sweeney about doing the same type of deal, and Sweeney replied, "No, I went through this once already." Meanwhile, Breen confronted Goldschmidt on his misrepresentation of Davis' agreement with Sweeney, but the agent told Breen he was too late—that Marge had given Davis the Corvette.

"Marge in a panic had given Eric the car because she was worried he would be the spokesman for the dealership," said Breen. "Then she tried to charge the car to the partners and pay herself back at the lease rate. The partners said, 'No way,' and it ended up in a lawsuit."

On the other hand, Marge also could be brutal to her centerfielder behind his back. Take the time general manager Tony Kiernan of Channel 5, the Reds' television station, approached the team about plans to establish Eric's Outfield Club with Davis. The station and the outfielder would split the cost of 500 tickets for about 10 games over the course of a season and give the tickets to the Cincinnati Youth Collaborative for inner-city kids as an incentive to stay in school. Kiernan also figured it would help Davis's standing in the community and make him feel more a part of Cincinnati, which could help convince him to stay when he became eligible for free agency. Kiernan wanted to see what kind of a discount the Reds could give him for blocks of 500 tickets in or around center field, even if it was midweek games against weak opponents. But Marge didn't want to do it. At different times, with different employees, she offered excuses such as: "I'm already giving that nigger a million dollars; I'm not going to make him any more famous here" and "We just traded one million-dollar nigger [Dave Parker], why do we want to promote another one?" and "If you were sitting in the outfield seats, would you want a bunch of black kids sitting around you, getting up and down and buying hot dogs? It's not why people are coming to the ballpark." Even though her attitude vetoed the idea at first, the plan was resurrected for another season, whether she liked it or not.

As Davis's salary reached seven figures, the slur changed from "trouble-making nigger" to joining Dave Parker as a "million-dollar nigger." Levy says he heard Marge refer to them both that way. Levy also heard her make a disparaging remark against a Jewish person, one of the few times Marge would slur a certain race or religion in front of a member of that group. It happened when Marge was getting into a heated discussion with Levy pertaining to Gold Star Chili's plans to sell its product at the stadium, and she lashed out at Gold Star chief executive officer Larry Horwitz.

MARGE: You sneaky goddamned Jews are all alike.

LEVY:	I can't believe you said that.
MARGE:	Well, that's how I feel.

Levy walked out of the office, floored by what had come out of Marge Schott's mouth. "Whatever you think and whatever you believe is one thing," he said. "But when you're so blatant as to insult someone and toss it up in their face because you feel you have that right because they work for you, that's another thing all together."

Actually, Marge slurred the Jewish people again in front of another member of the religion, but she didn't realize it or didn't care. Some Reds front-office types were invited to a special breakfast at the Hyatt hotel, after which Marge was standing with Hyatt general manager Sheldon Fox, and they were looking over a railing at the Reds' gift shop below. About 15 feet away from the Reds' gift shop was another shop that also carried some Reds merchandise, and the competition angered Marge. She asked who owned it and was told the man's name was Gary Fisher.

MARGE:	Is he a Jew?
FOX:	Yeah, I think he's of the Jewish faith.
MARGE:	It's typical. All he wants is to chase a buck. They ought to send the son of a bitch back to Israel with the rest of them.
FOX:	I don't think that's fair for you to say. You know, Marge, I'm of the Jewish faith.
MARGE:	You're not like him. You're one of the good ones.

With that, Marge walked away. To those who weren't used to Marge, it could be shocking to hear such language; but to those who had to work with her every day, it was nothing unusual. Breen had heard her use slurs, of course he had; in fact, she used to refer to Levy as "that beady-eyed Jew" around Breen, and she would tell Breen, "Charlie told me it's OK to hire a Jew, but to watch out for people with beady eyes." To Breen, Marge wasn't a racist or a bigot or an anti-Semite, because she didn't discriminate—she was nasty to everybody at some time. And he found some of her slurs to be merely a reflection of the way she was raised rather than a show of vindictiveness. Marge used to tell Breen, "Blacks like me. I relate to them well. They like my car [because of all the chrome]." She also used to say, "I eat a lot of chicken, you'd think I was black." And "The way I watch my money, people would think I was a Jew." Breen teased her and said, "The way you drink, they would think you were Irish."

Breen doesn't want to discuss the extent of Marge's drinking, per se, but does say, "Her consumption of alcohol may have made her more cranky at times; at times, it also made her more friendly. Either way, I don't really think that significantly affected her ability to operate the club one way or another. It would be unfair to say that problems with the Reds were a result of her excessive consumption of alcohol."

Neither will Breen discuss whether Marge was more apt to be intoxicated during her trademark late-night calls—although he concedes that she certainly called him late at night. Sometimes, he would be on the phone with someone else when the operator would cut in and say, "We have an emergency interruption," whereupon Breen would immediately end his conversation. There was no mistaking the voice on the other end. "Don, who the hell are you talking to?" Breen would reply, "Marge, what the hell are you doing?" She didn't care. She wanted what she wanted when she wanted it.

Other times, Marge would call looking for Breen and get the babysitter and suddenly start picking the babysitter's mind about whatever issue couldn't wait: "Well, what do you think? Are you a fan?" Eventually, Marge would get around to asking the babysitter where Breen was and say, "What's he doing leaving you home with his kids?" Then the babysitter would track down Breen at a restaurant or wherever, and Breen and Marge would match screams and yells over the phone.

"She would just drive you crazy," said Breen. "When the team was on the West Coast, the phone might ring at 11:00 or midnight because Marty and Joe made some wisecrack thinking she wasn't listening—and, of course, she was—and my wife would hear the phone ring and would always go, 'Don't answer it. You know who it is.' The phone would ring 20 times, then stop, then five minutes later ring again and keep ringing and ringing and ringing. So I'd get out of bed and go in this little office off my bedroom, and Marge would go, 'Do you know what that son of a bitch said?!'"

One night, when the Reds were in San Francisco, Marge heard Nuxhall say goodbye to Roger Blaemire in the booth, and she flipped out. She called Breen and screamed, "He's got Roger Blaemire in there, and I want to know how he got in there!" Finally, Breen got fed up with the late-night calls, and one night told her off. "Listen," he said, "if you were a man, I'd come over to your house, and I'd deck you." Marge screamed back at Breen, and Breen slammed the phone down on her. She didn't talk to him for weeks. Even if he needed something signed or approved, he'd get nothing. If Marge needed something, she'd tell chief administrative assistant Joyce Pfarr to get it from Breen but not to say it came from Marge. So Pfarr would go to Breen's office and say, "I'm telling you this, not Mrs. Schott, do you understand?" If Marge and Breen passed in the hall, they might growl or bark something at each other, but it was basically a cold war that was freezing the Reds' office. Papers were piling up on her desk. He needed an important agreement signed. She wasn't going to budge. He wasn't going to give her what she wanted (an apology), and this was another situation crying for strategy. This time, Breen decided not to use the dog. This time, he walked into her office, threw a box of saltwater taffy on her desk, and said, "I was in Boston yesterday and I saw this saltwater taffy, and I remembered your sweet tooth. So, here." And Breen left. Five minutes later Marge came into his office, and it was business as unusual.

"It was weird," said Breen. "It wasn't like you're dealing with the normal business environment where the boss comes in and says, 'If you ever hang up on me, I'll hang you.'"

Then again, dealing with this boss meant getting used to the unorthodox. Breen would sit with Marge for an hour or two every evening to walk her through the club's business issues, step by step, to make certain she not only heard but comprehended everything, because she signed every check. Some nights, it was more painful than others. One night, they spent half an hour arguing over a $1.59 lock for a desk at the Riverfront police room, where materials such as drugs confiscated at the games were kept. Marge wanted the police to pay the $1.59. Breen tried to explain to her that the police department didn't work for the Reds, that the Reds hired officers for the games. "Why are we paying them?" Marge shot back. "Why doesn't the city pay for them? For what we do for the city, what would they do if the Reds ever left?"

If it wasn't a lock, it might be the paint for the on-deck circle, and why did the Reds have to spring for that? It was very difficult to argue with Marge, because she made her decisions quickly and made them emotionally. Breen spent months negotiating a deal that would make White Way Electric Sign Co. the general contractor to sell scoreboard advertising, and he was having difficulty explaining to Marge all the benefits—until she learned that White Way executive Bob Flannery was a member of the Knights of Columbus (same as her late husband, Charlie) and that Flannery's wife went to a Sacred Heart Convent school (same as Marge). Suddenly, Marge was thrilled to do a deal. She went from referring to Flannery as "that salesman" to "that wonderful Mr. Flannery." And even when Flannery fell short in providing the revenue guaranteed to the Reds, and Breen went to Marge about it, she wouldn't push the matter.

"This wonderful Mr. Flannery is going to make it up to us," said Marge. "He's going to come up with an agreement to work things out."

Like Blaemire, Breen contends that for all the money the Reds made under Marge Schott, they could have made more. Shortly before Breen left the Reds he negotiated a seven-figure sponsorship deal, and a representative of the sponsor told him, "The only reason we're letting you get away with this is because we know that you're leaving and we're scared we'll end up dealing with her. It's worth paying you a couple hundred thousand extra just to have the deal in cement." Breen was elated when he came back to town after consummating the deal—until Marge refused to pay his expense report.

MARGE:	Why did you have to fly out of town?
BREEN:	Because it's a deal that is a million dollars in income, and they wanted me to go there.
MARGE:	Well, I don't agree with that.

Again, it was this idea of spending money to make money that galled her. If Marge were told she could make $500,000 and spend nothing or make $1 million and spend $25,000, she'd prefer the former. Breen wishes she had opened her private box and used it maybe for business leaders one day, inner-city kids another day, and have a good time with it. Not only could she have the joy of sharing her hospitality and spreading a little goodwill, she might secure a business deal or two. But he knew Marge would see that as "a sign of weakness" or "spending money that doesn't need to be spent."

The term "penny-wise and pound-foolish" has come up a lot from people who have dealt with Marge—and if the phrase itself doesn't, the idea behind it certainly does. Cal Levy met with resistance any time he wanted to spend a few dollars here or offer a discount there, even if it meant making more money in the long run. As director of marketing, Levy wasn't even allowed to spend money on a promotion. Just as Roger Blaemire found Kroger to sponsor the stadium fireworks following home runs when Marge decided it wasn't worth the expense, Levy had to find sponsors for giveaways such as sweatbands, watches, and the like at the ballpark. And even if he found one, Marge had to approve it.

"I thought it was unusual that the general partner wanted to sign off on what I considered to be piddly things, such as the cost of the giveaway items," said Levy. "We're big kids. This is what she pays us to do; let us do it. The items could cost as little as 89 cents apiece. The sponsors were able to do a giveaway day for the Reds for as little as $20,000."

Promotions that involved discounted or free tickets were predictably a hard sell with Marge. Levy saw them as ways to fill up seats that would go unused anyway, and the benefactors would inevitably be accompanied by friends or relatives, some or all of whom would pay full fare on their own tickets. Or if not, they might spend money on other items at the stadium. This is a 52,000-plus seat stadium that even in the best of seasons averaged some 40 percent unoccupied seats, the Reds surpassing the 2.5 million mark in attendance only three times (in the Big Red Machine era of 1976-78). And these types of promotions were for games with a predictably low turnout, so there wasn't much risk of giving away tickets that would otherwise be sold.

The Reds once had a promotion through the public libraries called the Reds Readers, which gave Reds' tickets, fast-food coupons, and other rewards to kids who read a certain number of books. It was similar to the Straight-A program, which awarded free tickets to straight-A students. But the Reds Readers program was cut off when the sponsorship level diminished to the point where Marge didn't want to offer it anymore. Levy called it a "warm-and-fuzzy deal," and he tried to push for its reinstatement. Marge said no. She didn't want to give away tickets. And she didn't particularly care for Levy pushing for it.

"I was branded as someone who wanted to give the store away," he said. "She said, 'I'm not here to give tickets away.' And on one level, she's right. But everything is not as black and white as Mrs. Schott sometimes sees it—or thinks she sees it."

Levy watched as Marge turned down money from other car companies for signage and for the Reds yearbook, which she justified by saying that baseball had a national contract with Chevrolet. But other teams had local car sponsors, and the Reds' failure to offer the same caused them to have a shortfall in signage.

"There's no doubt the club has made money, good money, with her as the general partner," said Levy. "But I believe it could be more from the marketing and the ticket-sales side. The two really intermingle."

The Reds also could not accept advertising from sporting-goods stores in the yearbook, because Marge felt they competed with the Reds' gift shop on licensed items. Yet Marge did little to make the Reds' gift shop stand out in the market. Even as baseball apparel was starting to become in vogue in mainstream fashion, Marge kept the Reds' gift shop as understocked as the gift-shop employees were overworked. In Cincinnati, you could go to the sporting-goods stores at the malls and find Reds' and other teams' apparel just as easily as at the gift shop—if not more so. The gift shop did sell the players' broken bats, which had a certain amount of appeal, but you'd never know about it unless you visited. The Reds' overall advertising and promotion ranked somewhere between poor and nonexistent, and Marge was to blame.

Levy watched in frustration as commercial time provided to the team as part of its local television contract went unfilled. Radio wasn't a problem, because Levy wrote the spots and Marty Brennaman recorded them. "But with the TV, you had to go and get production time, and it had to be either paid for or counted against a piece of the TV deal, and Mrs. Schott never wanted to do that," said Levy. "So except for a couple of years with the ads with her in spring training, you didn't see any TV."

The Reds commanded such a strong bargaining position, they could have run the spots in high-visibility time slots, too. And Marge could have used the time to put herself and the dog on the air to sell Reds baseball, if she so desired—and she undoubtedly would have. Upon joining the Reds, Levy was surprised that Marge didn't want players featured in promotions or giveaways unless there was no alternative. Marge and Schottzie were to get the publicity. "Mrs. Schott believes that she's the Reds," said Levy, yet Mrs. Schott lacked the foresight or savvy to better market herself with the available TV time. Marge believed the Reds were enough of an institution that they didn't need marketing.

"I don't think she understands to this day marketing—real marketing," said Levy. "Yet she feels she's the marketing maven of the world because she went out with the elephant and the dog in commercials and sold cars. She's a tremendous personality, and she never really used it the way she could have."

Her personality in the front office, however, was rarely described as tremendous. Former Reds employees who worked for Marge Schott talked about her the same way Superman talked about Lex Luthor—if only she had used her skills to help people instead of hurt them. Those who worked for her wanted to like her, wanted her to be the lovable eccentric the public saw. Instead, they saw trouble, although Levy says he can't remember when he first knew there could be problems with Marge Schott. "It might have been an elevator kick," he said. Indeed, whenever Marge wanted the elevator operator at Riverfront Stadium to pick her up at some floor on Reds game days, she would signal him by continually kicking the elevator. Wherever the elevator was, it had to immediately follow the banging noise or risk getting chewed out by the noisemaker.

"She carries her feelings on her sleeve with everything," said Levy. "If she's mad about something, you know about it. It's not very different than any other situation where there's a boss, and you know the boss is in a bad mood, so you try to avoid the boss. Only this boss seeks you out."

And if she couldn't find you, any employee would do. There were times when Marge was angry about something put on the scoreboard before the game or about someone being allowed on the field, and the first front-office type in her line of fire was Levy, in the tunnel under the stadium—so she'd launch her oral torpedoes at him. She didn't want to hear the facts, she didn't want to know the circumstances, she didn't care if the players' wives were watching—she just needed to imbed her footprints on someone's back. Someone had to be wrong, someone had to be blamed; it was never just fate, and it was never, ever Marge—even if it was.

Levy never forgot Farmers Night at Riverfront Stadium one year, an event that featured kids, a parade of animals, American flags and the like, and was a particular favorite of Marge's.

"She used to say people would drive 13 hours to come to Farmers Night from Wisconsin," said Levy.

Is that true?

"No."

Still, Levy liked the promotion, because it was something that separated the Reds from other clubs and the fans enjoyed it. But one year, the night was being spoiled by atrocious weather—rain, thunder, lightning, the works. It wasn't the easiest of events to coordinate anyway, and the weather was making it impossible to parade the animals around the field without an ark. Even though the weather let up in time to play baseball, the conditions and timing jeopardized the promotion.

"I remember her chasing around in the tunnel of the stadium, wanting to make sure the cows got to parade along the field, rain or not," said Levy. "After talking with the stadium-operations guy and the farm people, I told her the parade might not be able to happen. She held the game up and had the parade, anyway. The umpires got ticked off. And because I was the one who told her the game had to start on time and that they weren't going to do the parade because it was tough to get the cows on the field, she wailed on me, absolutely wailed on me—told me if I wanted my job, I should do what Mrs. Schott wants me to do, and she doesn't care about what time the game starts because all these people came to see the cows parade on the field. So she opened up the right-field fence and had the cows walk through before anybody was prepared for it, while players were coming on the field to warm up. It was a mess."

Levy had no choice but to stand aside and watch. Although they went head to head at times, he would have to do—as he said—what Mrs. Schott wanted him to do. Levy says Marge often referred to herself that way, in the third person—a malady often befalling athletes who talk too much about themselves and have an overinflated view of themselves.

Another time Levy felt the wrath of Marge was when the Reds staged their annual father-son-daughter game for the players and their children. These annual pregame exhibitions had already caused some distress for the owner, who thought the Reds were spending too much on it. The uniform, for instance, already had been reduced to just a shirt and a hat for each kid, and she wanted to stop providing hats. Once, during Levy's last year of staging the annual event, Marge complained that the frozen ice cream proved to the kids by the stadium concessionaire was too hard, which suddenly became the fault of the team's marketing director. "She stood in the hallway outside with all the wives and kids and screamed at me," said Levy, "because she thought it was my job to get the ice cream unfrozen."

Marge screamed at her employees for the same reason an explorer might try to scale Mt. Everest—because they were there. Levy might be on the phone with a prospective client, and she would storm into his office and start railing on him for some reason or another. Levy also learned it didn't do much good to seek her out and try to convince her of something she didn't want to do, because she wasn't going to change her mind. One of their biggest areas of disagreement was one of Blaemire's also—the Reds' logo. Levy and Marge clashed over how much to charge for its use in advertisements or promotions. But Marge didn't do discounts.

Marge didn't do long tenures among the front-office staff, either. Not many, at least. Cal Levy was fired in August 1989 and was told the team didn't need to give a reason. So he packed up his desk while director of stadium operations Tim O'Connell watched, presumably to make sure he didn't take anything. "Probably because they didn't want me to steal the samples of the mugs," cracked Levy, who believes he lost his job for speaking his mind to Marge and to the new head of business operations, Steve Schott. By then, Don Breen was already gone.

"I've looked through history," said Breen, "and history says that nobody lasts too long with Marge Schott. Or if they do, they're a puppet."

Breen had resigned a year earlier. Just before he left was one of his more pleasurable and memorable moments with Marge.

They had driven back from Columbus in connection with a deal for a spring-ending exhibition between the Reds and the Cleveland Indians, and when they got back to Cincinnati, she invited him into her house. She knew he would be leaving the Reds in a couple of weeks, and the mood was particularly friendly.

"I'll tell you, I drank more beers than I probably should have, and she had a couple of beverages, and it was one of the most pleasant conversations I've ever had with her," said Breen. "She told me I ought to have my own business, I shouldn't go to work in corporate America, what a good business guy I was—the best business guy who'd ever worked for her. She told me all this great stuff and made me feel great. We talked about life and families, and I was there until about 10:00 at night, constantly calling my wife saying that I would be home in another hour. We ended up hugging in the driveway, and she was just as nice as nice could be. My last couple of weeks there were pretty good, she was nice to me, and then I left.

"And then it took me three months to collect my last check— she was holding up my money on me."

— Chapter Seven —

Too Cute to Trade

Nineteen eighty-seven figured to be the Reds' year. After two straight second-place finishes and the emergence and maturation of young players who became known as the "crown jewels" of general manager Bill Bergesch, the Reds' expectations for their first division title of the decade seemed not only realistic but probable. Marge Schott knew it. The little patience she had was waning, and though she had learned something about making predictions or guarantees, she wasn't going to sit back and take another runner-up finish.

Indeed, the Reds got off to a strong start, only to unravel in the second half. While the trigger-happy San Francisco Giants were making trades for the likes of Rick Reuschel, Don Robinson, and Dave Dravecky to solidify their pitching staff, the gun-shy Reds were standing pat, which not only hurt them in the personnel department but in the morale of the ballclub. Bergesch, the man who was honored as the league's top executive for his brilliant transactions just two seasons earlier, took a lot of heat from the media and the clubhouse for failing to pull off deals when they were most needed, and Marge ended up firing him after the season.

In fact, during late August, when the team was in full bellyflop mode, Marge expressed disappointment that the team had not acquired Reuschel, who was a key to the Giants' division title run and whom the Reds had tried but failed to secure from Pittsburgh before San Francisco snagged him. She also said she did not turn down one request for a deal, that "not that many" had been presented, and that she had approved a deal for Reuschel. "We didn't think we needed anybody, I guess," she said. "You always like to improve your pitching, but it's hard to do at the last minute. Maybe this is something we should have done a year ago."

For all the flak Marge brought on herself when she tried to comment on baseball issues, this was a particularly astute piece of analysis. Not what you'd expect from an owner whose ideas for helping the team through its collapse included sending the team a good-luck cake from Schottzie and posting a "Don't Quit" ditty submitted by an 83-year-old fan. No, the type of comment more characteristic of Marge came in that very same interview concerning Reuschel, in reference to her leaving the baseball decisions to her "baseball people," Bill Bergesch and Pete Rose: "The only good thing about it is, if it doesn't turn out, it's not my fault. I've told that to Bill and Pete many times." That evoked one of the most memorable headlines of her tenure, one that captured not only the owner's feelings about the collapse but also one of her unofficial mottoes: "It's not my fault . . ."

But the fact was, Marge wasn't telling the whole truth about the Reuschel situation. Bergesch says he met with Rose, the coaches, and minor-league head Chief Bender a few times to talk about getting a crack at Reuschel, whom the Reds had turned away for a tryout request before the season because Rose told Bergesch, "I don't even want him. I don't think he can pitch anymore." Reuschel proved Rose wrong with the Pirates, and it would have cost the Reds some of the "crown jewels" to get him this time, so the Reds braintrust felt it wasn't worth making a deal.

"We kept up our discussions about possible trades, then I got a telegram from [Marge's attorney] Bob Martin when we were on the road," said Bergesch. "She was concerned about the Reuschel thing, that we would be adding some payroll. She didn't want to take on any payroll. She told us that she didn't want us to get Reuschel. The telegram said, 'Marge says do not make any trades or assume any contracts without her written permission. Effective immediately.' I showed it to Pete, and we were kind of shocked. I never did anything without telling her. In fact, one time Pete and I drove out to her house and told her what we were thinking about doing and literally talked her into letting us have the money necessary to do it."

Bergesch believes that was the deal that brought Buddy Bell from Texas. Other times, Bergesch worked at making his deals not only good for the Reds, but fiscally sound. When he acquired Bo Diaz from Philadelphia, the Phillies paid for part of his contract. When he snagged John Denny from the Phillies, "we made them take back" high-priced reliever Tom Hume.

"It was fairly late in the season when we got this telegram, at a crucial moment," said Bergesch. "It was just another little stumbling block that we had."

Bergesch is convinced he and Rose could have talked Schott into making another deal if it came to that, telegram or no telegram, and perhaps he is right. But for her to order Bergesch not to acquire Reuschel and later to say publicly that she had approved a Reuschel deal is outrageous. "I thought the Reuschel deal was going to be made," she said. "Apparently, they turned around on us and wanted to switch players, which wasn't good."

Later that season, Bergesch made a trade too late to save his sliding ballclub, acquiring pitcher Dennis Rasmussen from the New York Yankees for pitcher Bill Gullickson. Bergesch initially wanted to trade pitcher Ted Power instead, but Marge said no. Among her reasons: (a) Power was one of the few players who would go over and sign autographs for kids; (b) he had a new house in Cincinnati; and (c) he did charity work in town. Now it wasn't unusual for players to be deemed untouchable, but not for these types of reasons. Bergesch says he'd never seen anything like it—but he would see more of it from Marge.

Infielder Kurt Stillwell was another of her favorites, and Bergesch was working on a deal with Kansas City toward the end of that season that involved Stillwell or another infield prodigy, Barry Larkin, for one of two Kansas City pitchers, Danny Jackson or Mark Gubicza. The Reds zeroed in on Jackson because he was left-handed, and Kansas City gave the Reds the option of which infield prospect they would deal. Bergesch rightly considered Larkin a better prospect, but there was this issue of Marge.

"Naturally, we were thinking we would trade Stillwell," said Bergesch. "That's when she said she liked him so much. She didn't really say, 'Don't trade him' so much as she said, 'Oh, I'd hate to see him get traded. He's one of my little favorites. He's such a cute little guy.' She did that about some of the players. She would adopt her little-girl attitude about it. But that doesn't mean she didn't like Larkin. The one thing about Larkin she liked was that he was a native there, the whole family and all."

Bergesch never tested whether he could go through with a Stillwell trade. After going back and forth with Kansas City, they decided it was "too big of a deal" for both sides to consummate at that point, and they would wait until after the season. Indeed, the Reds made the deal over the winter, trading not only Stillwell but Power, too, for Jackson and infielder Angel Salazar. But Bergesch didn't make that one for the Reds. After the season, Bergesch flew to Tampa for the annual organizational meeting when the news came. "I had just gotten into my hotel room," Bergesch said, "and had a call waiting there from Bob Martin."

Bill Bergesch was fired.

No explanation given.

He came back to Cincinnati and decided to remain in town and continue residing at the Vernon Manor hotel for the time being. He liked the city and he had developed good friends in town, so he made it his base. His wife lived and worked in New York, so Bergesch would go there on weekends, or vice versa. Bergesch even had use of the Reds' company car until the end of the year—or so it seemed. Then one day, Bob Martin called.

MARTIN: Marge would like to have that car back.

BERGESCH: Bob, I have in my contract that I can use that car for now. I'm going to give it back to her. At the very latest, she'll get the car back at the first of the year when my contract runs out. And if I decide to leave town before that, she'll have the car back before that.

MARTIN: I know it's in your contract. Don't worry about that. You go ahead and use it. She just said that if she could have it back, she would like to get it back.

BERGESCH: Well, as soon as I'm finished with it,
                       I'll give it to her.

About a week later, Bergesch left the hotel one morning, went out to his car, and found the glove compartment emptied and all of his belongings dumped out onto the seat and the floor. He opened the trunk, and it looked like someone had been rummaging through the contents. The car also appeared to have been moved slightly, as though it wasn't quite where he'd left it the night before—close, but not exact.

"It was," said Bergesch, "the damnedest thing you ever saw."

He asked the doorman if he had noticed the car being moved, and, sure enough, he had. The doorman thought it was an employee of the car wash behind the hotel coming to get it—as Bergesch had arranged in the past—and an hour or so after taking it, the guy brought it back. Problem was, Bergesch hadn't arranged for any car wash. Bergesch knew right away what had happened. *Marge.*

He went upstairs and called Bob Martin.

BERGESCH: Bob, are you aware of what just
                       happened with my car?

MARTIN: I'm so embarrassed. Am I aware of
                       it? I'm the reason you got it back.
                       She had her guy go down there and
                       pick up your car and bring it back
                       out here. She was just going to take
                       your car.

BERGESCH: Bob, do you know what I would
                       have done? I would have turned it
                       over to the police as a stolen car. Do
                       you think that would be good
                       publicity for Marge? Maybe that's
                       what I should have done. It's a mess
                       what she has done.

MARTIN: I'm really sorry about it. I apologize
                       about it. I really told her how wrong
                       she was, that she could have gotten
                       herself in trouble. I had the guy take
                       it back.

BERGESCH: Well, he brought it back, but, boy,
              he left it a terrible mess.
MARTIN: I'm sorry. She got scared and told
              the guy to take it back. I guess he
              was trying to do it as fast as he
              could and get out of there before
              you came.

Bergesch was sad that things didn't work out with the Reds. He enjoyed the city, the people, and the team, and he never did get any explanation from her as to why he'd been fired. In the following years, it became clear that three years was about the life expectancy for any general manager under Marge. When something went wrong, someone had to be blamed.

"Somebody had to be the scapegoat" after the 1987 season, said Bergesch, who was exactly that. It certainly wasn't going to be Pete Rose. The manager is normally the first casualty of a disappointing team, but this manager was not going to be fired by this owner. "She couldn't fire the manager," said Bergesch. "Oh, no, she couldn't do that." He wasn't being sarcastic, he was being sincere. Marge was concerned that firing the legendary Rose would turn the masses into a mob, and that she would become an enemy to the people whose love she so needed. So any general manager who took the Reds' job had to understand that there were three givens—he'd have to work with the owner, the dog, and the manager.

The new general manager was Murray Cook, who came to the Reds from Montreal. When he came to Marge's house to interview, he found her pleasant, outgoing, positive, and "a little cutesy—which she does when she is not terribly comfortable with something or when she is trying to impress somebody and disarm them." Cook talked to confidante John McHale, former Montreal president, and was warned about the asylum he would be entering in Cincinnati. "Hey, it's a crazy situation," McHale told him. "Know what you're getting into." Still, it was a chance for a general manager's job in baseball, and there weren't many of those, so Cook took it.

His first sign that this wasn't exactly Eden came after talking to some of the veteran scouts he knew, such as George Zuraw and Chet Montgomery, who filled him in on her budgetary salvos.

Cook was used to frugality from his time working for Pittsburgh—but this wasn't Pittsburgh. Cook watched as valuable members of the scouting staff left, and though he could take solace in knowing they were leaving for better jobs he also realized the reason they left was an obstacle he'd have to deal with: Marge Schott.

"She just wears you down," said Cook. "The lack of respect and the lack of appreciation for people who were busting their tail to do a job for the organization just wear you down."

Still, on the major-league level, Marge gave Cook the freedom to operate when he first arrived, and he quickly made an impact. The previously untouchable Ted Power and the beloved Kurt Stillwell were traded, as was the greatest presence on the field and in the clubhouse, Dave Parker. Considering Parker's status, his deal to Oakland for pitchers Jose Rijo and Tim Birtsas may have been more noteworthy with the press and the public; but Stillwell and Power were more beloved to Marge, her two favorite players.

"She never did get over that," said Cook. "She wasn't mad about it. But one thing I found out as I went along, whenever you propose a trade to her, she never, ever supported you on it, even though she wouldn't say no. She would always say, if it doesn't work out, 'I told you so.'"

There was one player Marge stopped Cook from trading—Eric Davis. Twice during Cook's tenure, he was working on deals to trade the productive but injury-prone outfielder. The first time was right around the end of the 1988 season or just into the off-season, with Atlanta, but Marge nixed it before negotiations started. The second time was in 1989, when Cook was working on a deal with Boston for outfielder Ellis Burks; but again, no deal. Cook sensed Marge's fear of public opinion over trading the controversial Davis.

"She would say how important he is and 'I really like him,'" said Cook. "Then in the next breath, she would be pretty critical. But that was her."

And that was what made it so hard for people to categorize Marge Schott. One minute, she might be down on the field before a game embracing Eric Davis in a sincere display of adoration, and it didn't matter what skin tone he is. The next minute, she might be calling Eric Davis a "million-dollar nigger" and being as deeply a racist as she'd been color-blind the previous minute. The two sides just came out at different times. The public rarely got to see the bad side of Marge; the front office rarely got to see the bright side.

Murray Cook heard Marge use slurs.

Murray Cook heard Marge use the word "nigger."

"She's used all the words, and she's ridiculed or vilified every group of people imaginable," he said. "But it's not a personal vendetta-type of thing that she hates these people. She's not bigoted toward any group of people. She at one time lets everybody have it, either personally or as a group."

Some argued with her about it. Most, like Cook, let it go and moved on. It was such a part of her everyday vocabulary that her employees just ignored her. "You spend so much of your time trying to avoid being around her, because it's almost always uncomfortable and nonproductive," Cook said. "As a result, you don't spend a lot of time with her unless she demands an audience."

Cook tried to convince her that she would be much happier if she would simply let people do their jobs; if they failed, she could step in then and fire them if she so desired. But Marge wouldn't listen, because that wasn't Marge's style—either listening or allowing her employees to have the freedom to make their own decisions. To Cook, she was neither as unpredictable nor as omnipresent nor as interfering with on-the-field activities as his former boss with the New York Yankees, George Steinbrenner; she was more of a kibitzer, who tended to look at the dark side of everything. But she did share Steinbrenner's penchant for trusting those who didn't work for the organization more than those who did. Ironically, one of the outsiders she trusted for advice was Steinbrenner himself.

"She lacks trust in people," Cook said. "It's a defensive trait, because if you don't trust somebody, they can't hurt you."

Generally, Cook found he could successfully avoid Marge and run the team as he chose, but he watched the abusive way she treated others and that overshadowed everything else. Her slurs were offensive and her stinginess, ridiculous; but to watch her abuse her employees was to see the worst of Marge Schott. The players never saw that. When she came onto the field, she was downright lovable. And when she was in the clubhouse, she could be downright laughable.

Marge couldn't get over thinking that she could rescue the team when it was slumping by delivering an inspirational speech. Cook knew that as soon as she left the room, the players would let loose with their snickers. Cook tried to talk her out of these "clubhouse appeals," but to no avail.

"They were embarrassing situations," said Cook. "You try to be supportive of her, but, hey, I've been in clubhouses, I know what it's like. It's a raucous group, and they're very insensitive. Hell, if they were sensitive, they couldn't be successful in what they're doing. And Marge is a very, very sensitive person—and I'm not sure people realize that. For all her brusqueness and her attempt to be a man in a man's world—or a woman/man in a man's world—she is extremely sensitive. Extremely sensitive to the press. She reads every word. She hates to be criticized."

Marge began fighting back at sportswriters by taking away their bread and butter. When reporters wrote the wrong thing about her, she responded by revoking their dining-room credentials at Riverfront Stadium. Frankly, it was a rather silly sanction from Marge and one that hardly deterred any media member hungry for a story. After a while, it became almost a badge of honor to be press-ona non grata, and they took to wearing hats that read "Barred by Marge." When *Post* reporter Jerry Crasnick quoted Reds pitcher Tim Belcher in an exclusive story criticizing Marge for letting the dog roam around and defecate on the field, Marge penalized Crasnick by taking away his dining-room pass. When Belcher found out, he had pizzas and submarine sandwiches sent to the pressbox for Crasnick to share with his fellow scribes who had been "scooped."

As much as Marge detested being the subject of media criticism, she loved being in front of their cameras. When the 1988 All-Star Game was held in Cincinnati, she had a chance for endless photo opportunities, and, more importantly, an opportunity to exert control. Despite having a national spectacle in her domain, Marge decided to bar Don Breen, the head of her business operations, from participating in All-Star preparations. And she came dangerously close to disaster.

She was already missing marketing director Cal Levy, who needed a back operation, a spinal fusion, but was trying to put it off at least until after the All-Star Game in July. He realized in May he wouldn't make it, as the pain was incredible. In June, Levy's doctors told him there was an opening to have surgery at the end of the month; otherwise, he'd have to wait until mid-August. And though Levy made certain he had taken care of all his responsibilities for the All-Star Game, Marge was angry. "I don't know why you can't wait," she told him. "Did we know you had a back problem when we hired you?"

"I really believe she took it personally for two reasons," said Levy. "She thought I'd drive the insurance bills up, and she felt I was walking out on what I had to do. But she didn't understand I had no choice. I have nerve damage in my right leg and foot today because I waited too long to have that surgery, and my right leg will never be as strong as my left leg. I made that choice; I was excited about working on the All-Star Game."

To Levy, Marge's reaction was an example of her insistence that somebody had to be wrong, somebody had to be at fault, life couldn't just happen. The fact was, with Marge calling the shots, problems could turn into full-scale disasters, and this All-Star Game had all the warning signs of one. Cal Levy was out of the mix, Don Breen was shut out of the proceedings, Marge was headed off to Rome to see the Pope to give him a Reds jacket emblazoned with "John Paul 2," and there were thousands of tickets that Marge had hoarded while procrastinating over how to divvy them up. Most of the tickets nobody even knew about until the last minute.

Breen, Reds ticket-sales personnel, and Bonnie Paul jumped in and handled the matter on their own. Some sponsor requests that had been turned away, for example, were suddenly filled, but that still wasn't enough. A few days before the game, Breen discovered approximately 3,000 tickets that Marge had set aside, and the ticket office didn't know what to do. Breen called Bryan Burns, broadcasting executive for Major League Baseball, who responded, "Oh, my God, she did what?" So Breen and the Reds saved face by skirting the truth and announcing to the Cincinnati public that tickets had been returned from other teams and a variety of sources. Problem solved. Once again, Marge's front office bailed her out.

But there was never any appreciation. Not even for Bonnie Paul, who acted for so long simply as a friend before being put on the payroll for a short time. In fact, with Marge paying Bonnie, Marge had even more reason to treat her like the rest of the employees, which probably spelled the end for their association.

Finally, Bonnie quit. Cook said it had been building for a while, and Marge felt that Bonnie was getting too much notoriety. Marge always had to be in the foreground.

"Bonnie would have done anything for her—anything," said Breen. "Marge had made a point of trying to belittle Bonnie or just be outright nasty to her. She'd exclude her from parties and events Bonnie might have been involved in setting up. But it was beyond her to say thank you."

Because of the work of the people under Marge's employ, the All-Star Game went off without any major disasters. The closest probably was the flap over who would control the elevator: Marge or the Secret Service protecting vice-president George Bush at the game. "It was an I'm-as-big-as-you-are kind of thing with her," said Breen.

The All-Star Game turned out to be the only national baseball event held in Cincinnati in 1988, as the Reds once again did the limbo under expectations and finished in their familiar position of second place. Cook's job was spared, but Marge fired one of Cook's first hires with the Reds, Branch Rickey III, the minor-league director who seemed to get along so well with the owner at first. OK, so she didn't know about his grandfather; he appreciated that at least she was trying to be complimentary. And during that same initial conversation, she was thrilled to find out that he had family involved in the dog-food business. She grabbed him by the arm and took him on a tour of her office, spending a half-hour showing him all of her Schottzie paraphernalia and exhibiting a true affection for animals. It was a scene Rickey remembers as the best of Marge, as he saw her.

"Marge has an ability to charm people," said Rickey. "People warm to her very quickly. It seems such a shame she seems so uncomfortable with her employees in not knowing how to trust them."

Which brings us to the worst of Marge, as Rickey saw her.

Which he'd rather forget.

"It is a reluctance to accept a responsibility for her actions in firing large numbers of people," he said. "The sadness is, she doesn't equate that with any sense of cruelty. Perhaps the way that she is insulated with money, it's difficult for her to appreciate some of the compromises that she causes to minor-league field staff—at least during my time—with some of the salaries."

Farm-system salaries were a source of disagreement between Rickey and Marge. Rickey noticed that the Reds were paying among the lowest salaries to minor-league personnel in the business. Having worked with another relatively small-market, small-budget team in Pittsburgh, Rickey understood austerity; but the minor-league players' salaries were even lower here than at the Pirates. In fact, he says, the Reds were so low in this area that right after he left the Reds, minimums allowable in minor-league baseball were pushed ahead of what the Cincinnati organization was paying. Rickey also opposed Marge over the pay for the Reds' minor-league managing and coaching staffs. According to Rickey, the organization had a manager and coach in Class A making less than $13,000 each, when the industry generally paid a wide-ranging salary of roughly $15,000 to $30,000.

But Rickey couldn't talk her into more than a minimal increase in the entire pool to pay minor-league staff, and she didn't want to bother about individual cases. Rickey was basically dealing with Marge alone, because he and Cook realized Marge viewed the idea of chain-of-command as somewhat of a ball and chain. This was the result, essentially, of her divide-and-conquer mentality that often caused feuds among employees. But Cook and Rickey seemed to find a way to work through it. In fact, one of Rickey's proudest accomplishments in his short tenure was in not firing anybody, even though some former and current Reds employees wanted to eliminate some factions that had developed and grown counterproductive under Marge.

"My perspective was that so many changes were occurring, the one thread that needed to be pursued was to try to develop some kind of consistency," said Rickey. "I just felt that disruption was the norm in the organization. And that doesn't define an organization, that defines disorganization."

The disorganization continued with the firing of Rickey and his assistant, Tom Kayser. Meanwhile, Marge found a replacement for Breen from within her family, convincing her late husband's cousin, Steve Schott, to give up his job on Wall Street and become her new executive vice-president in September. They had first talked about the opening in the early summer of 1988, with Marge telling Steve that she didn't feel comfortable walking down the halls of 100 Riverfront Stadium, she didn't trust anybody, and she needed someone to come in and help her with a number of contracts that needed renegotiating. Steve found it interesting but left it at that, because he was happy in his position as senior vice-president of Shearson Lehman Hutton/ American Express. After the All-Star break, Marge again talked to Steve about the job, and this time she made the offer more attractive. She told him that if he accepted the offer, he would succeed her within three years as president and chief executive officer of the Cincinnati Reds; and, in time, there would be provisions for him to become a partner in the team. Steve felt comfortable with Marge, who told him he was the son she never had, and the offer was intoxicating.

"It was an offer," he said, "I could not refuse."

On the major-league level, the pressure was on in 1989 to break the pattern of second-place finishes, and Cook attempted to shake up the team by trading enigmatic first baseman Nick Esasky and standout middle reliever Rob Murphy to Boston for first baseman Todd Benzinger and pitchers Luis Vasquez and Jeff Sellers. Youth no longer could be used as an excuse, with Eric Davis, Kal Daniels, Barry Larkin, and more having become full-fledged proven commodities.

Before the season started, two of the team's top stars, Davis and Daniels, became embroiled in heavily publicized contract disputes. Davis' agent, Eric Goldschmidt, and Cook were having trouble coming to terms, and Davis appeared headed for salary arbitration. But instead of quietly and professionally seeking satisfaction through arbitration, Goldschmidt took the low road and Davis followed, complaining publicly that Cook was mistreating the Reds' best player. Worse, Davis threatened to boycott spring training—hardly endearing him to a Cincinnati public that already saw him as an underachieving crybaby, a result of his missing too many games and taking too much advice from Goldschmidt. In this case, the agent realized he could go around Cook straight to Marge and play them against each other. Marge fell for it. Instead of supporting her general manager or telling him she'd be willing to pay a higher figure, Marge decided to play White Knight and sign Davis herself, showing up her top baseball employee.

"Some of these agents, if they can get to an owner, they can wrap them around their fingers," said Cook. "Marge and I communicated on it, but once Goldschmidt found out he could talk to her, he wasn't going to talk to me. Does that undermine the general manager? Yeah, it does."

Then came Daniels, who hadn't been in the major leagues long enough to be eligible for arbitration and walked out of spring training because he refused to accept the club's $300,000 offer. He wanted $325,000. In came the White Knight again. Marge decided to stage a coin flip to determine whether Daniels received his proposal or the Reds'. The cameras rolled as the Reds and Daniels let the coin arbitrate. And Daniels won. Actually, Cook doesn't find that undermining; he calls it "a rather unique and kind of humorous way to solve an impasse." It wasn't universally accepted, however. Benzinger, who had just signed for $160,000 when his talks reached a stalemate, was ticked off that Daniels got his way by walking out while Benzinger stayed and ended up signing for less than he felt he deserved. "I won't forget this," he said.

National League president A. Bartlett Giamatti, who was about to succeed Peter Ueberroth as commissioner, wasn't pleased, either.

"We do not consider it a form of gambling," he said. "However, if what I read is right, it is a ridiculous way to negotiate a contract and trivializes the whole process and demeans the participants. I'm sorry anyone thought it was a good idea. I look forward to talking with Mrs. Schott about it."

Gambling got to be a pretty hairy issue between the Reds and baseball during that time, for it was at that same spring training that baseball revealed it was investigating Pete Rose for misconduct related to gambling, the likes of which made a coin flip for $25,000 quickly forgettable. We're talking about the game's golden rule: Never bet on baseball games. Because Rose ignored it, 1989 turned into a disaster for the sport, the city, the team—and the owner—who took the whole thing personally.

— Chapter Eight —

Rose's Fall, Marge's Gall

It was one of baseball's ugliest episodes. Pete Rose, the sport's centerfold for hard work and determination, accused of betting not only through a bookmaker, not only on professional sports, not only on baseball, but on his own team. It dragged on through the end of spring training and much of the season. Everywhere Rose and the Reds went, the cameras played follow the gambler, wanting one more closeup, asking one more question, addressing one more allegation. Only in the Reds' home city, Rose's hometown, did people shut their minds to the possibilities and, inevitably, the truth.

From the beginning, when Rose was first called to the commissioner's office, Murray Cook implored his owner not to pretend that nothing had happened. "Hey, here's your manager who's going to be gone for a day," he told her. "You can't stick your head in the sand and pretend that nothing's happened." But it was no use. The longer the scandal dragged on, the more Marge Schott distanced herself from her team. "She wanted to hide," said Cook. "She wanted to separate herself from it."

Not only was Rose's guilt becoming more and more evident, the Reds began sliding as a team, from first place on June 10 all the way down to fifth by July 23. It wasn't just the scandal, although the specter of it always hovered, the wondering if the next day would bring a new accusation—or a new manager. Injuries decimated the team. And Rose, the Great Communicator when it came to the media but a Silent Knight when it came to his players, was the wrong manager to keep this team from crumbling.

As baseball deliberated, Marge adhered to a directive from the commissioner's office that she let outgoing Peter Ueberroth and incoming Bart Giamatti handle it. Cook felt it was important to give some degree of support to his manager; he said that the club would presume Rose innocent until proven guilty and that he hoped the team could get on with the business of playing baseball while the case was pending. Cook was trying to deflect the Rose affair away from the team as much as he could, but Marge didn't like it. She didn't care for what he said about the embattled manager and didn't even want him to talk about the Rose situation publicly. Cook believes she resented any support he gave Rose, because she was so offended that Rose was putting Marge Schott through this. "She took it personally that Pete was doing this to her and the Reds—and she really does believe in the Reds," Cook said. "She thinks that everybody should bow down to the Reds and her, simply because it's the Reds, and that's not healthy."

Finally, on August 24, 1989, the case of Peter Edward Rose vs. Major League Baseball was over. The agonizing months of investigation and injunction and accusation that had elicited such emotion in Cincinnati ended when Rose and Giamatti reached an agreement. Rose was suspended for life for misconduct related to gambling. There was no official finding, but neither was there a gag on either side, and Giamatti expressed his opinion concerning the obvious: Rose associated with bookmakers, gambled on baseball, and gambled on the Reds.

Baseball did Marge's work for her, because Marge would not have fired Rose. At various times during Cook's tenure, she told him she couldn't do it. Even after Rose was banished from baseball, Marge admitted that she would have let him come back if Giamatti hadn't removed him. She simply lacked the guts and feared the repercussions. She knew Rose was great for the gate, and she was worried that firing Rose would turn the city against her. The fact was, firing Rose would have had some immediate backlash from zealots but would not have caused the mass hysteria Marge envisioned—and certainly not many diatribes within the media and inside the game.

"To be very honest with you, when a manager's been there five years and had four second-place finishes and one fifth-place finish, more often than not he's not gonna get another chance," said Reds broadcaster Marty Brennaman. "I'm of the opinion that, at that time, the public reaction against her would have been minimal. I think there were enough fans in this town who were ready to see a change."

With all the time and all the talent Rose had, there was no excuse for him not to have brought back home at least one division title, a situation made worse as it became clear that he had spent too much time calling in his bets and too little time talking to his players.

"Pete had an enormous amount of detractors in the game," said Cook. "Pete was not perceived by very many to be a good manager. For a long time, it didn't improve. He didn't get any direction. He had never managed, and Bill Bergesch was such a fan of his that Pete just did whatever the hell he wanted. I think Pete was crying for some direction. I thought that my first year [1988], he was starting to realize that some of the things that we talked about were important, the communication, the motivation, the instruction. He had a lot of good traits as a manager. He could have been an excellent manager, because he has a great memory and he can get along with players if he tries. And I thought he was getting better."

Marge said that if Rose had escaped suspension and returned she would have warned him to change his ways. She claimed to be saddened by the whole mess and what it did for the fans.

"The only thing I feel bad about with Pete—and I'm sure he does, too, in his heart—is that he had a very strong image to give to the children," she said a month later. "We're so family oriented with the Reds. Some of the children at Riverfront can't say hello or goodbye, but they can say, 'I wuv Pete Rose.' It's sad that Pete doesn't feel he did anything wrong."

By the time Rose was gone, replaced on an interim basis by coach Tommy Helms, Marge had essentially stripped Murray Cook of much of his power. With the team out of contention, she told Cook not to make any more trades, or any personnel moves unless it involved a minor-league player, or any expenditures that weren't absolutely necessary. So Cook, who already had secured infielder Mariano Duncan and pitcher Tim Leary from Los Angeles for outfielder Kal Daniels, was prevented from making any deals for much of the second half of the season.

Granted, it was too late to salvage 1989; but it caused Cook to cut off negotiations he had going with other general managers on deals that could have helped the team in the future.

"She just lost confidence in my/our/the baseball people's ability to perform effectively," said Cook. "It was terribly frustrating."

About the only notable event for the rest of the season occurred toward the end, when the Reds were slumping along toward fifth place and the only point of interest seemed to be whether Cook and Helms would retain their jobs for 1990. The World Wrestling Federation was coming to Cincinnati for a performance on the same day the Reds had an afternoon game at Riverfront Stadium, and Reds broadcaster Marty Brennaman was asked if he and partner Joe Nuxhall would like Randy "Macho Man" Savage to sit in the booth with them for a few innings. As Marty and Joe were WWF fanatics, as the Reds were in a season-ending stretch that Brennaman called perhaps the worst two months he'd experienced with the team, and as Savage was a former Reds farmhand named Randy Poffo, Marty jumped at the opportunity. But Marty and Joe didn't realize that Savage would show up in full costume and go into his "Macho Man" routine, tearing up a life-size poster of nemesis Hulk Hogan and causing the fans to glare at the entertainment coming from the broadcast booth. Some of the players got into the act, peeking out from inside the dugout and even playfully flexing their muscles to impress the visiting dignitary.

Everybody loved it. Except Marge.

She sent Steve Schott, her executive vice-president and her late husband's cousin, to put an end to the theatrics. He ordered the engineer to take Savage off the air—or Steve would find another broadcaster. When the engineer relayed the message to Marty, Savage went off the air and Marty went off on Steve. While Joe was broadcasting, Marty went looking for Steve and confronted him in a vacant room behind the booth. Marty was so mad, he was literally shaking.

"Let me tell you something," Marty told him. "Don't ever threaten me with my job. Ever. As long as you live, never threaten me, because I can't be intimidated."

After the game, Marty got a message that Marge wanted to see him in her office, and when he arrived, roughly a dozen people were waiting for him. Marge started chastising her broad-caster, saying that Savage wasn't conducive to the family atmo-sphere she was trying to create at Riverfront Stadium. Marty tried to argue that professional wrestling was a big hit with the kids, that Hulk Hogan was a great role model, and that he was just trying to add a little entertainment to a game that was anything but pivotal in the standings. Marge didn't want to hear any of that. She just wanted to make sure it didn't happen again. Still, Marty's greatest memory from that meeting came not from Marge but from the portly Steve, who delivered what Brennaman calls "the greatest line of all time" in reference to Randy Savage.

STEVE: Well, Marge, I did my best to get
                him out of there. In fact, I thought I
                was going to have to get physical
                with him at one time.

MARTY: You've gotta be kidding. He'd have
                pinched your goddamned head off.

Outside of that incident, Brennaman says he never had a problem with Marge. In fact, Marty says Marge consistently supported him, which is admirable considering his type of broadcasting. For a home-team announcer, Brennaman is one of the most objective voices you will find, willing to criticize his team's foibles while other broadcasters shamelessly shade the truth and cheer. And when NL president Bart Giamatti and commissioner Peter Ueberroth reprimanded Marty and Joe and accused them of making comments that helped to incite a riot at Riverfront after Rose had shoved umpire Dave Pallone, Marge backed her voices completely.

Another time, one of the Reds' wives complained to Marge that Marty was being too critical of the players. Shortly thereaf-ter, Marge approached Brennaman about the subject, and when she did, Marty interrupted her.

MARTY: Now if you're telling me to back off
                of being critical of the players, you'd
                better go find yourself another radio
                announcer. I have always main-
                tained that if I'm going to praise
                them when they play well, then I

	maintain the right to be critical when they're not.
MARGE:	Oh, no, no, no. You misunderstand. I told this person that if they felt strongly enough about it, to write you a letter. You keep doing what you've been doing. I'm not telling you this because I want you to change anything.
MARTY:	Well, if there's a letter written, there will be copies sent to *The Enquirer* and *The Post*, and there will be one put up on the bulletin board in the clubhouse for all the players to see.

Brennaman never got that letter, and he claims Marge has continued to back him. He is savvy enough to understand that being critical doesn't equate to being stupid, and he knows better than to take off on Marge over the air—although he got on her for allowing the dog to run around and relieve itself on the field. And Marge is careful not to say anything publicly against Marty and Joe, whose popularity in Cincinnati rivaled Rose's. In fact, when the pair started splitting up for some television broadcasts on Opening Day 1986, the talk-show lines lit up with complaints from fans who didn't seem to care that the team had won, 7-4. Marge never forgot it and later refused to let the pair split up for TV again, although eventually she relented.

While Brennaman and Nuxhall claim that Marge is good to them, Marty seems more willing to judge her by that while Joe appears more disturbed by the way she acts toward others. "The way she treats her employees—that's always been my gripe," said Nuxhall. "But I give her credit for what she's done, too. I guess everybody has their way of running a show."

Nuxhall remembers one run-in he had with Marge when he had three baseballs autographed by such celebrities as Phyllis Diller, Marie Osmond, and Andy Williams to be auctioned off at Nuxhall's annual charity golf tournament. Nuxhall got someone to approach Bob Hope, who was in town attending a function at the Montgomery Inn restaurant, to add his signature to the baseballs. While the comedian was signing, Marge walked up and asked whose baseballs they were. When she was told, she remarked that Nuxhall worked for her and walked off with one of the balls.

"I wasn't happy," said Nuxhall.

As for Steve, Marty says he never had a problem with him after the Macho Man fiasco—that Steve apologized for threatening his job and eventually proved an ally for him in contract negotiations. However, Steve's presence at Riverfront Stadium was not so universally appreciated. Four years as a financial consultant on Wall Street did not educate him in the ways and means of a major-league baseball team, and his ignorance became an inside joke that occasionally made it outside. The classic story was when he asked Nuxhall, a Reds legend and the youngest major leaguer in history, what he did before he was a broadcaster. Steve, feeling misunderstood, only made it worse when he tried to approach the subject with Nuxhall again.

> STEVE: I meant, what did you do between
>   the time you played and the time
>   you became a broadcaster?
> NUXHALL: You mean the 45 minutes in be-
>   tween?

But Steve's ignorance about baseball wasn't as bad as the politics. He came to the Reds referring to the owner as "Aunt Marge" and alienated himself from the front office by assuming the worst and reporting on the staff back to the owner. Cal Levy, who believes he was fired for standing up to Marge and Steve, referred to Steve as Marge's sentinel: "He was her eyes and ears in the office, and she trusted him completely. That may be because she never wanted to believe anything positive about the staff, anyway. I think he did what he thought she wanted him to do, and I don't think he understood the dynamics of that situation at all."

Certainly not in the beginning.

But, to his credit, he learned.

By the time he learned fully, Murray Cook was gone, fired at the end of the 1989 season. Cook believes it was nothing personal, that Marge lumped him together with Rose and simply wanted a fresh start for 1990, and that his relationship with Marge was so good she fired him personally instead of sending her attorney, Bob Martin, to do it for her. Actually, Cook was destined to be a short-term general manager even by Marge's standards, because she didn't like his wife, Pamela, and she hated the way they got together—and Marge ranted that she didn't find out about it until after hiring Cook. Pamela was married to Montreal Expos president and general partner Claude Brochu when Cook was that team's general manager.

"I'd been separated for several months, and Pamela was in the process of separating from her husband," said Cook. "We fell in love. It's nothing very deep and dark. It was rather untimely, but it was just one of those things that happens between people. It was a very difficult situation, and we decided it was better separating from the Expos. So I resigned."

When Cook interviewed with Marge, she asked him if there were any problems she should be aware of, and Cook told her that he and Pamela were both in the process of getting divorces at the time. Shortly after Marge hired Cook, she learned the details of Cook's relationship with Pamela, and Marge started carrying on about feeling betrayed and how someone in baseball should have told her. To any other owner in a sport that once saw pitchers Fritz Peterson and Mike Kekich swap wives, this would have been nothing more than a little cocktail talk. To Marge, it was catastrophic, and she would call Pamela Cook names behind her back.

"We weren't the only people who've ever been divorced," said Cook. "I don't know why that should be such a dramatic deal in your professional life, as long as you're fulfilling business obligations and doing your job well. There was never anything to be embarrassed about here. But this is part of Marge's M.O.—she liked to get involved. And that's her right as an owner. She can do what she wishes, and you have to respond accordingly."

Howie Bedell almost had a similar problem with Marge, although she at least confronted him about it. Bedell ran the Reds' farm system beginning in 1990. He was out on the road checking out some of the organization's teams, when Steve called him and told him to come back to the office, even though he was supposed to be on the road for another two weeks. Steve told him that Marge wanted to see him "today or tomorrow," that it was "very important." Bedell called then-general manager Bob Quinn to find out what was going on, and Quinn said, "Howie, I don't know, you got to settle it yourself." The next day, Bedell drove five hours to Riverfront Stadium from Charleston, West Virginia, wondering if he was going to be fired or just what was the problem. When he got to the Reds' offices, Quinn reiterated his ignorance in the matter and refused to go with him into Marge's office. Bedell then confronted Steve, who put him off for a half-hour then told him he was a little busy right now. Bedell backed Steve through the doorway and closed the door.

BEDELL: Sit down, we're going to talk.

STEVE: What are you talking about?

BEDELL: Why was I called up here?

STEVE: No matter how things turn out, I
            will always be your friend.

BEDELL: Steve, what are you talking about?

STEVE: I don't know. You're going to have
            to talk to Marge.

BEDELL: There's something going on here.
            We've got a great year going. The
            minor leagues are fine. I had hoped
            I could come here and retire. I like
            this city an awful lot. I have a lot of
            friends out here, and baseball is
            baseball. But something's not right.

STEVE: I just wish you luck, and I'll always
            be your friend.

BEDELL: That's really nice. I appreciate that.

STEVE: When are you going to see her?

BEDELL: I'm going in right now.

STEVE: Can I go with you?

BEDELL: Be my guest.

So Howie Bedell went in to see Marge Schott, who spent the first 45 minutes or so talking at him and around him but not getting to the point. Finally, Bedell spoke up and said, "Look, I don't understand what this is all pertaining to. If it's the matter of me traveling too much or doing something you're not comfort-able with, just tell me." But Marge didn't respond. She just looked at him. So Bedell said, "I've offered Steve the chance to travel with me a number of times to learn what baseball is all about. But all he wants to do when we go away on a trip is find out when the cocktail hour is and where some of the nice places are so he can meet some female companions, and what time the golf course opens."

At that point, Steve sank in his chair.

And Marge finally got to the point.

MARGE:	Where do you live?
BEDELL:	Sometimes in a hotel. Most of the time in Dayton.
MARGE:	Do you know a woman named Janet?
BEDELL:	Sure.
MARGE:	Where is your wife?
BEDELL:	She's at home [in Pottstown, Pa.]. She broke her foot.
MARGE:	This Janet person, how do you get away with that?
BEDELL:	What are you talking about?
MARGE:	Are you living with her?
BEDELL:	Janet and Pam are very good friends. She's from Pottstown, and when her parents passed away, she had no real family, so she lived with my wife's family for two years until she graduated high school. When she learned I was going to be in Cincinnati, her and her husband, Jim, who's a retired officer in the Air Force, asked me if I'd stay in their home . . . Marge, how did you ever get this idea?
MARGE:	Lois [Schneider], your secretary, told Joyce [Marge's secretary] about this lady you were talking to who would call and ask if she should hold dinner for you. Joyce told me you had a girlfriend.
BEDELL:	No, I don't.
MARGE:	From now on, I'm going to bug the ladies' room.

BEDELL: You can't do that. It's against all
               principles.
MARGE: I can do it. It's mine.
BEDELL: Don't do that. It's just a misunder-
               standing.

With the other-woman issue behind them, Bedell ended up spending the entire afternoon in Marge's office talking politics and just about everything else now that the air was cleared—at least figuratively speaking. "She smoked so many cigarettes," said Bedell, "if I end up with a cancer problem, I have every reason to believe I could trace it back to that day alone." When they were finished talking, he and Marge embraced, and Marge surprised him by squeezing him hard and giving him "the wettest kiss on the lips" before telling him, "Go out there and do what you need to do, honey." Marge paraded Bedell down the hall, past Quinn's office, and Quinn told him later, "Everyone was betting you were fired."

He wasn't. Not yet, anyway. But Bedell's encounter was indicative of Marge's reliance on judging her male employees by their marriages and their wives and her insistence on focusing on their personal lives. In fact, for as much of a role model for working women as Marge appeared to be, she was not above telling married women she met that they should quit their jobs and stay at home and make babies.

The end of 1989 brought a change in general managers, farm directors, and managers—and a change in team physicians. Dr. Warren G. Harding III had been with the team since 1987, having been the orthopedic consultant for roughly a decade and becoming even more involved in 1986 when team doctor George Ballou became sick. Ballou had been with the Reds since 1953. When Harding took over on a full-time basis, Marge took away Ballou's complimentary tickets and refused to allow him to purchase them. Harding was also struck by her refusal to ensure top medical care for her players, and it was left to him and trainer Larry Starr to take care of it themselves.

Marge displayed very little understanding of what would seem to be common sense—that you spent the money necessary to keep your high-priced players healthy and in top physical shape now or paid more in the long run in time on the disabled list and games in the standings. The concept of having a doctor there in case of an emergency didn't quite sink in, either. Even though the rules dictated that a team doctor had to be present to take care of the home and visiting teams, Marge asked Harding if he really had to go to all of the games. "I think she never really understood what I did," said Harding. "She had no idea why I was there."

And she became impatient with the players getting hurt and not coming back to work as quickly as she would have liked, figuring it was the doctors' responsibility and that he was concerning himself more with the players' well-being than with the team's. One of Marge's favorite questions when she'd run into Harding would be "Why isn't Eric playing?" or "What's wrong with Eric today?" Yet for all her pushing, she did little to meet her requirements as owner to make certain that the best treatment and rehabilitation were available.

The problems ranged from little nuisances to major obstacles. Marge wouldn't approve the purchase of medicine by Harding because she couldn't understand why a baseball player needed an antibiotic, for example. But take a case where a player would come to Harding after a game with a sore throat that turned out to be infected. Harding didn't want to send him out looking for an all-night pharmacy—he wanted to get the player started in the recovery process right away, so he'd give the player penicillin. To do that, Harding had to provide the medicine himself.

With a little help.

"I would get free samples from the drug representatives, and I'd tell them, 'We need some of these to keep in our medical bag at the stadium,'" said Harding. "And they were always happy to give you starter supplies."

Rolls of tape were another problem. There was a budget for tape, and if the team ran out, it was a nightmare trying to get more. Notes came back saying, "How could you possibly need this much tape?" But what was the medical and training staff supposed to do with such cases as first baseman Terry Francona in 1987, whose knees needed taping every night?

"We'd have to buy extra tape ourselves," said Harding. "It was kind of embarrassing. After a while, you get kind of gun-shy of going back to the same source and getting insulted, so to speak."

Harding said sometimes he would pay for it out of his own pocket, and sometimes his medical practice at Wellington

Orthopaedic and Sports Medicine provided some. They didn't have to do that, but the alternative was to watch the players get less than the proper medical care, and they weren't going to allow that to happen. And those expenditures were minuscule compared to the care and therapy Wellington provided for the Reds free of charge, because the Reds wouldn't do it and certainly wouldn't pay for it. The staff at Wellington was as cooperative as the ownership of the Reds wasn't, understanding that the proper rehabilitation after injury can equate to an extra start for a pitcher or another 10 at-bats for a player, and it made the therapists and doctors feel as though they were a part of the Reds' effort.

"Every time the team would go out of town, the players who were left at home on the disabled list would continue their therapy at Wellington because there weren't any other provisions made for them," said Harding. "Larry and the assistant trainer would be on the road, and the players required the care of therapists."

Even when the Reds were in town, sometimes Wellington would help out by allowing players to use its equipment, either at Wellington or at the stadium. The Reds simply didn't have the same equipment as Wellington or as some of other major-league teams, and some of the equipment they did have was not exactly state-of-the-art.

"It would have been nice to have the latest things, but we got pretty resourceful at getting things fixed for the 10th and 12th time and doing a lot of maintenance and repair work," said Harding. "You make it work—that was the attitude that carried us through."

Having Larry Starr helped immensely, a trainer Harding proclaims was "without peer." But after 1989, Harding no longer worked with Starr or the Reds, because Marge decided to hire an acquaintance, Robert Heath, as the new team doctor. And that was it for Warren Harding. He was sad about leaving, but in retrospect he felt worse for some of the members of the Reds' front office, who didn't have regular jobs and had to endure her insensitive treatment or face unemployment.

Harding's successor was out of a job almost as soon as he was hired, once the Reds learned more details of his background. Later, in fact, Heath's license was revoked in 1991 after a state medical board examiner concluded he had had sexual contact with several teenage boys, among other charges.

With the season nearing, Marge approached Dr. Michael Lawhon, a former Louisville University basketball player who also happened to be an associate of Harding's at Wellington. In fact, Lawhon had been assisting Harding with the Reds, going to some 30-35 games a year. Marge first talked to Lawhon at a charity basketball game and took a shot at Harding—and, in effect, at Lawhon, considering he was assisting Harding—but Marge obviously had no idea of that. "We need a doctor who is not a wimp with the players," she told Lawhon, "somebody who can make them play."

It was an awkward situation for Lawhon. But being a former athlete himself, the opportunity to work for the Reds was intoxicating, and he told Marge he believed he could be beneficial to the team because he understood what it was like to be a ballplayer and he had the medical background for the position. Lawhon talked to Harding about it, and they agreed it would be good public relations for their medical group to keep the Reds. "He was," said Lawhon, "a perfect gentleman."

Before long, Lawhon was seeing and hearing the same things Harding had seen and had warned him about before taking the job: Marge had no understanding of what went on in a locker room, what happened on the field, and what went on when players had injuries. In fact, she questioned Lawhon about having to come to all the games, just as she had with Harding.

"Why the hell do you come to all these games?" she asked Lawhon. "Every time you come, one of our players gets hurt."

Lawhon insists that she was not kidding, that she was "very serious." So, just as Harding had done, he explained to her that baseball rules dictate that a doctor be present at every game in case someone is injured on the home or visiting team. It was a concern Marge Schott did not share.

"I don't give a goddamn about the goddamn players," she told Lawhon. "They're a bunch of babies."

End of conversation.

And Marge repeated to Lawhon at other times her assertion that his appearance at Reds games meant one of the players would get hurt. She also told him, "I hate doctors." Lawhon got her to laugh about that by responding, "I don't like all of them, either." Getting her to understand his role as the team physician and purchasing what the team really needed to update the equipment was a much more hopeless task.

Lawhon wasn't looking for Marge to spend six figures on high-tech weight-lifting equipment. He wanted the Reds to purchase electric-stimulator machines and ultrasound machines—equipment that would aid in the everyday rehabilitation and conditioning of players. Lawhon and Starr recommended the purchase of an electric-stim machine to help the treatment of sprains and strains and were told not only that their request was turned down, but that Marge ripped it up and threw it in the garbage.

Sometimes the Reds would end up borrowing equipment from visiting teams. Sometimes players would purchase equipment themselves. Sometimes players would end up back at Wellington for treatment before games. The situation was so bad at Riverfront Stadium, Lawhon at times saw players line up at 4 p.m. until near gametime for treatment.

"A lot of the players just skipped treatment because they didn't want to stand around and wait," said Lawhon. "They felt they should be out on the field practicing."

But that increased their chances of further injury and slowed down the rehabilitation process. Here Marge was investing millions of dollars in her players in terms of salaries, yet she wasn't paying the thousands necessary to make sure those investments were performing up to their capabilities. The Reds had a knee-rehabilitation machine that Lawhon said had to be repaired every couple of weeks: "I mean, the thing was archaic." The Reds lacked a computerized machine that measured the leg strength of a player's healthy leg against the leg strength of a player's recovering leg to learn how far a player had to go in rehabilitation. Lawhon had to send a player to his ofice to get such a reading.

Although Lawhon insists that he and Starr were able to provide the Reds with quality care, he knew better equipment would have helped the players not only physically but mentally. It was only natural that when players saw some other teams emphasizing the best possible treatment for their players—when they might provide a team physician, an orthopedic surgeon, an internal-medicine doctor, a team psychiatrist, a strength coach, and all the equipment necessary to protect their players—it preyed on their minds. As a Reds player, you come to feel second best. And when you're rehabilitating, you don't have the type of positive attitude that can help you heal faster.

"Mentally, it puts the players at a disadvantage," said Lawhon. "These guys bounce from team to team now. They know what the other teams have. They know what the other management does for the other ballplayers."

One case in point was Eric Davis. He was constantly getting sidelined with injuries, at least partly because of his penchant for diving in the outfield after fly balls and because of his frail frame. But Lawhon wondered if the mental aspect didn't play some part in all of that.

"I don't think you can lay it all on equipment," said Lawhon. "But I think we could have developed a better workout atmosphere for Eric that would have made his rehabilitation much easier."

Eventually, Lawhon concluded that he could no longer work for the Reds because he didn't feel he could provide first-class treatment for the team. So he resigned in December 1991, not wanting to do anything to damage his reputation and citing in a statement "a lack of support and honesty from the front office . . . continued second-guessing and misleading reports about injuries . . . refusal to provide equipment necessary for the treatment of common, everyday injuries . . . refusal to provide rehab equipment to the players to facilitate strength and conditioning programs . . . lack of coordinated medical training programs for the minor-league system." He knew the instability of the medical staff for the team was detrimental to the trust and therefore the health of the players, but he just couldn't put up with it anymore, as much as he loved being part of the Reds.

But at least he was there to see their one magical season, the one during which they stayed in first place from wire to wire during the regular season and later pulled off a shocking four-game sweep of the Oakland Athletics. It was a great moment for Lawhon and the Reds and the rest of Cincinnati.

But not for Marge Schott.

— Chapter Nine —

Wire to Wire
Without a Net

There was a different feel to the Cincinnati Reds in 1990.
Gone were the trauma and melancholy of the scandal that
strained the emotions of the city and claimed the baseball
career of its favorite son. Gone with Pete Rose was a manager
riding the glory of his past accomplishments, who proved once
again that great players rarely make great managers, because
they expect too much of themselves to appear in their players.
Gone also was the burden of lugging around the unfulfilled
expectations and anxiety produced by four consecutive second-
place finishes, the fall to fifth place tantamount to a plunge into
obscurity.

This was a fresh start. A new manager and new general
manager. A new look and new outlook.

For a general manager, the animal-loving owner of the Reds
went shopping for an inmate of the Bronx Zoo and selected Bob
Quinn. Steve Schott says he got Quinn's name from National
League President Bill White and received permission to talk to
Quinn from Yankees owner George Steinbrenner— who could
always find another figurehead. Marge sought the advice of
another former Yankee type, Dallas Green, who raved about
Quinn's work ethic, loyalty, and honesty when it came to the
club. But as much as he tried, Green could never convince Quinn
to show the same devotion to the truth when it came to the media.

For a manager, Marge asked Green if he was interested, and
he told her to hire a general manager first. When she did, he

decided he would pass, hoping to land a position with one of the expansion clubs instead. So it was back to the Yankees, and this time the Reds settled on Lou Piniella, a fan favorite in Gotham as a player who ended up in Steinbrenner's inner circle of revolving managers, general managers, and broadcasters. Piniella was everything Rose wasn't and everything the Reds needed. He was a disciplinarian, intense and explosive—quite a contrast to the laissez-faire managing style the Reds had endured. This job was important to Piniella, his third stint as a manager after two under Steinbrenner, and he was intent on proving to Boss George that he could indeed be a championship manager.

When Quinn was announced as general manager, he said all of the things that the owner wanted to hear. He said he had a one-year plan for the Reds. He said Marge's ownership entitled her to certain "proprietary rights." He said he could work with her. On the other hand, it took Marge just a matter of minutes before she was undercutting her new general manager. She was asked at the press conference about the primary player issue of the moment, whether any player was worth the $3 million a year Eric Davis was seeking, and she replied, "If they can play every position—and do it all at once." Such words would put Quinn in a somewhat awkward position, considering he'd have to negotiate with a player who felt he was worth $3 million, and over the years the Reds-Davis negotiations had been characteristically ugly. Only this time, if the talks failed, the Reds' marquee player could exit via free agency after the season.

As it turned out, Marge's stand predictably didn't hold, and Davis received his $3 million per year—$3.1 million, actually, for three years. Once again, Marge got involved in the negotiations, this time with Quinn and Steve in the mix, as well. The final negotiating session was held at Marge's office, and new farm director Howie Bedell waited in the GM's office for Quinn, his temporary hotel roommate. Each of the participants came out of the office separately and filled Bedell in on the details. Steve told him he believed it could get settled. Marge told him she believed she could end all of this by raising the offer from $9.3 million to $9.8 million. Goldschmidt came out and indicated that if he agreed to $9.3 million, Davis would take it. They agreed to talk again the next day, Goldschmidt telling Quinn he wanted $9.6 million.

When Quinn and Bedell got back to their room, they were invited to a party across the street for Barry Larkin, in honor of his impending marriage. When they got there, Davis looked at Quinn and said, "I guess we have a deal," and Quinn responded, "We have a deal." So Quinn put the $9.3 million figure on a napkin, and Davis signed the napkin.

"It taught me a lesson," said Bedell. "You need to see the player somewhere along the line."

It was something Murray Cook had realized, but perhaps too late to save his relationship with Davis. Quinn, at least, was off to a good start by signing Eric Davis. And he managed to save Marge some money because she let him handle the negotiating in the end. But it was a rare victory for Quinn, who would turn into the biggest whipping boy Marge Schott ever had during her tenure as general partner of the Reds. She once even told a limited partner, "I don't know what Bob Quinn does."

Quinn had the type of personality that Marge devoured. A recovering alcoholic, he acted as though every day was a gift from God, smiling brightly and handing out his wife's cookies in the press box, even readily and sincerely quoting Barbra Streisand—that people who need people are the luckiest people in the world. Quinn, a third-generation baseball executive, certainly knew the game and was a nice and decent man, whose biggest faults in public were never admitting to mistakes and habitually lying to the media. But his main drawback came behind the scenes in not standing up to Marge. And with Marge, that was like putting a bull's-eye on his back. The more she pushed him around trying to get a reaction out of him, the more intent he was not to give her one.

You just can't survive that way with Marge. Those who lasted for any length of time did so by trying to avoid her whenever possible, knowing that to be near her was to be a potential outlet for whatever was bugging her. When you have to be around her, employ strategy whenever possible, using Schottzie or family or the notion of how tough it is for a woman to succeed in a man's world to get Marge in a better and more receptive mood. The local media learned that a long time ago, realizing that the best way to get an interview with Marge was to put a female reporter on the job and/or to call Marge after 10 p.m., when she seemed a little more talkative and a little less sober. For employees who had to deal with her on a more regular basis, it was necessary to be straightforward, detailed, clear, and firm—but careful, because if you got to the point where you butted heads, your butt could be headed out the door. Not that any approach was foolproof, but the worst was to let her walk all over you, and Quinn never seemed to realize that. Or perhaps the years of working under Steinbrenner desensitized him to the point where it almost didn't matter.

Still, Marge would make him sweat for the most ridiculous of matters. Quinn was only there a few months when he asked Bedell to sit in on and offer his support for a presentation Quinn was making to Marge and Steve for new copy machines. Bedell was amazed. The old ones were broken and couldn't be repaired, and here was the general manager of a major-league baseball team having to compile an extensive report on why it was so important to have functioning copy machines. So Bedell sat in on the 7:30 p.m. meeting, watching his general manager who had been at the office since 6 a.m. make this thoughtful presentation on copy machines—and Bedell couldn't keep from smiling. Marge looked up, snuffed out a cigarette, and confronted Bedell.

> MARGE: Howie, you think this is funny, don't you?
>
> BEDELL: Yes, I do. I think it's a real waste of our time and your time. Bob's a busy man trying to accomplish a great deal here for you. I know he worked hard on this report. I'm not smiling because of that. I just think it's amusing that for less than $10,000 we spent this much time on something the office needs. It's what they use. It's a part of office procedure. These cannot be repaired. They are many, many years old, and we're spending all this time on this.

Marge turned in her chair, and looked at Quinn and said, "Howie's right."

After the meeting, Bedell assured Quinn he was not trying to show him up and that his smiling did not reflect his attitude toward him, only what Marge was putting him through. Quinn understood and was impressed by the way Bedell seemed to have Marge's ear, telling his farm director, "Maybe your approach was the right approach." He suggested Bedell go straight to Marge with requests or concerns instead of going through him. Bedell didn't like that. He preferred to follow the chain of command, whatever that was. It was in constant flux beginning in 1990. One day, Quinn and Steve were on a par in the company flow chart; the next day, Quinn might be under Steve. But every day, Quinn seemed to be attached to the bottom of Marge's shoe.

"Often, Bob would talk about how Marge was walking all over him," said Bedell. "I said to him, 'As a person, you don't have to take that.' But he said, 'I don't have any choice.'"

Actually, Bedell felt as though he himself got along pretty well with Marge from the beginning. When they first met, Quinn took him out to her estate in Indian Hill at about 10:00 a.m. As they were going up the driveway, Quinn warned him not to get out of the car, or it could be dangerous.

QUINN: The dogs will bite you.

BEDELL: I have a good way with animals. I'm
                not worrying about them biting me.

QUINN: Well, just stay in the car until we get
                the indication that we can get out.

So they pulled up to the house and waited there a minute or two until Marge appeared at the window, saw them, went to the door and opened it, looked around, and said, "All right, it's OK to come in."

Bedell didn't have any strong preconceived notions about Marge before he entered her home. Oh, he'd heard some stories about her, understood she was eccentric, but had heard nothing to dissuade him from interviewing for this job. After all, Bedell felt good about the idea of working for Quinn, a long-time acquaintance who was the general manager of Reading, Pennsylvania, more than 20 years earlier, when Howie played there. In fact, Quinn drove Bedell to the airport when he was called up to Philadelphia in 1968; and a few days later, Bedell hit the sacrifice fly that ended Don Drysdale's record scoreless-innings streak at 58 2/3. Quinn's father, John, signed Bedell to his first professional contract.

But entering the world of Marge was a trip into uncharted territory.

"I could see she was living alone for the most part," Bedell said. "She had a large, spacious home that was not as tidy as you might expect. It was unkempt. Things were not dusted. There were ashtrays full of cigarettes in the room we went into. It was cold—it was a cool day, anyway, and the house didn't have a lot of heat. It was dark, kind of drab."

And Marge?

"She was not well kept, groomingwise, when I met her," he said. "But I truly felt that she could pass for anyone's grand-mother if she fixed herself up a little bit and she minded some of her personal habits."

Quinn, Bedell, and Marge talked through most of the after-noon. Marge's biggest concerns were that (a) Bedell expressed an interest in someday being on the field again as a major-league coach, and he assured her it would not interfere with his job for the Reds, and that his on-the-field knowledge would actually help him as a farm director, and (b) Quinn and Bedell were friends. Bedell didn't quite know what to make of it then, although later he would realize that Marge's style was to pull people apart instead of wanting them to pull together. Friend-ships made it difficult to divide and conquer.

During the course of the conversation, Quinn wanted one of his trademark cigars, but had left them in the car—which meant a possible showdown with the dogs. The St. Bernards had been out of sight, and Marge told Quinn it might not be a good idea for him to go out there—but that if he did, she'd keep a lookout for the dogs. So they walked to the front of the house, Marge kept watch for Schottzie and Siegie, and Quinn made a mad dash 15 feet to the car, worried that at any second one of those Volkswagen-sized canines would turn him into yesterday's general manager before Marge would get the opportunity. He grabbed the cigars, hightailed it back inside, and proclaimed, "Well, I made it, Marge."

When the interview was over, Marge hugged Bedell. Quinn and Bedell started out the door again, when suddenly the sound of loud barking hit them from the end of the driveway, and the two dogs came barreling toward them. Quinn raced to the car for safety. Bedell, who had a dog himself at home, was not about to run from a pair of dogs. Schottzie and Siegie came right up to him and rubbed up against him, as docile as can be, and he kneeled down and petted them. Impressed but cautious, Marge warned him to be careful, "They're liable to bite." But the only casualty was Bedell's black pants, which were covered with St. Bernard slobber. Bedell then got in the car, and he and Quinn drove away.

"I thought you were a goner," Quinn told him.

Bedell was offered and accepted the job, and it wasn't long before he started to see the house of horrors he had entered. Quinn agreed to a two-year contract for Bedell calling for $40,000 the first year and $42,000 the second, plus the club would provide the use of a car and would pay his health benefits. Bedell signed the contract. Quinn gave it to Marge to sign, and she put off doing it. When Bedell would ask Quinn about it, he would say it was "on her desk." Bedell quickly learned that "on her desk" meant there was a problem. Bedell implored Quinn to sign it, as he was the general manager and had agreed to the terms, but Quinn assured him it would be taken care of. It wasn't.

The Reds were paying Bedell his salary, but they were deducting the health-care premiums from his check, they were not providing him with a car, and they were questioning his qualification for the pension program. Bedell kept pushing Quinn, but was getting nowhere. Frankly, Quinn and two other new-comers—controller Tim Sabo and administrative assistant for player development and scouting Jim Bowden—were in the same situation as Bedell, having to pay the premiums the club was supposed to pay. Finally, Sabo came into Bedell's office and told him the health-care matter had been solved by increasing his salary enough to offset the price of the premiums, which would continue to be deducted from the paycheck. The same solution was offered to Quinn and Bowden by Steve. And although Marge didn't understand the pension setup, Sabo checked with the commissioner's office, learned that Bedell was correct, and assured Bedell the dispute was over.

As for the car, Steve called Bedell into his office one day and told him Marge wanted him out at her dealership in an hour. There, Marge took him on a tour of the place, introduced him to her employees, and finally showed him a maroon 1990 Chevrolet Lumina. Bedell would get the car, but with one catch. "She wanted me to understand that if anybody asked me where this car came from, that I bought it," said Bedell. It was a strange request, considering the club was *supposed* to provide Bedell with a car, and he reminded her as much. But she told him, "I would just prefer that these general people in our office complex didn't know about it," so he agreed.

Meanwhile, Quinn was having his own problems securing an automobile from Marge. Eventually she gave her general manager a Corsica, which is a lower-grade car than the Lumina she gave her farm director.

Along with Bedell, Bowden was one of Quinn's first hires with the Reds. Bowden was a prodigy of general manager Syd Thrift in Pittsburgh. He had followed Thrift to the Yankees and had earned a reputation for being overambitious, but bright, hardworking and adept at computers. When Quinn was general manager of the Yankees, Bowden was alleged to have been part of a plot to rip off computer information from the Pittsburgh organization. Even though Bowden was eventually cleared, George Steinbrenner had Quinn fire him. But Quinn told Bowden that if he ever had the opportunity, he would try to help him out. This was the opportunity.

"Bob told me that he had agreed to bring in this fellow from the Yankees that had been with Pittsburgh," said Bedell. "He told me the story, and I knew a little about it. He said he was a computer whiz but—in his words—'he's a pain in the ass but if you take him and work with him and direct him, he could possibly be a pretty good baseball person someday.' I asked Bob, 'What kind of baseball background does he have?' And he said, 'None.' I indicated to him that that would be a very difficult job to make a baseball person out of him, considering he didn't have any baseball background. And Bob said, 'Well, he's very impatient, and it will be your responsibility that he gets assignments.'"

One of Bedell's first assignments as farm director was to fire Sheldon "Chief" Bender, who had been with the organization since 1967, after having been with the St. Louis Cardinals' organization since 1948. Quinn relayed the directive from Marge, after Chief had fallen on the wrong side of Steve and Marge. But Bedell wouldn't do it. He had played for the Cardinals organization when Chief was there, and he hoped that, if he ever got into this type of situation, somebody would do for him what he was about to do for Chief. Already, Chief had been kicked out of his office and told to work out of his home as a "special player consultant," but he showed up in Bedell's office with tears in his eyes.

CHIEF: You're not gonna fire me, are you?
BEDELL: I've known you for a long, long
                time. Chief, I have no intention of
                doing that.
CHIEF: Well, I know they're trying to fire
                me.
BEDELL: You may be right about that, but
                Howie Bedell's not gonna fire you.
                Right next to me, there's space
                behind the secretary, why don't you
                just consider moving everything
                right down there?

Even with all the typical chaos going on in the front office, Quinn was methodically making a series of moves that would deepen and strengthen the Reds for the upcoming season. He drafted pitcher Tim Layana out of the Yankees' minor-league system and traded pitcher Tim Leary and outfielder Van Snider to the Bronx for first baseman Hal Morris and pitcher Rodney Imes. Right before the season, Quinn dealt shortstop Whitey Richardson and pitcher Butch Henry to Houston for outfielder Billy Hatcher. But no trade was more controversial than the one with the New York Mets that sent All-Star reliever John Franco for reliever Randy Myers. Marge was already second-guessing it after the Reds had committed to the deal. Quinn and Piniella talked to her and tried to ease her mind.

"The trade had been made, and she got cold feet about it," said Piniella. "I said, 'Marge, we already made a commitment, we gotta go through with it.'"

Learning just how well the trade would work or how the Reds would play that season ended up being delayed, because an owners' lockout of the players postponed the beginning of the schedule. As a result, the Reds had to open the season on the road, in Houston, breaking a Cincinnati tradition. Marge was outraged. How dare baseball take away what was so important to Cincinnatians? How dare baseball rob her of one of her greatest moments in the spotlight?

Marge was determined to make the best of it, and she wanted to turn the Reds' first home series into a celebration. She wanted all the same festivities that Opening Day normally had, from the parade to the afternoon game—but the game that would be the Reds' home opener was scheduled at night. Marge wanted to poll the public to see if the fans wanted the game changed to the daytime, but National League president Bill White ordered her not to do it. So her media mouthpieces at WLW Radio and Channel 5 did it for her.

Frankly, the city wasn't on the verge of rioting in the streets over this issue. With the tradition already messed up and the season underway, there was no great groundswell of support to manipulate the ritual and turn the home opener into quasi-Opening Day. But Marge was so determined to get the game switched to daytime, she had Reds employees call up the poll number to pad the total supporting an afternoon game. Even so, 50.8 percent voted to keep the game at night, with 49.2 percent wanting the game moved to daytime. "It appears I'm damned if I do and damned if I don't," she said. But Clint Brown, the president of Alliance Research in nearby Crestview Hills, Kentucky, proved to be Marge's savior by calling her with the results of an unsolicited but scientific poll his company had conducted of 260 baseball fans, which said 51 percent wanted a day game, 33 percent wanted a night game, and 16 percent had no preference. It was the excuse Marge needed.

"I think God hired you," Marge told Brown.

By the time the Reds' home opener came around, the Reds themselves had become a much bigger story. They swept their six-game opening road trip and kept up the pace back home, going 9-0 before they were finally beaten. A team that had been fundamentally impaired under Rose was doing the little things, such as hitting to the right side of the field to advance runners, under Piniella, whose fire was rubbing off on his players. Plus, the Reds had an unparalleled bullpen, with three relievers of closer quality and explosive fastballs—Norm Charlton, Rob Dibble and Myers—who adopted the nickname made famous by an undercover police unit in Las Vegas and by a Janet Jackson hit song, "The Nasty Boys." The Reds would stay in first place all season, the first National League team ever to accomplish a 162-game wire-to-wire act, although at times the Reds appeared to be teetering on a tightwire instead. Piniella helped by instilling his lack of complacency into the team. Quinn did his part with a couple of finishing touches, acquiring outfielder Glenn Braggs and second baseman Bill Doran during the season, not only improving the personnel, but lifting the morale by showing the team that the front office was committed to a title, too.

By this time, the positive publicity from Marge's hiring of Quinn had erased all of the negative publicity surrounding her firing of Murray Cook, and of Bill Bergesch before him. Although she might not have understood the role of the press—or why a general manager should get so much recognition, for that matter—she seemed to understand the media's attention span. "She has a knack for realizing that no matter how bad a situation is with the media, by the second week, it's gone, it's history, that things go away whenever she would do anything unpopular," said Cook. "And she's right."

Cook was long since forgotten by the time Marge got into another run-in with the media over the controversial handling of Ken Griffey, one of the most respected Reds inside the clubhouse and the closest thing Cincinnati had to a leader among the players. At age 40 and on his second tour with the club, the former Big Red Machinist was a father figure to his teammates, offering insights on everything from how to handle a championship run to how to deal with Piniella's intensity—not to mention the manager's daily shuffling of players on the field. At its best, Lineup Du Jour keeps the hot players playing and the entire roster involved; at its worst, it keeps the semi-regulars perpetually looking over their shoulders when they believe they should be in the lineup every day. On a talented and deep team, Griffey as much as anyone was getting lost in the lineup shuffle, relegated to occasional pinch hits, so when the Reds were in desperate need of pitching help, Quinn looked at Griffey as expendable. On a Saturday morning before an afternoon game, Piniella told Griffey he wanted him to go on the disabled list, but Griffey insisted he wasn't hurt and so would not go. With no choice, Piniella and Quinn delivered Griffey one: Either he could be released or he could retire, but he had to decide before the game. Unable to reach his agent or the players' union, Griffey had to make a snap judgment. Griffey still felt he could play, but he didn't want to play just for the sake of playing. The idea of playing in Seattle with his son, Ken Griffey, Jr., was alluring, but he hadn't talked to Junior and didn't know how his son would feel about it, especially with Junior in the running for the batting title. And he worried that his release might cause a stir with the Cincinnati players and media and disrupt the Reds' championship run. Plus, Piniella and Quinn told Griffey that if he retired, the Reds would guarantee the remainder of his salary for the season. So Griffey decided to retire, figuring he could always change his mind. Problem was, once you're on the retired list, you can't come off of it for at least 60 days.

When Griffey's agent, Brian Goldberg, found out what had happened, he acted quickly. He discovered that not only did Junior want his father with him, the Seattle Mariners wanted Griffey there, too. Goldberg talked to National League President Bill White and was told Griffey's retirement had not been filed yet. White said given the questionable circumstances of Griffey's departure from the Reds, and the positive effects for baseball if Griffey could join his son in Seattle, White would change Griffey's status to "released" if the Reds approved it. So Goldberg contacted Quinn, who said he would talk to Marge. When Quinn didn't call back, Goldberg called again the next afternoon, and Quinn told him Marge wanted compensation for changing Griffey's status. Goldberg told Quinn that the Reds already were responsible for the rest of Griffey's salary for the season, about $85,000, and he wasn't even on the team now. Goldberg said that if Quinn would give him permission to talk with the Mariners, he believed he could get them to claim Griffey on waivers and therefore assume the $85,000 left in the salary. (If Griffey cleared waivers and was released, any team could sign him for the prorated major-league minimum salary—about $15,000 in this case—and the Reds would be responsible for the difference.)

"Brian, you don't understand," Quinn told the agent. "Marge assumes the Mariners will claim him, and the Mariners have told us they will; but Marge wants something more. She wants to know, 'What's in it for me? What the hell do I care if a father and son play together in Seattle? I want something more.'"

Goldberg was schocked. Seattle paying the rest of Griffey's contract seemed compensation enough, especially because Marge was angry at Piniella and Quinn for guaranteeing Griffey's salary for the rest of the season. Goldberg asked Quinn what else she wanted, and Quinn said Marge was looking for a cut of the gate on games in Seattle that Griffey and his son played together. "Bob made sure to tell me he thought this was ridiculous and he wanted to do the right thing, but Marge wouldn't let him," said Goldberg.

When nothing had changed by the next day, four days now after Griffey's retirement, Goldberg decided it was time to try embarrassing the Reds into doing what was right. He went public with Quinn's "What's in it for me" message from Marge, most notably on WLW. When WLW sports talk show host Cris Collinsworth heard Goldberg's remarks, he went ballistic. *"What's in it for me? What's in it for me? What's in it for me?"* he kept repeating in disbelief, chastising Schott. Marge heard it and erupted—at everyone involved. When contacted later, Marge characteristically denied making such a comment, claiming she'd been "put in front of the bus"—one of her favorite expressions. And when Quinn also was contacted later, he characteristically backed her up publicly, claiming Mrs. Schott had been "put in front of the bus." They accused the agent, one of the truly decent members of a sometimes indecent profession, of trying to force the issue. But Goldberg's plan worked, because two days later, Quinn called him and said that if the agent and Griffey would allow the Reds to say this was being done at Griffey's request, the team would release him.

Done.

So the Reds put Griffey on waivers for the purpose of giving him his unconditional release. Goldberg, free now to negotiate with other teams for Griffey's services, called Mariners general manager Woody Woodward, who said the timing of the release surprised him a little. The Reds and Mariners had not come to an agreement yet that Seattle would claim Griffey.

"Woody said he was furious over Marge trying to extract extra compensation—that he was so mad, they might not even claim Ken on waivers, thus forcing the Reds to pay all of Ken's salary except the prorated minimum," said Goldberg. "Woody's only question to me was, if the Mariners didn't claim him and Ken Jr. play together—would we agree to go with the Mariners an not pursue other teams? After speaking with Ken, I told Woody that I had no intention of being involved in any dispute between them and the Reds, but we would not pursue other teams."

Woodward followed through and stuck it to Marge, allowing Griffey to pass through waivers unclaimed. Goldberg assumed as much when he called the Reds when the three-business-day waiver period had expired to see if Griffey had cleared. A secretary put Goldberg on hold, then came back and said, "Brian, I've been told to tell you that you are to find out from the Mariners." Goldberg told her that the rules specifically state that the team waiving the player is required to provide that information, but the secretary just repeated her message. The rules also say that the player can call the team that waived him (collect, if he's out of town, which Griffey was), and Griffey did just that— only the Reds refused to accept the call. Goldberg then called the Mariners, who said they had not claimed Griffey. And Griffey later signed with Seattle.

Marge got no cut of the gate, no compensation at all. In fact, her greed *cost her* about $70,000 in Griffey's salary. Marge was so mad, she complained to Bill White. As a goodwill gessture, the Mariners made a contribution to the Cincinnati Zoo in Marge's name.

Meanwhile, WLW gave the former Cincinnati Bengals wide receiver a written reprimand for his on-air attack of the team owner—an unjustifiable transgression when you want to work for The Voice of the Reds/Marge. Collinsworth was told he should have talked to Quinn or Marge to get the Reds' side of the story before lashing out at Marge, which might appear to be journalistically sound, but went against the norm at the station, which was notorious for stirring up the masses while knowing only half the facts—if that much. When University of Cincinnati basketball star Louis Banks was on trial for rape, WLW sports-talk show host Andy Furman convicted him before the jury gave its verdict—which turned out to be *not* guilty—and Furman says he didn't even get a written reprimand for that.

WLW was a wonderfully entertaining and lively talk-radio station that basically owned the Cincinnati market during Marge's tenure. There was no more powerful or influential sports voice in the city than the self-proclaimed "Big One." But the station's foundation was the Cincinnati Reds broadcasts, and Marge held WLW hostage with contract provisions that basically sucker-punched the First Amendment. Witness this excerpt from the deal signed in 1988 for 1989-91:

The parties recognize that it will be in their mutual interest to engender a good working relationship between them during the term of this Agreement. Consistent with this, Jacor (owner of WLW) shall instruct the Station's employees that as a matter of policy, they should not make any remarks on the air that assail the personal reputation, morality, integrity, or character of any of the Club's partners, officers, or agents.

This policy, however, shall not be deemed to restrict or prohibit the Station's employees from expressing opinions, fair comment, and true statements of fact in making remarks on the air or to inhibit or stifle the Station employees in the course of their rights of free speech from engaging in legitimate broadcast journalism or in the exchange of ideas and views with the Station's audience.

In the event the Club believes that any remark on the Station by any of Station's employees has violated the foregoing policy, the Club will have within 10 days thereafter to notify Jacor and Jacor will promptly investigate the matter. After said investigation, which shall take no longer than five additional days after said notification, Jacor will take such remedial action as it deems appropriate to control the likelihood of reoccurrence by the offending employee. This action may consist of, without limitation, a warning or reprimand, an apology, fine, suspension, or termination. If in the opinion of Jacor, it does not feel that its policy has been violated, it will provide the Club within the said five-day period a written explanation of the basis for its conclusion and/or remedial action taken, if any.

In the event violations of Jacor's policy occur on a repetitive basis, as opposed to isolated occurrences, and Jacor has failed to act reasonably or in good faith in its efforts to control compliance with its policy, the Club shall have the right to terminate this Agreement immediately; whereupon, all rights and obligations of either party shall be null and void. Notwithstanding the foregoing, the Club shall have no right to terminate this Agreement for the acts of any Station employee who, for repeated violations of the policy, has been fined, suspended, or terminated.

Now perhaps lawyers can argue that the second paragraph in that excerpt ensures free speech, but it never got to the point where it is tested. WLW continually proved it would rather cower to Marge than risk upsetting her, fearing that even if the contract wasn't broken, Marge could bolt to another station when the radio deal expired. So edgy was WLW over the

Collinsworth incident, it killed a taped commentary concerning Griffey that avoided the "What's in it for me?" issue and focused solely on the loss of Griffey as a clubhouse leader. WLW program director Vance Dillard explained at the time, "There was absolutely nothing wrong with the commentary, and under normal circumstances it would be perfectly fine. But after what happened the other day with Collinsworth, things are pretty tense over here and Marge is threatening us with the contract, so we figured anything involving Griffey was just too hot to handle right now."

Gary Burbank, the satirical funnyman at WLW in the 2 p.m. to 6 p.m. time slot, so agitated Marge that he was asked not to even mention her name on the air anymore, much less mimic her voice. So he simply referred to her on the air as "St. CEO."

Burbank's first problem with Schott came when he played a song on the air to the tune of Allan Sherman's classic "Camp Grenada," replacing such lyrics as "Hello, muddah; hello, faddah" with "Schottzie's pregnant, who's the faddah?" The next thing Burbank heard, a Reds employee told him that Marge had called a group of them together to listen to the tape and had told them how horrible it was. All the while, however, the employees were trying to keep from busting out laughing. Burbank remembers this as one of the two or three times she asked the powers that be at the station for his resignation. Too popular to fire, Burbank drew his first "Boy, we'd hate to lose the Reds" look, which basically encouraged him to back off.

Burbank would target anyone of any importance in town at some time, and normally there would be no problem. But Marge would hear what he did or, perhaps more likely, hear *about* what he did, and she'd fume, such as the time during the 1986 partners meeting when it appeared she would be ousted, and Burbank started playing, "Ding Dong, the Witch Is Dead." And she used to hate Burbank's regular bit on the Reds that he called "Schott's Landing," in which he did a classic spoof on Marge's voice, referring to everybody as "You's babes." After more not-so-subtle urging from management, Burbank ended up changing the title to "The Hunt for Reds October."

But the greatest dispute he ever had with her came from a bit he said actually was favorable to Marge and was supposed to show how the media—and he includes himself in that category—would go overboard to take swipes at her. According to Burbank, one character in the bit said, "How's Marge going to treat her employees on Earth Day," and the media type responded, "Like always—treat them like dirt."

"She got a letter from one of her employees, and I got a copy of it, about what a wonderful, kind person she is, and how she really is Mother Teresa—in drag," Burbank said. "No, really, it was the same kind of letter you saw some kid write a teacher that he loved in the sixth grade."

After that, Burbank was told it was probably best not to do her voice at all. So out went his impersonation. Then after some other complaints, he was told it was probably best not to even mention her name on the air. These were not orders, mind you. They were more like suggestions, after summing up the situation, and explaining to him that what he was doing could lead the station to lose the Reds—or at least force station management to have to beg and plead and grovel to Marge not to leave WLW.

"I was never pointed at and told, 'Don't do it,'" said Burbank. "It was more like being told it would probably be a good idea not to do it. According to my contract, I could do it all day, and no one could say a word. If anybody is guilty about being wimpy about his Constitutional rights, it's me. But I don't want my radio station to lose the Reds because of me."

After Burbank started referring to Marge as "St. CEO," his loyal listeners caught on to the not-so-subtle nickname and even helped him out by calling in with an impersonation or two of Marge, since he couldn't do it. Collinsworth, too, became so obvious in his hands-off treatment of Marge that it spoke volumes about what he couldn't say. When a caller criticized Marge, Collinsworth would stay out of the argument or play it down the middle, politely saying something to the effect of, "I just can't comment on something like that on this radio station." He'd already been excluded from "The Hot Stove League," a one-hour-per-week segment to his 6 p.m. to 9 p.m. show during the off-season that focused on the Reds and featured Marty Brennaman and Joe Nuxhall.

Others came more readily to Marge's defense, but no one more than late-night host Bill Cunningham, who was doing three hours of what Burbank compared to World Wrestling Federation on radio. During the scandal over her racial slurs, Cunningham used his media platform as the voice in defense of the embattled owner, although he, too, later admitted to hearing her use the word "nigger" to describe blacks. Cunningham had little credibility, switching back and forth on issues and even admittedly going against his convictions on the air if he thought it would generate more callers. "It makes better radio," he explained privately after one such incident.

The most raucous and controversial sports voice on WLW, however, was Furman. Although Furman also was not above changing his stance to elicit callers—or above brown-nosing Marge on the air—he said he had never been told to stay away from issues concerning Marge. He conceded that was probably because he'd never said anything against her to warrant such a warning. Even when it became more and more obvious that Marge's slurs were real, Furman did not attack her, even though he is Jewish and found her terms offensive. "She's a putz, a modern-day Archie Bunker," said Furman. "She has no clue what she's done. But I like her. If my father said the things she did, I'd pity him for thinking that way, but I wouldn't hate him. I pity her, as well."

As for Griffey, the Reds sent Jim Bowden to Goldberg's office with the release letter for his client. Goldberg had never met Bowden, but they talked for a few minutes about what had happened, the agent recounting how Quinn had said he wanted to do what was right and release Griffey, but Marge had given him the "What's in it for me?" number. Within 15 minutes after Bowden left, Goldberg got a call from Steve Schott. The executive vice-president said Bowden was just in his office, telling Steve of his conversation with Goldberg, and Steve wanted to know if it was true. Yes.

"Steve made it clear that was not the first time Quinn had said something like that to somebody—that he would like to do something, but Marge wouldn't let him," says Goldberg. "The purpose of all this was clear to me: No. 2, Steve was upset because he perceived Quinn as not backing up Marge; and No. 1, this young kid who was just in here is obviously out to make Quinn look bad and had the ear of Steve Schott in doing that."

Meanwhile and publicly, the Reds were looking bad for the way they handled Griffey, many of the players honoring him by writing his No. 30 on their caps or shoes.

The exit of Griffey was just another example of how the Big Red Machine was hardly treated as royalty or discussed with dignity by the team under Marge's reign, although sometimes the gaffes were not her fault, but rather just a reflection of her leadership. Her aforementioned slurs of Joe Morgan and her treatment of Johnny Bench were definitely hers. Marge liked Tony Perez because she loved his wife, Pituka, but the Reds bumbled his situation when they urged him to retire before he was ready, and one day made the embarrassing blunder of announcing on the Riverfront scoreboard a day to honor the retiring first baseman—only Perez was as shocked to see the message as anyone, considering he hadn't decided to retire yet.

Arguably the greatest Red of them all, Pete Rose, had to be conned off the active roster by Bill Bergesch after the 1986 season, age having diminished his effectiveness but not his stubbornness. Then Marge tried to step in toward the end of the 1987 season and turn the hit king into a novelty act by encouraging him to take a few swings for the team. He didn't.

"It's not exactly like she thinks," Rose said at the time. "She thinks I can walk out of the dugout and get a base hit."

"Oh, he can do it," said Marge. "He's Pete Rose. I think it would be wonderful. I think he could walk up there, get a base hit and slide into first."

Still, nobody from the Big Red Machine was treated like Bob Howsam. When the local CBS-TV affiliate, WCPO, staged a reunion weekend in 1990 to commemorate the 15th anniversary of the Machine's first championship, Howsam and the players were invited to the reconstructed Crosley Field in suburban Blue Ash for a game, then were honored at Riverfront Stadium before a Reds game on September 15. But when the team members gathered underneath the stands before the introductions, Howsam was pulled aside and told that his name wasn't on the list of participants, he wouldn't be introduced, and he wouldn't be part of the festivities. It could have been an ugly scene, but Howsam decided he was not going to let the actions of one person, Marge Schott, disrupt the honor his players deserved, and he told them it was all right to go ahead without him.

"I never thought I'd be in Riverfront Stadium and not be welcome," Howsam said at the time. "When you deal with small people, you have to expect this."

"It's wonderful he can have a woman he can put in front of the bus all the time," Marge responded. "I do enough for this city."

Marge was behind it, although she denied it, and Howsam found the matter that much worse when he saw the seats provided for the honorees and their families—way out down the third-base line, a little past the left fielder.

"Sitting them out there," said Howsam, "was a slap in the face of every ballplayer that had brought glory to the city and recognition around the world with the Big Red Machine."

But their recognition 15 years later was a threat to hers, and this general partner of the Cincinnati Reds walks behind no living being, unless Marge's carrying a leash. In 1990, Marge Schott and Marge Schott's Reds were the focal points, and nobody would upstage them, especially not Howsam.

Nobody did. By the time of the reunion, the Reds were well on their way toward their first World Series berth since the Machine Age, and they clinched the National League West division on a rainy September Saturday in Cincinnati. While the Reds were waiting for the inclement weather to subside, they learned that second-place Los Angeles had lost, prompting an extemporaneous celebration on the Riverfront field as the players and their emotions poured out of the dugout and into the rain, with the fans partying in the stands.

The celebration would resume when Cincinnati defeated Pittsburgh in six games in the National League Championship Series, but Marge's reveling turned to reviling when she didn't make it to the clubhouse in time for the NLCS trophy presentation. Steve Schott and Bob Quinn accepted the award, but Marge came down hard on Quinn for being there when she wasn't. From that point on, the Reds were headed to the World Series for a showdown with Oakland, and Marge's treatment of Quinn would go from bad to brutal for the rest of his tenure.

The trip to the playoffs would be memorable, although behind the scenes the risk of some very embarrassing moments were developing for the team's scouting and development personnel. Howie Bedell said he was out of town and involved with the instructional league when he got a call from Reds scouting director Julian Mock after Game 1 of the NLCS. Mock had attended Game 1 with scouting supervisor Gene Bennett, and Mock was "despondent." It seemed Marge was sticking by her plans not to invite many scouting and development personnel to the playoffs, or to the World Series if the Reds made it that far, and

Mock found this a travesty. Mock had been through the playoffs before, during the Howsam years, and Bedell had been through it with the Kansas City Royals and Philadelphia Phillies, and they both knew it was standard procedure to reward your behind-the-scenes personnel by taking them and their families to the games and festivities. They also knew how degrading it would be for Reds personnel if they were excluded.

Bedell couldn't stop thinking about Mock's phone call. At 2 a.m. he jotted down some notes and decided he was going to put them in the form of a letter to Marge. In the morning, he called Quinn, who told Bedell it would be difficult to get Marge to do anything at this point and that he wasn't going to get involved. So Bedell called his secretary, Lois Schneider, and dictated a letter. In it, he told Marge it would be a serious mistake to exclude scouting and development personnel, that it would be viewed poorly by the rest of baseball and by the media and fall back on her shoulders. Bedell also wrote that he had talked to Quinn, but that Quinn wasn't going to come forward. Bedell dictated the letter at about 9 a.m. At about 10 a.m., a panicked Steve Schott called to tell Bedell that the letter had worked, that Marge was surrounded by office personnel deciding who should or shouldn't be invited. Steve said, "I'm going to the bar to have a drink."

As it turned out, scouting and development personnel *were* included on the World Series guest list, as Lois Schneider and Joyce Pfarr, Marge's chief administrative assistant, sat down and determined who would go to which games. It avoided another postseason public-relations nightmare for Marge, who had been blasted by the Pirates for putting their wives in faraway seats during the NLCS.

Bedell hadn't planned to attend the World Series at first, but his invitation said he not only was invited but *requested* to go, and so he did, one of the few people in scouting and development at all of the games. The Series started in Cincinnati, and before Game 1, Bedell and his wife and their two guests—none other than their friends from Dayton—ran into Marge and Schottzie in the hallway. Bedell introduced Marge to all of them, and then Bedell's wife spoke up.

"Marge, it's really a pleasure to meet you," she said. "I've heard so much about you. And by the way, Janet is 'the other woman.'"

It was meant to be funny, but Marge just looked up and said, "Nice to have met you" and walked away. This was about 20 minutes before Marge would go on the field just before gametime to make a speech, and Bedell noticed Marge was a little bit off.

"She was not steady then," Bedell said. "In my opinion, she had a certain something to drink."

Before long, the rest of the nation would know about it, too.

In 1956, shortly after her 28th birthday, Marge posed in her formal gown. Marge's soft appearance back then is a sharp contrast to the distinctive features that life chiseled into her face during the turbulence of the past four decades.

The Cincinnati Post

In 1952, Marge married Charles Schott, a member of one of Cincinnati's wealthiest and most influential families. Their marriage had some happy moments, but Charlie's alcohol abuse and infidelity had brought the marriage to the brink of divorce when he died in 1968.

Marge and Charlie with Marge's parents, Charlotte and Edward Unnewehr. Marge was always her father's favorite, and after she dropped out of the University of Cincinnati, Marge worked for a few years at her father's cigar box business in a job she referred to as "Heir apparent, manufacturing."

Before Charlie's death in 1968, Marge (shown here at her Indian Hill estate in 1967) channeled most of her energies into volunteer activities and raising her beloved St. Bernards.

The Cincinnati Post

Marge resented Pete Rose's popularity with the fans and even questioned his baseball knowledge. At one point she complained, "Why did they have to name a damn street after Pete Rose?"

The Cincinnati Post

Marge and former Reds manager Lou Piniella were all smiles after the team clinched the National League West title in 1990. But the smiles soon faded, and, after several disputes with Marge, Piniella left for the Seattle Mariners.

Marge often referred to Reds sta[r] Eric Davis as one of her "million-dollar niggers." Once, when she saw "Davis" on the back of a visiting player's uniform, she asked, "What's Davis doing in a Pittsburgh uniform?" Bill Bergesch, the team's general manager, responded, "Marge, we're playing the Giants, and that's not *our* Davis, it's *Chili* Davis."

Marge always loved to be involved in promoting the Reds, especially if the promotion involved animals. It has been said that the quickest way to get on Marge's wrong side was to get between her and the cameras.

The Cincinnati Post

Plant City, Florida, had always been a fun time
he fun times were overshadowed by baseball's
wner.

As a result of her suspension, Marge missed Opening Day for the first time since becoming general partner. Despite the embarrassment and condemnation that followed in the wake of revelations about Marge's racial and ethnic slurs, fans at Cincinnati's Opening Day Parade showed their continuing affection for the banished owner.

The same day that Major League Baseball suspended Marge (February 3, 1993), she and her new manager, Tony Perez, were busy introducing the team's new uniforms to the public at the Reds Caravan. Only a few months later, Perez's stunning firing sent shockwaves through all of baseball.

Even when she was cutting back on almost all expenses for the Reds, Marge spared no expense to promote Schottzie — from Schottzie hats to Schottzie calendars to Schottzie pencils. Said Roger Blaemire, the Reds' vice-president of business operations, "I was a goddamned shill — a court jester playing to a dog."

— Chapter Ten —

The Mourning After
the Series Sweep

With American troops stationed in Iraq and Operation Desert Shield soon to be upgraded to Operation Desert Storm, the schedule of President George Bush precluded him from throwing out the ceremonial first pitch of the 1990 World Series. So Barbara Bush was called in to pinch hit for the former Yale first baseman. Before she arrived at Riverfront Stadium, a dozen or so dignitaries, including commissioner Fay Vincent and his wife, were gathered in Marge Schott's private box waiting for the arrival of the president's wife, while Marge paced back and forth, chainsmoking her cigarettes. Finally, the telephone rang. Marge barked a few orders, and a few minutes later Mrs. Bush arrived. She walked over and greeted the Vincents, whom she knew well.

But the First Lady of the national pastime did not bother to go over and greet the First Lady of the nation. Instead, Marge continued to pace.

A few minutes later, the door to the suite opened and a man in a Reds jacket and cap walked in with a leash bearing Schottzie. Suddenly, Marge's face lit up and she came to life. She half-dragged, half-walked Schottzie across the living-room area of the suite to where Mrs. Bush was seated and finally introduced herself and the dog.

"Barb, this is Schottzie," said Marge. "Schottzie, say hello to Barb—this is Millie's mom."

Millie, of course, was the Bushes' dog.

Schottzie then put her head on the lap of Mrs. Bush, saliva drooling down the dog's jaws as Mrs. Bush tried to half-pat and half-push Schottzie's head away.

But this was only the beginning.

Later, Mrs. Bush was ready to go onto the field to throw out the first ball when Marge approached her.

"Barb, I've got a great idea," said Marge. "Why don't you take Schottzie out on the field with you? The fans will love it."

Mrs. Bush declined and threw out the ball unencumbered.

But Marge had some other ideas. Just before the national anthem, Marge decided she wanted to address the fans—again. Roughly a half-hour earlier, she had given a speech out on the field, the commissioner having given her the OK as long as she did it just after batting practice and did not interrupt any of the scheduled proceedings. During this speech, Marge dedicated the World Series to the troops "in the Middle West."

The television cameras and microphones did not pick this up, however. CBS not only had choreographed every second of television time leading up to the start of the game, officials of Major League Baseball and CBS had worried going into this World Series about what Marge Schott might do or say that could diminish this showcase event for the sport and the network. So the television audience was spared that gaffe. But it wasn't spared the next one.

Realizing her earlier mistake and that television had not caught that speech, Marge saw this as an opportunity to get it right this time. She was ready to walk out onto the field from the entrance behind home plate, but Schottzie wouldn't budge. Marge started pulling the leash, and one of the umpires gave Schottzie a poke with his foot to try to get her to move. Finally she and the dog were on their way, only to be stopped again. Dave Dziedzic of the commissioner's office who was coordinating the event with CBS, tried to talk her out of proceeding.

"The commissioner doesn't want you to go out there," said Dziedzic.

"Fuck the commissioner," said Marge.

And Marge stormed right past him, with Schottzie in tow, and headed toward the microphone on the field as Reds public-relations director and public-address announcer Jon Braude began to make another introduction.

"Now, ladies and gentlemen," said Braude, "we ask you to please rise and face the American flag in center field and join United States Air Force Captain Alan Boykin in the singing of our national anthem."

Instead, there was silence. Almost 10 seconds of silence, actually, as Marge stood before the microphone, a sight that elicited terror inside the CBS-TV truck. "We said, 'We're in trouble,'" remembered Ed Goren, who was producing the pre-game show for CBS. After all, here was CBS in its first year of televising the World Series as part of a billion-dollar contract with baseball, trying to make certain everything went flawlessly. Baseball had pressured the network to start the game on time so as not to throw off the starting pitchers who were warming up in the bullpen, and CBS wanted to hit the schedule so the game wouldn't run into the local news if possible.

"We had hit everything," said Goren. "Now we get to the point where all we do is turn it over to Major League Baseball to introduce the anthem, and that's it, we've got it made. And up to the mike steps the owner of the Cincinnati Reds. And we're sitting in the truck saying, 'Please, don't.'"

First came a voice that said, "Test."

Then came Marge.

"We're dedicating this World Series to our wonderful women and men over in the Far East that are serving us, and they're the greatest, and we're gonna stand behind them, and this Series is for them," said Marge, slurring her words and leaning so awk-wardly that this came off more like a toast than a speech at the World Series. Marge then waited out the applause at the stadium, oblivious to the millions of jaws simultaneously plunging in front of televisions everywhere—and perhaps also oblivious that the war with the Japanese had ended almost half a century ago, her daily battles against Toyota notwithstanding.

"I would like," Marge continued, then continued again, "I would like a momava s-s-s-s-ilence [translation: *moment of silence*] or prayer, for our people over there. Please bow your head."

And heads indeed bowed.

Perhaps out of embarrassment.

"Good deal, OK?" Marge concluded.

And now she was done, the spectacle complete. CBS focused on Vincent, who had a sheepish grin on his face, and then came the national anthem, a commercial, and the game. The start was late, but nobody could blame CBS (although CBS sports president Neal Pilson later complained to baseball about its inability to control its personnel). At the time, everyone was stuck.

"All we could do was go with the flow," said Goren. "It's live television. You're more embarrassed for the game—and for her. Every major-league executive had to be saying, 'My worst nightmare has just come true.'"

But Marge's display on the field would live on in the whispers and rumors that she was drunk when she delivered her speech, but nobody wanted to say it publicly at the time. In retrospect some of those who were around her will admit as much, concurring with the assessment of then-Reds controller Tim Sabo, who said, "She was plowed," and who claims he saw her "stumbling down the hall." This was just the first time the world saw an example of a problem some members of the Reds organization had seen on occasion and certainly had heard if they received one of her late-night phone calls. Reds officials say they have seen her retreat to her private box to drink, or stumble into the parking garage and fumble with her keys for literally minutes before backing her car into a post, or be driven home by security because she was in no condition to drive herself.

"I'm not a doctor, but alcohol played a part at least in her overall appearance and her decorum and her attitude," said former farm director Howie Bedell. "Examples would be times when we needed to see her on matters and we were told that while she was there she was just not available—she wasn't feeling well. From what I observed over the years and the atmosphere that I have been in, there were signs that she was drinking. There were signs on her face. At times, it was her speech."

This time, it was her speech during her speech at Game 1 of the World Series. Still, it would be quickly overshadowed by the game itself, won by Cincinnati in a surprising 7-0 rout over an Oakland Athletics team that was being called a potential dynasty and was expected to demolish the underdog Reds. The overshadowing was certainly helped by WLW (the same station that had endlessly replayed and mocked Roseanne Barr's controversial rendition of the national anthem from a Reds–San Diego Padres game) which was predictably avoiding the issue. "We kind of shrugged our shoulders," said talk-show host Andy Furman. "If it had been anybody else, we probably would have killed her."

The next night, the Reds again knocked off the A's, although this time it was 5-4, and this time it took 10 innings. It was a game that developed a rather unusual twist, when Cincinnati manager Lou Piniella examined his shrinking list of available relief pitchers and noticed that scheduled Game 3 starter Tom Browning was missing. Debbie Browning had gone into labor at the stadium and was leaving for the hospital when Tom received the news, from clubhouse worker Rick Stowe. Tom then took off in full uniform to be with her. Unaware of the situation, Piniella looked for Browning on the bench, couldn't find him, and got word to radio announcer Marty Brennaman to put out an All Points Bulletin over the airwaves for Browning to return. As it turned out, Piniella didn't need him, and it became one of the most told and retold stories of the Series.

The only missing chapter to the tale happened when Debbie Browning went into labor. This being her third child, she knew she had to leave, and she knew she had to leave now. When she got to the elevator, she had to wait for a while to get on because it was filled with Secret Service agents and Mrs. Bush. Finally, she boarded the elevator and went to the Reds' offices on the third floor to use the restroom. There, she met Marge in the hallway.

MARGE: How are you feeling? Are you tired?

DEBBIE: The baby may be coming tonight.

MARGE: Let's get a win first before you go.

Debbie Browning says Marge offered her the use of her office if she wanted to lay down, but she declined. She had a baby to deliver. "I guess she did what she thought she should do in a case like that," said Debbie. "For someone who's never had a baby, it's pretty typical."

Later, Marge told her if she had realized the baby was coming, she would have had a helicopter primed to take the pitcher's wife to the hospital. In retrospect, Debbie Browning doesn't look poorly upon Marge for that night or even think of it as insensitive, just Marge being Marge. "That's just her way," she said. Debbie has learned to laugh such things off and has grown fond of Marge and her sense of humor. She knows Marge will make seemingly derisive comments about the players in front of their wives, but Debbie claims Marge is only kidding and some people just don't know how to take her—same as the time in a wives' meeting when Marge was talking about all the players' babies and said the problem with the Reds was "Too much off-the-field production and not enough on-the-field production."

In the World Series, Tom Browning came through in both departments. After Debbie delivered her baby, Tucker, at the hospital on October 18, Tom delivered a victory for the Reds on October 19, an 8-3 decision in Oakland that virtually ensured a championship for the Reds. The next night, two of the Reds' most important players of the Series would be forced to go to the hospital themselves. Billy Hatcher, who had broken Babe Ruth's record for batting average in a four-game World Series by going 9 for 12 (.750), was hit on the hand by a Dave Stewart pitch in the first inning. Later, Eric Davis displayed his ability and courage when he tore his kidney making an acrobatic catch that was wrongly ruled a hit—and stayed in the game to complete the inning despite his pain. Even without them, the Reds were able to complete the improbable sweep, silencing the mighty A's, 2-1, and igniting a party back home in the streets of Cincinnati.

After what happened following the team's clinching of the pennant, Marge made certain she was in the locker room this time when the championship trophy was being presented. She did not want general manager Bob Quinn to be there during the ceremony with her and Piniella. If it hadn't been for Fay Vincent, she might have gotten her way and denied Quinn a deserved spoil of the victory.

In the end, however, Quinn was a mere afterthought considering the other news she would receive after the Reds' World Series sweep, the information that would enrage her. It was bad enough the team couldn't have done it at home, where she would have been Queen for a Day of the Queen City instead of just another face in Oakland. Now she was told that when a team sweeps the World Series, the two owners lose their opportunity to make big profits. Indeed, through the first four games, 60 percent of the gate receipts go to paying the players' shares of the World Series money, with the remaining 40 percent split equally among the two clubs and the commissioner's office. The owners don't prosper unless the Series goes beyond that, when the gate receipts are divided evenly among the two teams and the commissioner's office with no payout to the players. This setup helps ensure that the players won't try to throw a game or two to purposely extend the Series—but it destroyed the celebration for Marge Schott. She couldn't enjoy the championship now, knowing all the money she could have made, and she let everybody know how furious she was.

Marge didn't want to have any type of traditional victory party for the players, and instead was going to have just a small get-together in her hotel suite for a few people, such as Piniella and his wife (Quinn, of course, was not invited). When it became clear nothing was planned for the players, staff, and the rest of the Reds contingent, the limited partners came to the rescue. Jack Meier went to the management of the Parc Fifty-Five hotel where the Reds were staying and asked what could be done. The hotel closed off a restaurant and set up an open bar, and the party was on. The restaurant was willing to keep the kitchen crew late to serve whatever the Reds wanted, but Marge stepped in and insisted there be no food. Limited partner George Strike says he would have made sure the bill was paid—on his own if Marge tried to keep the team from doing it—but Marge had already made her decision so he backed off, not wanting to get into a fight with her. Instead, some of the Reds went on a hamburger run to a nearby fast-food place and brought back the team's victory feast.

"You win a world championship," said Lou Piniella, "and you just expect a little more."

Marge attended this fete herself, but had a much more difficult time leaving than arriving. She was so drunk, she was about to jackknife to the floor, when Steve Schott caught her, and Marge was helped back to her room. Meanwhile, some of the players hit San Francisco. Steve Schott, Jim Bowden, Lou Piniella, limited partner Bill Reik, and a few others ended up at Carl's Jr., another fast-food place, for a celebratory meal at about 3:30 in the morning. When Reik saw Billy Hatcher there, the man who had broken Babe Ruth's record and was forced to revel at Carl's Jr., Reik said, "Can I at least buy your hamburgers?"

The conversation at Carl's Jr. inevitably turned to the woman who had made this type of celebration possible, Marge Schott. They were trying to decide when the Reds' plane should leave later that day, either at 11 a.m. or 1 p.m. Steve said Marge told him she wanted to leave at 11, but Joyce Pfarr said she had scheduled an interview for Marge around that time, so it would have to be 1. Others jumped into the conversation, and Steve was told, "Don't worry, she won't remember it, anyway."

Her loss of income, she certainly wasn't going to forget. And sure enough, on the plane trip back, Marge still was fuming over the Reds' having swept the World Series. Nobody wanted to be around her, and those who tried to reason with her, telling her that everybody in the world would *pay* to be in her position, found it was no use. Her obsession with money was robbing her of what could have been one of the finest moments in her life. Still, she wanted to put on her game face for the public, getting into an argument with the charter airplane crew about where the plane would land. The airport back home was going to have the plane taxi up to a gate, because a big crowd was gathering outside. Marge wanted the plane to land out in the open, so the television trucks could be there and Schottzie could be waiting at the foot of the stairs. Marge won, and the team deplaned in open view, where the suddenly vivacious owner grabbed the camera lens with her smiles and pride in her championship.

As much joy and satisfaction as everyone else involved with the Cincinnati Reds truly felt about winning the world championship, Marge's furor over the sweep somewhat dampened it. And though Marge would try to defend her actions at least in terms of the lack of a party to Lou Piniella, saying everything happened so fast that things just sort of "got away from her," her anger about the sweep would hurt her manager. He called it his least favorite story about Marge Schott.

"It took a little of the luster out of winning," Piniella said.

Chapter Eleven

"I Hope You Guys Lose"

For putting together the final parts of the World Series champion Cincinnati Reds, Bob Quinn would earn The Sporting News' Executive of the Year designation, while his owner was trying to find ways to keep him in the background of the city's celebration at Fountain Square. As it was, Marge Schott tried to crop him out of pictures from the event—and to edit Quinn's cameos out of the videotape chronicling the championship season.

Perhaps worst of all, Marge tried to make Quinn responsible for what quickly became a public-relations nightmare with outfielder Eric Davis. It was Davis, remember, who tore his kidney attempting a catch in Game 4 of the World Series and ended up hospitalized while his teammates were completing the sweep. Davis' condition forced him to stay in Oakland when the rest of the Reds' contingent returned to Cincinnati. When Davis was able to leave the hospital, he wanted to go back to Cincinnati immediately, but doctors didn't want him flying just yet, at least not in a normal airplane seat, because he needed to lie down. Unable to contact the Reds and unwilling to wait until he heard from the club, or until he could fly back on a commercial airplane, Davis chartered an airplane and hired medical personnel for it. When the Reds did not offer to foot the bill, he paid it himself and began a one-man campaign against the club for its insensitivity.

For once, Eric Davis had the ear and the shoulder of Cincinnati. This most maligned of Reds, whose every injury had been doubted and whose heart had been questioned, had earned the Red badge of courage with the city for staying in the game despite a torn kidney. Yes, maybe Davis had rushed back from Oakland and should have stayed a little longer until he could fly back without needing such special care. But any other owner would have made certain Davis was treated royally at this point—even carried piggyback halfway across the country, if that's what he wanted.

Marge needed some major-league damage control.

Which meant Quinn would take the fall.

For the benefit of her public image, Marge held a powwow with Davis at his home in suburban Amberley Village. While the cameras rolled, Marge once again pleaded her great love for Davis, said of course she would pay the bill, and claimed the mix-up was caused by her baseball people, namely Bob Quinn. So Davis got what he wanted (coming back to Cincinnati quickly and having the Reds pay for it), Marge got what she wanted (positive publicity for her and another set of her footprints on Quinn's back), and Quinn got what he wanted (continued employment). But the truth was, Quinn once again got blamed for Marge's antics.

"It was not Bob, it was Marge," said former Reds controller Tim Sabo. "I was involved in the negotiations for who was going to pay for what. Marge clearly said she didn't want to pay it. At one point, Bob asked me to try to resolve it, and I told him I was already attempting to. Eric was not without some responsibility here. If Eric had waited another two days out there, he could have traveled first class, and the cost would been less than half as much. But it was certainly handled badly by the Reds, and it was Marge's decision initially not to pay for it. Her specific instructions were basically to put it back in my file and hope it goes away."

Marge did give Quinn a new contract, but she would have faced an onslaught of criticism if she hadn't rehired the general manager of the World Series champions, the Executive of the Year. And don't think that designation escaped her or pleased her. Quinn's recognition for 1990 would only increase her abuse of him for the rest of his tenure, which his new contract guaranteed only through March of 1992.

Meanwhile, there would be more target practice on the GM. Marge became angry when Quinn took a cruise before contract negotiations with free-agent pitcher Tom Browning had concluded. Even though Quinn had made Browning's agent aware of his trip, and even though Quinn told her he didn't believe Browning would leave Cincinnati, Marge was enraged without her human dartboard around. Browning didn't leave after all, giving the Reds one last crack before taking San Francisco's offer and coming down from his insistence on a five-year deal while Marge stepped in and upped the offer from three years. Browning received a four-year deal (plus a fifth if he pitched 200 or more innings in 1993 or 1994, or a $583,000 buyout).

Lou Piniella also got a new contract. At first, Steve Schott said, Piniella informed him he didn't think he was going to come back for 1991, that he was going to go out on top. "It's like catching the prize marlin in Florida," Piniella told Steve. "Once you catch it, then you go on to the next adventure." Piniella claimed he could make as much or more money focusing full time on his outside business interests. But after talking with Steve and then with Marge, the owner agreed to increase his salary for the final two years of his contract from $350,000 to $650,000. Marge knew she couldn't lose Piniella, that it would be far more disastrous to her image than losing Quinn. Despite his occasional explosions, Piniella was a generally amiable sort, but his persona and instant success had made him very popular in Cincinnati. As with Rose, that would intimidate Marge.

Still, being champions had its advantages. Marge and the Reds were invited to the White House to get the official kudos of President George Bush. Marge could have taken a number of front-office staffers with the team, but she told Reds controller Tim Sabo, "Why should I do that? You're not deserving of the honor."

The off-season also would contain one of the scariest times for Marge Schott, who was hospitalized with cellulitis. "She was very seriously ill," said her friend, Mary Clair Torbeck. Still, a weakened Marge was out of the hospital in time for Opening Day and to pass out the World Series rings, often foregoing if not forgetting the first names of some recipients as she called them onto the field, one by one, in a pregame ceremony. Naturally, she had one for Schottzie, as well, an oversized contraption to be worn as a dog collar that somehow seemed to cheapen the entire affair.

And if that weren't bad enough, the rings were hardly befitting a World Series champion. A number of players had their rings redone because: A) The diamond chips were falling out; B) The red-gemstone background was not top quality; and/or C) The gold C wasn't the Reds' wishbone C but an oval with a red line through the right side that some of the players called "nail polish" and didn't even match the red of the gemstone.

According to Tim Sabo, some of the non-playing personnel who received rings actually were given versions with cubic zirconia instead of diamonds. "It was done on a person-by-person basis," said Sabo. "When the rings finally came in, there were two different appraisals, one for the diamonds and one for the cubic zirconia, but Joyce and Marge gave out the diamond-ring appraisals to everybody, so everyone thought they had real diamonds. When those who didn't found out, they rushed out to get them changed."

As it was, Marge hesitated to allow some of her scouting and development people to get any rings at all. Farm director Howie Bedell, for instance, at first was told he and a number of others on his level would have to pay for the rings, but she eventually backed off on that. Bedell then made a list of all the minor-league personnel who deserved rings, as well, but Marge gave them to all the field managers in the system and not to all of the coaches. So Bedell again wrote her a letter asking her to do something about this. Only this time, it did no good. Quinn told Bedell that Marge not only wouldn't approve the rings, she would cancel any further orders with the ring company if she heard of anything being done without her approval. Bedell says Marge gave in on the scouts, but still was holding back on the development end — his end. Finally, Quinn called him one day with a plan.

"Howie, make a list of those people who didn't receive rings who would like rings," Quinn told Bedell. "They're going to have to pay for them, but just quietly take their ring size and get the commitment that they'll pay for them, and call so-and-so and give him the order. I don't want you to tell anyone about that. Don't even tell Lois [Bedell's secretary], because that will be the worst, and it will get back."

Unfortunately, it did. One day, roving coach Jose Cardenal came to Cincinnati to work with first baseman Hal Morris on playing the outfield, and Cardenal made the mistake of admiring Lois' ring and saying he couldn't wait to get his ring. Lois said he wasn't going to get one, but Cardenal insisted that Bedell had taken his ring size. So Lois called Joyce Pfarr, and about a week later the ring salesman called Bedell to tell him the ring orders for Cardenal and others like him were canceled. Cardenal apologized to Bedell and told him what had happened. But the story had a happy ending. After Bedell and the Reds parted, Cardenal told Bedell he and some of the others later went to Jim Bowden, who acceded into Bedell's job and later into Quinn's, and he secured Marge's approval for the rings.

Perhaps nobody during Marge's time with the Reds has had a more open ear from her than Bowden. His good standing with Marge left him in bad standing with many of his coworkers, who believed Bowden was playing politics and backstabbing them to get ahead. Everyone knew the way to Marge's heart was through her office door, and members of the Reds brass believed Bowden was going to Marge with information and ignoring the company flow chart. In 1991, Bedell tested this theory by setting up his 29-year-old assistant.

Bedell told Bowden, and only Bowden, that he had rented a red Cadillac at the club's expense—a lie—while in Plant City, Florida, for extended spring training. Sure enough, word got back to Marge, who told Quinn to check into it, so he called Bedell.

QUINN:	I understand you rented a red Cadillac.
BEDELL:	Do you believe that?
QUINN:	Well, I'm asking you a question.
BEDELL:	Why should you be so serious about something like that?'
QUINN:	Because Marge asked me to ask you.

Whereupon Bedell filled Quinn in on his little scheme.

QUINN:	This is one good example of where the problem is in the office.
BEDELL:	You knew that before you hired the guy.
QUINN:	Yes, I did. I told you it was going to be difficult.

Bedell even confronted his assistant about the incident when Bowden and a group of others arrived in Plant City and came into the office. Bedell greeted them, then went in for the kill.

"Look, as long as you're here, you're going to need transportation," Bedell told them. "That red Cadillac is right out in the parking lot. Pick up the keys. I've got them in my locker. You guys go ahead and use it while you're here."

They all looked perplexed, because there was no red Cadillac out there, and Bedell walked away, pleased that his plan had worked. Before he left Plant City, however, Bowden approached Bedell on the matter.

BOWDEN: Look, that red Cadillac thing, I'm
            sorry about that.
BEDELL: What do you mean? What are you
            sorry about?
BOWDEN: I know that Bob Quinn called you
            about it, and I'm real sorry about it.
BEDELL: As a matter of fact, Jim, he did. Now
            let me say something to you. You
            better remember to get the full
            story. If you don't get the full story,
            and you do what you did, all it does
            is cause a lot of heartache and
            embarrassment.

But Bowden emphatically denies Bedell's allegations, saying he never backstabbed—that, if anything, he might get in trouble for being too open with his opinions—and he finds the charge of his former boss insulting.

"That shows you what a liar he is. That event did take place, but his intention was to set up Brad Del Barba and Lois Schneider," Bowden said, referring to the Reds' coordinator of scouting and player development and to Bedell's secretary. "I'm not going to get into bashing Howie Bedell."

"You can't trust Jim Bowden," said Bedell. "Jim Bowden does not tell the truth. He's a total opportunist. He will slant the facts to meet the occasion and has done that numerous times. During the first year he served under me, we had a session on this regarding him and Brad. They were both vying for what they thought would be some turf, and he would constantly create situations for Brad that made it quite difficult for him to overcome in the office situation. I tried to bring the two of them together on numerous occasions to iron out their differences. But from the very beginning, Jim Bowden had his own agenda."

Del Barba says he can't remember what exactly happened and whom Bedell was trying to catch. To the best of his recollection, he and Schneider knew about the car, but only after they were called into Marge's office and she asked them about it. If Del Barba does remember anything, it was the poor relations in the department, saying he didn't get along well with Bedell or Bowden. "It was just an interesting situation between Howie, Jim and myself," he said.

Unfortunately, this is the kind of atmosphere that Marge encourages at 100 Riverfront Stadium and beyond. Her desire to have everybody come to her with a problem instead of to supervisors, her refusal to trust that employees are not trying to bilk her out of time and money, and her breeding of insecurity within the ranks with her abusive language and her senseless firings have left the team a breeding ground for politics. Bedell, who once had implored Quinn to pull the organization together, realized it was hopeless. Bowden was just another example, right up there with Bedell's secretary telling Marge of Bedell's supposed extramarital liaisons.

"So now I've got Lois doing what she's doing," he said. "I've got Chief Bender hoping that something happens and he can come back into some kind of job. And I've got Bowden, probably the one person I thought was bright enough after a couple of years to learn about this thing and become a legitimate director, doing what he's doing."

Now add to the mix the two top management types — Steve Schott, who's doing the Big Brother routine to the employees for Aunt Marge, and Bob Quinn, who refuses to stand up for himself much less anyone who works for him — and it's amazing there weren't any fatalities other than morale in the front office. The irony is, here were the Cincinnati Reds, champions of Major League Baseball on the field yet never in more disarray off it. Where once the employees used to look out for each other, now they had to look over their shoulders to keep an eye on each other. It was sad, really. You wonder how many of these people would have fared in a more healthy environment, but more than that you wonder how the front-office types had managed to pull together so well here during the 1980s. Indeed, Marge may never realize this, but she benefited from a number of good people who were left over from the Howsam administration and a number of others who came into the organization even after she began. Most of them had bonded together through the misery, becoming friends and remaining productive despite the odds and the owner. In fact, many of them who left called themselves the Cincinnati Reds Alumni Association and got together for a 1990 World Series party and another soiree that Christmas. Cal Levy held both parties at his house, and he estimates 25-30 alumni made each of them, exchanging war stories and job updates. They even had "CRAA" buttons made up.

"We formed relationships there," said Levy. "We all worked hard, and it was a good bunch of people. We got along. And because we got along, things got done."

But it didn't last. How could it last? Marge's distrust was becoming contagious, and it kept people from effectively doing their jobs. Bedell decided to work out of his home and on the road instead of in the office. To Bedell, this allowed Bowden to take care of business at the office and gave Bowden an easier route to Marge. To Bowden, this showed that Bedell wasn't in the office enough to know how it or Bowden was operating.

Being away from Marge didn't mean being away from her influence, though. Marge started trying to renege on three of the deals Bedell had negotiated—with Quinn's approval—for his minor-league personnel. Marge thought Bedell had agreed to pay Triple-A Nashville manager Pete Mackanin too much money, so she had Quinn renegotiate it—and Mackanin ended up making $3,000 more in the new deal. Marge was upset when Single-A Charleston manager Jim Lett wanted to leave his West Virginia hometown to become a coach at Triple-A Nashville, and Marge accused Bedell of coercing Lett into the decision. "She couldn't understand why someone in his own hometown wouldn't want to manage there," said Bedell. Steve Schott even called Lett, with Bedell sitting beside Lett, to make certain Bedell was telling the truth. Lett assured Steve he felt he had accomplished all he could in Single A and had decided himself to move on.

With P. J. Carey, whom Bedell wanted as a coach, the Reds at first tried to delay his startup date, and Bedell ended up paying

Carey's first month's salary out of his own pocket, roughly $2,000. "My first year with the Reds cost me a little over $10,000 when you add meals and calls and everything," said Bedell. "My accountant wasn't too happy about it."

Bedell agreed to sign Carey for $30,000 the first year and $32,000 the second year, Carey having made $28,000 the previous year with the Seattle organization. Marge questioned whether the Reds were tampering with Mariners property, and Quinn told her no, that Seattle general manager Woody Woodward had said he wanted to offer Carey a contract, but Carey wanted to move on. Marge didn't buy it. "Woody's one of your friends, Bob, why should I believe you?" she said. At one point, Quinn tried to get Bedell to sign Carey for $26,000 the first year, but Bedell refused. Quinn told him that he couldn't get anything more for Carey than $28,000 the first year and $30,000 the second year, so a disgusted Bedell went back to Carey and told him the deal they had agreed upon would have to be lowered. Carey took it anyway.

At the same time Bedell tried to hire Carey, he was trying to hire Frank Funk and Moe Hill to minor-league positions, with Quinn recommending that all three be submitted at the same time. They were. Carey and Funk were hired; Hill was not. Carey and Funk were white; Hill was black. Bedell believes that it was more than a mere coincidence.

QUINN:	I don't think the thing with Moe Hill is going to fly at all.
BEDELL:	Why?
QUINN:	The guy hasn't been working—she questions that. Besides, it just might not work.
BEDELL:	Can you give me a reason beyond that?
QUINN:	No, I can't, and I would rather not. You can't have him. Just drop it.

With Hill out, Bedell had to find a new manager for Class A Charleston, but he wasn't happy about it. Bedell says the concern about Hill being out of baseball wasn't valid, considering it was not unusual for baseball personnel to leave and then return to the game. Bedell says the race issue was never discussed directly because he didn't want to put Quinn in the awkward position of having to address it. But one comment Quinn made about Hill left him wondering.

"He never indicated black or white, he just said he didn't think Moe Hill would be right for West Virginia because it's a Southern town," said Bedell. "Bob would not have made that kind of statement on his own."

Where it came from is not clear. Maybe there were concerns from Charleston that were passed on to Marge. Maybe they were Marge's concerns. In any case, it was the Reds' call and not Bedell's, no matter how much he didn't like it or the motivation behind it. Bedell can't think of any reason outside of race why Moe Hill wasn't hired.

Besides, Bedell saw how Quinn handled another such matter during spring training. When Bedell sought approval for making African American minor-leaguer Darrell "Doc" Rodgers a player-coach, Quinn approved it himself. The money was the same, and only the designation was different. "We don't have to run this through Marge," Quinn told him.

Again, there was no specific mention of color.

Again, Bedell later would wonder.

At other times race was more clearly an issue. Bedell says he heard Marge use the term "nigger" a few times, and "Jew bastard" once or twice in discussing money. "I don't know that I'm qualified to say she's a racist," said Bedell. "She is insensitive, very much so."

Bedell's second season, 1991, was turning into a nightmare. It was becoming apparent his tenure in Cincinnati wasn't going to last very long, and one of the final incidents would convince him. Bedell complained to scouting director Julian Mock that the Reds were not bringing in enough players to properly fill Bedell's six-team minor-league system—that Mock had signed about 18 players in Bedell's first year and about 25 in 1991. Mock told Bedell, "It sounds like you not only want to develop them, but to sign them." Mock said he would take this to the Reds and get the matter straightened out, and Bedell figured that meant to Marge. About two months later, in August, Quinn told him to come to the office for a meeting, but that there was no problem.

"It was like leading me to the guillotine," said Bedell.

Indeed, when Bedell arrived to meet with Quinn, Bob Martin—Marge's attorney and normally her one-man firing squad—was also there. They told him he was relieved of his duties, that sometimes changes have to be made.

BEDELL: Can you give me any clue what I might have done incorrectly?

MARTIN: No, Howie, baseballwise, I can't say a thing to you. She just asked me to do this, and I hope you understand. Do you have the keys to the car?

BEDELL: Yes, and I'm gonna keep them.

MARTIN: You're gonna what?

BEDELL: I'd like the right to purchase the automobile.

MARTIN: Oh, OK.

BEDELL: I'd like to go in and see her.

MARTIN: I would advise against that.

BEDELL: She hired me, and I'm going in to see her.

So Bedell left that meeting and created a new one. He went to see Marge, and she was rather startled to see him.

BEDELL: Marge, I just had my meeting with Bob and Mr. Martin, and they informed me that my contract will not be renewed. I just wanted to come and thank you for the two years. It's been a most enlightening two years. I hope that we accomplished some of our goals that we outlined originally to you. I personally am very proud of the World Series we won and some of the successes we've had at the minor-league level. I wish whoever follows me and wish you and the organiza-

	tion nothing but the best in the future.
MARGE:	Howie, I really appreciate everything you've done for me, and I thank you for that. I'm gonna give the job to Jim Bowden. I think he's gonna have some problems because he's not very mature. The ballplayers might make it rough for him, but let's see what happens. And besides that, I like his wife.

And so, they worked out the terms of the car purchase. Bedell went out to the dealership to meet Marge and to take care of the final details of it, and that should have been the end to their dealings. It wasn't. Marge and Martin said there would be no problem paying him through the rest of the year, when his guaranteed deal with the Reds expired, and at first she followed through on that. But, with about a month and a half to go, Bedell received a letter from Martin saying the team would not pay him anymore, that Marge believed she didn't owe him any further paychecks because Bedell's two-year agreement was with Quinn and not her. Bedell called Quinn and asked him to talk to Marge. Quinn refused to get involved and instead advised Bedell to get an attorney. Bedell tried to reason with Quinn, explaining he had no means of support and didn't want to have to pay for a lawyer. But Quinn wouldn't budge, saying, "Just get an attorney. You'll be fine."

So Bedell went to an attorney, who wrote two letters to Marge, the first of which elicited no response, the second of which threatened legal action and prompted the Reds to pay him in one lump sum. Meanwhile, Bedell was out $1,500 in legal fees.

But his ordeal still wasn't over. Bedell was unemployed for about a year, and about six months into it decided to give in to reality over pride and applied for unemployment compensation. While he continued searching for a job, he was approached about putting together a group of former ballplayers for a USO tour. With time on his hands, Bedell was eager to do it and contacted such old friends as former Red Bobby Tolan, along with Dick Allen, Andre Thornton, and former Reds minor-league coach

Ray Rippelmeyer. When they were in Milan, Italy, for a clinic, Bedell got a call from Paul Archey, director of game development for Major League Baseball.

ARCHEY: Oh, by the way, I received a call today from Jim Bowden. He wanted to congratulate yourself, Ray Rippelmeyer, and Bobby Tolan for representing Cincinnati in such a wonderful cause.

BEDELL: Why would he do that?

ARCHEY: I don't know, but he seemed quite enthusiastic.

Bedell put the issue aside until the USO tour was done and he came home, when he talked to Archey again. Archey told Bedell he had talked to "your good friend in Cincinnati" again, meaning Bowden.

ARCHEY: I called him in reference to another trip we might be taking. Because he had shown so much enthusiasm for the USO, I asked him for any cooperation and if he wanted to be with us in the future. And he basically said, "I don't really care what you do with the USO. I was just calling to get information for my data base."

BEDELL: What questions did he ask you?

ARCHEY: He wanted to know if there was a salary being paid for these trips.

Even though Bedell had written to the proper authorities in Ohio with all of the provisions of the trip, for which his expenses were paid but nothing else, Bedell received a questionnaire from the Ohio unemployment compensation authorities concerning the trip. The Reds were looking into his compensation from the USO, and while the matter was being examined, Bedell's unemployment checks were stopped again. Again Bedell went to his attorney, and this time it cost another $1,000 to get the Reds off of his back and restore the checks. Bedell has no doubt that Marge was behind it, because Quinn told him so.

"You ought to be aware that Mr. Martin, Marge Schott, and Mr. Bowden were here in front of me today," Quinn told Bedell, "and during the conversation, Marge said to Jim, 'I want that Howie Bedell checked out where the unemployment compensation is concerned.'"

In retrospect, Bedell—employed in a minor-league managerial position with the expansion Colorado Rockies and seemingly finally rid of the burden and the fallout from his tenure with Marge Schott—looks at the power of Marge and contends there is absolutely no reason for her to have done the things she did.

"I believe, deep down inside of her, there's a real lonely spot there," said Bedell. "I don't feel sorry for her, but I'm not angry at her. She has created some pain for people, maybe without even knowing it. I'd like to think she doesn't do it deliberately. But I believe she recognizes that people take her abuse because they need a paycheck, and she uses it, and that's sad.

"I can no longer see her as that grandmotherly type I thought she might be. She can be as sweet as can be one moment, portraying something that makes you want to spend time around her; the other side of the coin is, I couldn't wait to get away from her. Life's got to be more than this. Patting boys and girls on the head in the stands is not really what it's all about. I see all these other things, her excessiveness with alcohol, her being alone and looking for love and companionship. And it's like she's crying out for help."

Instead, she often goes out her way to distance, if not alienate herself from people, particularly her employees.

But just when you think you have her pegged, she'll do something wonderful. She treated Jim Bowden as well as anybody, particularly when he needed it most, when his newborn baby boy almost died. Tyler Bowden was born July 7, 1991, in an emergency caesarean, his lungs malfunctioning, machines keeping him alive.

"This was the most tragic thing that's ever happened in my life," said Bowden. "I usually don't get emotional, but I broke down crying. I called every minister and priest we knew across the country and asked for prayers. And Mrs. Schott called. I was very upset, and she said, 'Let me make sure you have the best doctors in the country. I'll make some calls for you.' She made several calls and came up with Dr. Ed Donovan at Children's Hospital. My son was life-flighted from Mercy Hospital to Children's Hospital. Forty-eight hours later, I was told to make burial plans.

"In the meantime, Mrs. Schott was the first person from the Reds to go see my wife, who was in a different hospital from the baby, and she said, 'My prayers are with you' and was really sensitive to how my wife was doing. I kept going between the chapel and Tyler and my wife. It was the hardest time in my life. But because we had Dr. Ed Donovan and because we were at Children's Hospital, they had a drug that had just been legalized eight months earlier. They gave it to Tyler as a last-ditch effort—and it worked. Today, he is as healthy as can be. It was a blessing from the good Lord.

"But the thing that will always stick in my mind is that Mrs. Schott was the first one to call for the best medical help she could find and the first one to personally visit my wife in the hospital."

It didn't stop there. After Bowden replaced Bedell as director of player development in August, a job that requires a lot of travel, Marge would often call his wife when he'd be on the road and say, "Amy, how are things? I know these hours in baseball are crazy, but for him to do his job, he's got to do that. But if I can be of any help to you, let me know." Another time, when Bowden told Marge his older son was going to sing Christmas carols with his kindergarten class at the school, Marge asked if she could come. And she did.

"She has been very warm to both of my children," said Bowden. "When the person you work for treats your family that way, in a first-class fashion, it makes you feel wanted and makes you want to do your job right."

Piniella, too, raves about Marge's treatment of his family. She was even good to Quinn's family. But when the families would leave, that was when the trouble could start—especially for Quinn. She took away his general manager's box at the stadium, leaving him to find unused radio booths to watch his team at home. At the 1991 All-Star break, with the Reds stumbling on their way to the worst follow-up ever recorded by a World Series champion (74-88), Quinn made arrangements to go to the All-Star Game in Toronto to explore trade possibilities. After Quinn had made his reservations and submitted his down payment, Marge put out a memo saying no one with the team was authorized to attend the All-Star Game. Of course, this was aimed at Quinn—nobody else from the Reds would be going on club expense. So Quinn had to pay his own way and, worse still, was forced to use vacation days for the trip.

Not that Quinn was allowed to do much in the way of transactions, anyway, for 1991. Marge decided she didn't want to break up the championship team of 1990, preventing Quinn from making any type of major deal, and Quinn didn't want to part with the major prospects left in the organization for a quick fix. And so, such available pitchers as Luis Aquino, Ron Darling, and Dennis "Oil Can" Boyd were passed on by the Reds. Meanwhile, they lost a pair of pitchers in Danny Jackson and Rick Mahler and a couple of second basemen in Mariano Duncan and Ron Oester— although Marge made a last-minute blitz to try to sign Jackson. When the Reds needed bodies, they had to comb through a once-proud and productive minor-league system ravaged over the years by Marge Schott's neglect. Actually, that was the one area where Marge finally gave in to Quinn, as she began to reemphasize the farm system during his administration, although too late to help for '91.

Meanwhile, Lou Piniella was losing his patience as he was losing not just games, but players. Injuries left Piniella searching for Band-Aid remedies, such as moving former closer Randy Myers into the starting rotation, when the club needed tourniquets. As the season wore on, Piniella began openly pleading for help, but to no avail. Worse yet, he lost one of his best prospects when rookie first baseman Reggie Jefferson was suddenly traded because a snafu by Quinn could have left Jefferson a free agent.

Quinn had tried to designate Jefferson for assignment, hoping to send him to the minor leagues, but the prospect still was suffering the effects of pneumonia. When a player is designated for assignment, the team has 10 days to release him, trade him, or send him to the minors; but a club can't demote a sidelined player, so the Reds were in danger of losing Jefferson. Quinn had hoped he could save some major-league service time off of Jefferson's resume — which could keep him from being eligible for arbitration and free agency a year longer — and had figured

Jefferson would be recovered in time. He was wrong. Quinn ended up dealing Jefferson to Cleveland for a less-ripened first-base prospect named Tim Costo, and Quinn met with a barrage of criticism. Then, word started spreading that the Reds could lose Costo, as well, because the Indians traded him before he had finished a full calendar year of pro ball (he was about a week short), and that's against the rules. Bedell says Bowden called the commissioner's office to get permission, and Bowden reported back to Bedell, "Thank heavens I did that, or Bob would have been in deeper." Baseball could have insisted the Indians part with another player, but instead OK'd the trade, figuring it would have placed more of a hardship on Costo to keep him with the Cleveland organization now that another first-base prospect would be ahead of him.

Before he knew for sure, Steve Schott was worried the Reds would be burned twice with Jefferson and decided to check into it before it was too late. Of all people, though, Steve called WLW's Andy Furman for help.

The executive vice-president of the Reds viewed the Don Rickles of local radio as a confidante and asked Furman off the air if he'd call around and find out if Quinn had erred again. Furman said he would. But what also transpired in that conversation is a matter of opinion.

"He told me that if the story were true to stir it up on the radio about Quinn, to make Quinn look bad," said Furman. "He used to call me before the show sometimes and tell me to stir things up. And a lot of times, when a player was signed and Quinn was on TV talking about it, Steve would call me and tell me he really got the deal done."

Steve emphatically denies asking Furman to blast Quinn if the Costo allegation were true. Steve points out that when a Cincinnati reporter began probing into the story shortly after it happened, Steve had his lawyer call Furman to find out Furman's side, and Furman backed up Steve's story.

"He went on record to the lawyer saying it didn't happen," said Steve.

What Steve didn't know was that Furman was the unnamed source who had tipped off the reporter, and the attorney so scared Furman that he called back the reporter and retracted everything, admitting he was frightened. The reporter didn't run the story, considering both parties of the conversation were going to go on the record saying Steve had never told Furman to "stir it up" about Quinn. But with time and Steve's tenure with the Reds having passed, Furman will not only say it did happen, he'll swear to it.

"I'd be willing to take a lie-detector test," said Furman, who admitted to others privately at the time of the incident that it was true.

One thing is certain. The person who was really getting hurt by all of this was Quinn, because this was his responsibility, not Steve's and not Furman's. Steve says he was afraid to wait on it for fear it could cost the team Costo. Furman says he wanted to do Steve a favor. In any case, after Furman hung up with Steve, he called Reds broadcaster Marty Brennaman, who was with the team in New York, and told him of Steve's concern. Brennaman assured him there were no problems with the deal. Brennaman then informed Quinn about what was going on, and Quinn, already feeling Steve was stepping on his territory, told Marge the story and told her he didn't appreciate Steve going behind his back. Marge decided to find out what was going on and called Furman.

She asked Furman who had put him up to this. Furman was hesitant to tell, at first, but he gave in when she pressed him.

"Between you and me, Marge," Furman said, "It's Steve."

Only it wasn't between Furman and Marge.

Steve was in the room with Marge when she made the call.

"Ten minutes later, Steve called me, and he was fit to be tied," said Furman. "Later, I learned Marge called the general manager of the station, Dave Martin, and commended me. Dave Martin called me in and said, 'What did you do?' I told him, 'I ratted on Steve Schott.'"

Steve downplays this whole scene as having nothing to do with his falling-out with Marge, which resulted in him leaving the team just before the season ended. The fact is, Steve and Marge were clashing more and more as Steve gradually realized that the complaints and concerns of the people inside the Reds' organization were valid, and he became more understanding and sympathetic to them. Marge was starting to come down hard on Steve, and the stress was showing on him as he continued to gain weight throughout his tenure with the team. Steve admittedly had come to the Reds ignorant of how to run a baseball team, but he earned some respect inside the organization for taking the time to learn it, watching everyone from the scouts to the ticket-takers.

"He improved somewhat as a baseball man as he went on," said Howie Bedell. "He was a well-meaning guy for the most part who truly wanted to be a part of the game and was making an attempt to do a good job."

"My relationship with Steve has changed since I've left the Reds," said former marketing director Cal Levy. "I told Steve when I was there what was going on. He didn't believe me. I told him how I felt Mrs. Schott treated people. He didn't believe me. And now he believes me."

What Steve Schott will say is that he and Marge had some philosophical differences when it came to relying on the limited partners and in supporting the player-development area. He believes he accomplished what he set out to do—to not only further advance the business operations of the Cincinnati Reds but to make Marge comfortable with her organization. And he says that after winning the World Series in 1990, she told him, "I do feel more comfortable now with the people in the organization." But instead of becoming less involved with the team, Marge started becoming more involved, and Steve quickly realized her oral promise of turning over the president and CEO jobs within three years—which would be September 1991—was not going to come true.

"In the name of family unity, I decided not to press the issue with her," Steve said. "I started to listen to other opportunities."

Steve contends they parted by mutual consent, but there is no questioning the relationship was strained by the time they actually split. When he left, Marge didn't bother to name a new head of business operations. She just took over those responsibilities, too, for the 1992 season.

On the baseball end, Marge freed Piniella and Quinn to shake up, if not break up, the 1990 team if that's what it took to contend again. Quinn became the talk of the off-season in baseball, acquiring Bip Roberts, Greg Swindell, Tim Belcher, Dave Martinez, and Scott Bankhead for the present and third-base prospect Willie Greene for the future. Even the once-untouchable Eric

Davis was dealt, as part of the Belcher deal to Los Angeles. Meanwhile, Bowden was turning Triple-A Nashville into a haven for borderline, journeyman major-leaguers, which gave the Reds some quick-fix options in case of injury during the season and kept some of the top prospects in the lower levels—probably inflating the system's overall record in the process, which helps explain the .570 winning percentage, best in baseball in 1992.

On the major-league level, injuries again struck the Reds hard in 1992. But the makeup of the team—the deepest, strongest contingent the Reds had constructed under Piniella and Quinn—was able to come away with 90 victories. Without the injuries, the Reds could have competed with Atlanta for the division title. Even with the injuries, if the Reds had gone after a missing piece or two during the season, they could have had a chance. But Quinn hung on tight to his prospects, even though Piniella warned him they wouldn't be his prospects for long if they didn't win again in '92.

He was right. It was the last season for Quinn—and for Piniella.

The question of whether the pair would return became a continuing saga as the 1992 season wound down. For Piniella, the issue grew as wearying as it grew infuriating. After all, hadn't he led the team to a world championship in 1990? And wasn't he in the midst of taking this modern-day M*A*S*H unit to another 90-victory season? Yet, there was not a word from Marge Schott, not a vote of confidence, not a pat on the back, and not a call to set up an appointment to negotiate a new contract after the season. Nothing. Piniella was left in limbo. To know Lou Piniella is to know that he wants to be wanted or he will find someplace else where he is. He is not one to beg or posture for a job, possessing enough of the ballplayer's confidence to know that he will succeed somewhere if he is treated right.

"I got left hanging there all of September," he said. "I had to answer so many questions, and it became a public issue in the papers. It got somewhat embarrassing to me."

For Lou Piniella, this was simply the event that solidified his decision to resign. So did hearing Marge on the car radio one night saying that Schottzie was more important than anyone on the team. But his main reason for resigning stemmed from an incident in 1991 when the umpires' union sued him over his comments that one of the men in blue, Gary Darling, was biased against the Reds. It was the wrong thing to say, and Piniella would admit that later, but that mistake was only compounded by the umpires' retaliatory legal action, an absolutely frivolous lawsuit. Meanwhile, Piniella was hurt and angered that the Reds refused to pay for his legal bill and wouldn't even offer any public support for him. One day, he pulled Steve Schott aside in the coaches' dressing room at Riverfront and started verbally undressing him, screaming that he expected the Reds to pay for his legal help. As of spring training 1993, Piniella was still waiting, still trying to work something out.

"The big reason that I left there was, when I got sued by the umpires, I was left alone," said Piniella. "I was one of her key employees, and the posture that I got was, 'You handle it yourself.' What I said was wrong, and I realize it, but I said it in the heat of battle and I said it for the good of the ballclub, not myself. And, hell, I never got any backing. When you work for people and you pour your heart and soul into a job, you expect more. I've got a ball team to concern myself with, and it's hard doing two things at once. The ballclub had liability insurance and lawyers working for it, but what I got was, 'Well, our insurance rates would go up.'

"What the hell do they have insurance for?"

There were times the manager was amazed by the things the owner was doing, and this was a manager who had experienced Steinbrenner.

"A couple of times, she called me right before ballgames, right before we went out on the field, and said, 'I hope you guys lose,'" said Piniella. "She was upset at things—at a player or whatever.

"It gets you down a little bit."

Still, Marge mostly let Piniella manage the way he wanted to manage, without interference, and he appreciated that. And if she wanted to come in and give an occasional clubhouse pep talk to the team, well, Piniella realized it was her prerogative as owner, and her heart was in the right place, and she would always check with him. "At times, I really didn't agree that it was needed," he said, "but if she felt that it was, so be it."

After the 1991 season, Marge did fire his pitching coach, Stan Williams, who had coached the World Series team, prompting

Williams to comment, "Broomhilda got me." Piniella says he talked to Marge a few times about that one and could never get a straight answer. She also was openly critical of third-base coach Sam Perlozzo for sending Tom Browning home on a play in which Browning tore up his knee in a collision at the plate. Piniella supported Perlozzo, and tried to explain to his coach that Marge was more of a fan than an owner and that she expressed her frustration as a fan would.

"She called me quite a few times and talked to me about some of the moves that I made—why I'd do this, or why is this guy here or that guy there?" said Piniella. "I guess she listened to the radio shows like everybody else, and being a fan, reacted that way. But she was polite about it. But she doesn't really get involved with who's on the team. If a good friend calls her about something, then she'll pose questions, but outside of that, no."

Other antics were more annoying. Her habit of rubbing Schottzie hair on the manager for good luck, for one. Watching Piniella be put through that type of public display was painful, to say the least.

"It was a little embarrassing," said Piniella. "The other clubs would laugh at me. At the beginning, I thought it was just a superstition, but it got a little tiring. She has her peculiarities, but what the hell? Like I told her when I left there, 'Marge, you own the ballclub, you have a right to do anything that you want to do. If I'm not satisfied, well, then I have an option. I can either stay or go, and I'm going to exercise my right just to go.'"

In their final meeting, Marge did finally offer a new contract, albeit for the same $650,000 Piniella already was making. But the salary was not an issue by that point. Piniella made his decision before he met with Marge, and he was not going to change his mind. He claims there are no hard feelings toward Marge.

"She's a tough old woman," Piniella said, "but with a lot of compassion. I liked her. She didn't mind smoking a cigarette and saying what's on her mind. I saw the good side of her the vast majority of the time. And she didn't bother me too much. She's moody, but you would get treated according to how she liked you. I probably had as good a relationship with her as anybody there, and I'm appreciative of that. She was good to my kids, she was good to my wife, she was good to my family. I did see some of the sides that I didn't particularly like, but when you're an employee, you go with the program."

Still, the program could be hard to follow when the fixation over nickels seemed counterproductive. When Piniella arrived at spring training in his new job, managing the Seattle Mariners, he was impressed with the "first-class" way the operation worked. "If you need equipment, you get it," he said. "It was hard in Cincinnati to get special equipment." How hard was it? Howie Bedell says that one spring the Reds had two working pitching machines and wouldn't pay to fix the roughly half-dozen broken ones.

"There's no penny pinching here," said Piniella (*here* referring to the Mariners, *there* to the Reds). "The Reds watch their dollars, and an organization *should* watch its dollars, but there are certain things you need to get the damn job done. You go out to dinner here with the general manager and talk baseball matters, hell, he [the team] picks up the check. Over there, when I took the newspaper people out in the spring or during the season, I [Piniella] would pay the damn bill.

"It's important to take the media out. It's not doing me any good, it's for the good of the ballclub. It's great PR, and you talk baseball, and you get to know the people you work with. But I'd talk to Bob, and he'd say, 'Marge isn't gonna like this' and 'Marge isn't gonna pay for this.'"

But Marge wouldn't do this just to single out Pinella or to give Quinn a hard time. Once when Murray Cook was general manager, he and other front-office types went out to dinner in Plant City with Reds limited partner Bill Reik. When Reik offered to pick up the check, Cook apologized for not being able to put it on the club's tab. "Murray, you don't have to apologize," Reik said. "I understand."

Piniella still would take media members out on occasion—but far fewer occasions than he would have preferred. And instead of going through the hassle of trying to convince Quinn to try to convince Marge, he just paid for it. It was easier that way.

"When we won a world championship over there, the woman really increased my salary," said Piniella. "I had to ask for it, but she did. It's a great organization with a hell of a lot of tradition. I didn't realize how much tradition, but it's just not run the right way, and it should be."

Piniella didn't like Marge telling him to go directly to her and to bypass Quinn when he wanted something. He says he wouldn't do it for Steinbrenner, and he wouldn't do it for Marge. So he told her he didn't feel comfortable doing that.

"He was my immediate boss upstairs, and how would it look if every time there was a problem, I would just exclude him and go directly to the ownership?" he said. "Supposedly, Bob is her first man, and sometimes Bob didn't even go to her."

Frankly, there were times Piniella wondered if Quinn was acting on her orders or just in anticipation of them. Piniella would get frustrated seeing Quinn protecting prospects instead of going after accomplished players who could help the team win now, especially if it could have kept the team in the hunt for the division title. But Quinn felt he owed it to Marge and the Reds to protect their future—even at the expense of his own future and of the team's present. In the end, Marge didn't appreciate it; at the time, she might not have even approved of it, considering her contempt for patience. Piniella tried to reason with him, telling Quinn, "Bob, you know we've got to do the things we've got to do. Whatever happens with you and me happens, but we've got to do what we feel is right." But it was no use.

And so, Piniella devised an alternate plan. Piniella didn't want to go directly over Quinn's head, so he did it indirectly, airing his grievances publicly to get Marge's attention. "Hell, it wouldn't work any other way, so I tried it a different way," said Piniella. "I could have probably gotten more things done if I had gone directly to her, but I don't operate that way."

Quinn never liked Piniella airing things in public and would say so privately, but he tried to explain Piniella's actions as those of a typical manager, always thinking about right now, in contrast to the general manager's need to think about tomorrow and the bigger picture. Quinn would constantly try to sugarcoat their differences in the media. Once, when told that he and Piniella didn't appear to be on the same page, Quinn said, "Not only are we on the same page, we're on the same paragraph and the same sentence."

Still, Quinn and Piniella genuinely liked each other and worked together in orchestrating some of their trades. And when Marge got panicky or angry about certain deals and lit into Quinn, such as his midseason 1992 trade of popular outfielder Billy Hatcher to Boston for borderline pitcher Tom Bolton, Piniella defended his general manager. Nobody pretended Tom Bolton was the next Tom Seaver, but the Reds were desperate for pitching help and Hatcher was rarely playing and had expressed a desire to move on if it was possible. The Reds wanted to accommodate Hatcher—an integral part of 1990 but now a bit player with a seven-figure salary—and the deal saved the Reds about $1 million in salary that could pay for someone else who became available. Despite Marge's constant harping on the payroll, she didn't grasp any of this. When Bolton didn't pan out, she told her baseball people, "You guys didn't make a very good deal."

Piniella got some of that, but Quinn got more—which was nothing unusual. Piniella didn't like the way Marge treated Quinn, and he tried to talk to him about it.

"Bob would come down to the office beaten up at times," said Piniella. "We'd sit down and talk, and I told Bob a few times, 'How in the hell can you put up with this? You probably don't know it, but if you're not here next year, it might be the best thing that's ever happened to you.'"

But Quinn didn't want to leave the job. Whereas Piniella always believes there's another position somewhere for him, Quinn didn't want to take that chance. Better to keep hitting his head against the wall than worry about what would happen if he stopped—he might feel better, but then what? He wasn't going to quit, and he wasn't going to quit trying. He was openly campaigning for his job in the media, and he called deputy baseball commissioner Steve Greenberg and asked him to help.

"Marge is going to make up her mind in the next week about my situation," Quinn told Greenberg. "Would you give her a call and put in a good word for me, because I know you have a great relationship with her?"

Greenberg started to laugh, because he thought Quinn was kidding. But then he realized he was serious. Somehow, Marge gave Quinn the impression she had a great rapport with the deputy commissioner, who didn't quite see it the same way. He didn't think his relationship with Marge was bad—"strange" was the term he used. He and Marge would talk maybe every six to eight weeks on some issue, say hello at meetings, but nothing special.

One conversation, however, did stand out, when Marge called Greenberg out of the blue after he'd been in office for about a year and a half.

MARGE: I didn't know you were Hank
              Greenberg's son.
GREENBERG: Yes, Marge, I am.
MARGE: Tell me the truth. Is that true?
GREENBERG: Yes, it's true.
MARGE: I've heard of him.

Greenberg assumed most people in the game knew he was the son of the baseball legend. But the truth is, considering Marge's limited knowledge of baseball, it is even more surprising she knew who Hank Greenberg was.

In any case, Quinn didn't seem to need Steve Greenberg or anybody else's help after Piniella departed. Marge had been saying privately she was going to keep at least one of the two, Piniella or Quinn. But after Piniella resigned, she fired Quinn anyway. One of the limited partners, shocked at the news, called her and asked her about it afterward.

"You told me you were going to keep one or the other," the partner said. "What am I missing?"

"I talked with one of the scouts, and he said I should just clean house, so I did," said Marge. "I'm gonna give Jim Bowden the job. The only thing that bothers me is, he's awfully young."

"It's the perfect situation because of David Shula," said the partner.

"Who's David Shula?" Marge responded.

None of this was out of character for Marge Schott. Not making a decision based on the advice of the last person she talked to, not failing to know the name of the Cincinnati Bengals' youthful head football coach (who was earning strong early-season reviews at that time). Not going back on her intention to keep one of the two people responsible for 1990.

She is not going to change, and she will be the first one to admit it. Nobody can tell Marge Schott she is wrong, and nobody can take her on. If so, that somebody risks recriminations.

That somebody risks becoming another Tim Sabo.

Chapter Twelve

The Man Who
Shot Down Marge

T im Sabo had never met Marge Schott. It was the winter of
1989 and he was at the Reds' offices for his final interview
to get the team's controller's job, when it was time to meet
the woman who had become such a dominant personality in the
local sporting scene—the woman who would make his life a
living hell for years to come. When the two future litigants met,
Sabo was a little surprised. He remembers that she wasn't dressed
very nicely and that she chainsmoked her way through the
interview. She talked to him about loyalty, about dogs, about the
terrible financial state of the game. Marge asked Sabo to tell her
about himself, and he told her he was not a yes man and not just
a bookkeeper. But she wanted to know more. She wanted more
personal information. She wanted to know about his family, for
instance, and which religion he followed (a question she was not
entitled to ask). Sabo was a bit offended, but he wanted the job
and wanted to get on her good side.

"I evaded the religion answer by saying my wife was Catholic," said Sabo, who was Methodist. "I knew Marge was Catholic,
and I knew that would score points with her."

During the course of the interview, a Reds employee Sabo
didn't recognize entered and gave Marge some information, to
which Marge said, "You tell that son of a bitch to . . ." Sabo forgot
the rest of her comment, but the tenor of it would stay with him:
This was not a boss who would couch her comments. That was
OK with Sabo, because he considered himself a hard-nosed type,

as well. Besides, this was the job he had dreamed of since he graduated from Miami University to work for Peat, Marwick, Mitchell & Co., where he helped out on the Reds audit. In fact, he says that's a major reason he went to work there.

"It was my favorite audit," said Sabo, and why not? He grew up a big baseball fan, albeit more for the Indians than the Reds, as he was from Madison in northern Ohio, about 45 minutes from Cleveland. Now the figures he was checking would tie into the Cincinnati Reds and not your everyday company or corporation. "It was exciting. When I was at Peat Marwick, I'd joke that someday I wanted to be chief financial officer of the Reds. Little did I know what a sick joke that was."

At that time, Lou Porco was CFO of the Reds, and Chris Krabbe was his longtime assistant. But in 1986, Porco retired rather than continue to deal with Marge. Krabbe drew the same conclusion in 1989, taking a job with Spring Grove Cemetery. After leaving Peat Marwick to work at Scripps-Howard and then the Student Loan Funding Corporation, Sabo kept in touch with Krabbe, and when Sabo read in the paper that Krabbe was leaving, he talked to Krabbe about the job. Krabbe warned him that this might not be the ideal position, speaking in generalities but obviously referring to Marge Schott. But Sabo didn't listen. He was smitten with the idea of working for the Reds. "I had blinders on," he said.

On December 15, 1989, Tim Sabo began working for Marge Schott.

In the first month, he knew this was trouble. His first day, Sabo looked at the Reds' finances and saw that the Reds made $19 million in taxable income for 1989—this, after Marge had claimed such poverty in his interview. And when Tim introduced his wife, Linda, to Marge for the first time at the company Christmas party, Marge shook a fist in his face and said, "You better do a good job for me." If that wasn't enough to startle Sabo, the first time Marge went over company salary increases with him certainly did.

Late one afternoon, she came to Sabo and said, "We've got to do the goddamn raises." Considering Sabo had only been with the team a couple of weeks, he was in no position to evaluate personnel. He watched Marge go through the Reds' yearbook and, in about an hour—with no input from supervisors—she was finished. The total raises and bonuses were less than $100,000, with no front-office employee getting more than a 3-percent increase. But it was the way she decided who got what that amazed Sabo. "Take Lois Wingo" he said, referring to the Reds part-time accounting secretary. "Marge said her husband's got a good job, so she doesn't need a raise."

Then on January 8, 1990, Marge bought two Chevy Celebrities from her dealership for the Reds and told Sabo to backdate the transactions to October 31, 1989. That way, Marge could lessen her taxable income for the 1989 audit, even if it was only "hundreds of dollars," Sabo said, "clearly not worth the risk." Three weeks on the job, Sabo struggled with how to handle it, but decided to go along with the boss's wishes. This time.

"That's the last thing I did like that," he said.

Bearing a confidence that sometimes bordered on overconfidence, and still failing to see reality through the stardust of Major League Baseball, Sabo thought that if he stayed he could make an impact on her and the organization. He tried fighting back. When he learned that he was being charged for half of his insurance premiums, even though he insists Marge and Steve Schott had clearly indicated when he was hired that they would pay all of it, he kept pushing them.

It became one of many battles between Marge and Sabo, two forceful personalities that would clash, but only one having the authority to act. And Marge's actions were horrifying Sabo, not simply because they were poor business policies but also because he found the practices unethical, if not illegal. He began jotting down notes of what he saw, turning his daily calendar into a diary. "It was for my own protection," he said, only wishing he had done it more methodically.

Some of the entries—which have been expanded from Sabo's shorthand notations and put into their proper context—are astounding:

Feb. 13, 1990—Marge cut back the number of Opening Day tickets to front-office staff members because she thought they were scalping them.

March 14—After Reds minor-league instructor Jose Cardenal was hit in the head by a ball, Marge said, "Jose Cardenal was probably screwing around. I wish it would have been one of my $3 million niggers."

Actually, Eric Davis was the only Red making $3 million at the time. Sabo says he heard her use slurs not only against Davis, but also Dave Parker. And when Major League Baseball offices shut down for Martin Luther King Day, Sabo heard Marge say, "I'm not going to shut down for 'Nigger Day.'"

But Sabo says Marge's attitudes weren't just reflected in her hiring—they guided it. When he was looking at a black candidate for an opening in the accounting department, Marge said, "I don't want their kind here. I have to put up with them on the field. I'm not going to put up with them in the front office."

Sabo says he argued with Marge about it, but to no avail. "She told me there were 100 resumes in her desk from people who wanted my job," he said. And it wasn't just him. Sabo also saw Reds marketing director Chip Baker hamstrung by Marge's racist hiring practices.

"Chip had to replace his secretary," said Sabo, "and he knew he couldn't get a minority. I saw him hang up on one person interested in the job as soon as she answered the phone. I asked him why, and he said, 'Because she sounded black.'"

Sabo says that when Clifford Alexander and Janet Hill of Alexander & Associates, hired by baseball to monitor minority hiring, came to inspect the Reds, Marge ordered him to stay away from them, and they didn't seek him out, even though he oversaw front-office personnel hiring.

March 19—Marge questioned the expenses of a scout who turned in a $2 ticket for a high school game. "Scouts don't have to pay admission to see games," she said.

"She thought all of the scouts and all of the employees were stealing from her," said Sabo. "She thought the scouts were getting reimbursed expenses that were invalid, that they were inflating mileage. Somebody might fly someplace and lose their airport parking receipt, and it was obvious the expense was legitimate, but she wouldn't want to pay it."

March 21-22—National League president Bill White told Marge not to let fans vote for whether Opening Day would be a day or night game. But Marge strong-armed WLW to stage a vote and had Reds public-relations intern Joe Kelly, on his first day on the job, and other employees call and pad the vote total for a day game.

June 18—Marge nixed the Section 125 (making medical-insurance premiums paid on a pre-tax instead of post-tax basis) and 401K (a pre-tax savings plan for the employees) proposals for her employees that not only would make them money, but the Section 125 plan alone would have made her about $5,000. "The employees don't deserve it," she said.

Marge eventually changed her mind on both after pressure by the employees. "There was widespread support through the staff of wanting the plans, including Marge's executive assistant, Joyce Pfarr, who often had Marge's ear," said Sabo.

June 22—Marge was trying to make a surcharge off the players' and employees' All-Star Game tickets, charging an extra $15 each.

Aug. 23—At least 10 people heard Marge scream, "What's in it for me?" when she learned Reds outfielder Ken Griffey, Sr., wanted his retirement changed to a release so he could play in Seattle with his son, Ken Griffey, Jr.

Sabo was in the room with Quinn when Marge came in, and Quinn recommended to Marge that she give Griffey his release. That's when Marge asked him, "What's in it for me?" Quinn replied, "Nothing. We'd just be doing the right thing." Marge told him to look into what she could get, anyway. Marge also railed on Seattle itself and Mariners owner Jeff Smulyan, saying, "The Jews control the club, and the Japs own everything else out there."

Aug. 29—Marge was accused of tampering with Kansas City assistant trainer Dan Wright. As a compromise, Marge told Royals owner Ewing Kauffman she would donate $6,000 to his favorite charity to make up for it, but she actually donated $1,000. "It's the principle of it," she said.

The Reds hired Wright in 1990 only because new rules insisted that each team have at least two trainers. At first, Marge wanted him to work in the ticket office during the off-season, but she gave up on that one. As it was, she refused to let Wright start until he absolutely had to be with the team, on Opening Day.

Sept. 4.—Marge refused to pay a vendor because a sponsor hadn't paid her yet in a totally unrelated matter.

Sept. 5—Reds gift shop employee Sylvia Buxton claims she put in more than 1,000 hours each of the last two years, but Marge and Steve refuse her benefits and vacation, even though 1,000 hours is the cut-off point. Steve accused Sabo of creating a problem at the gift shop.

Sabo says Buxton had "a lot more" than 1,000 hours, the federal criterion for a full-time employee, but had no luck getting her so designated when he approached Marge and Steve. "I later found out Steve had his hands tied," said Sabo.

Sept. 14—Marge tried not to give American League teams their allotted League Championship Series tickets and lied to the players about the number of tickets they could buy. Marge told one player, "I don't know if I'll even have a seat, honey, with all the tickets we have to give Major League Baseball."

Sept. 18—Marge and Steve intentionally didn't introduce Bob Howsam at the Big Red Machine Reunion Day at Riverfront Stadium.

"We discovered WCPO had left his name off accidentally," said Sabo, referring to Cincinnati TV station Channel 9, which had organized the reunion. "We discovered it in time to take care of the problem. But Marge said to omit him and blame it on Channel 9."

Unbeknownst to Sabo, the CBS affiliate had other problems with Marge. Channel 9 used to have a regular segment on the news with Reds outfielder Eric Davis, but Marge refused to allow Davis to appear in uniform without being compensated for use of the logo. But once, Channel 9 tried to photograph him from the neck up, and Steve called saying the V in Davis' uniform collar could be made out. Steve talked about charging the station for logo use, which would usually run about $3,000.

The Reds' logo was sacred to Marge, and she insisted that companies pay when they wanted to use it, without any deals. With one exception.

"When she ran her car dealership ads during my tenure, she never paid the club for use of the logo," said Sabo. "Technically, it's not correct to do that. When I approached her on it, she said, 'The Reds are lucky I don't charge them for the use of Schottzie.'"

Sept. 25—Marge was holding 1,500-2,000 League Championship Series tickets.

Sept. 26—All Reds business associates won't get playoff tickets.

Oct. 1—Major League Baseball urged Marge to give two complimentary tickets per employee. Two additional tickets per employee also were made available for purchase. To be mean, Marge won't allow those tickets to be alongside the complimentary two, even though those seats are available.

Oct. 4—Marge was drunk. Security wouldn't let her drive home.

Nov. 14—Marge ordered expenses backdated to fiscal year 1990. This reminded Sabo of the previous year, when Marge bought two cars in January and wanted them put in fiscal year 1989.

"I did not do that this time," said Sabo, "although she was probably unaware of it."

Dec. 11—Marge likes Cindi Strzynski, secretary for traveling secretary Joel Pieper and director of season ticket sales Pat McCaffrey, because "she is a mature woman who won't be having kids."

As much as Marge loves the idea of families, she wasn't always thrilled when women went on leave or left the business because of babies. It got to the point, Sabo says, that she told him not to hire any more women of childbearing years.

Dec. 20—Marge told Steve to call on the sly about getting Columbus as a farm team.

The Ohio capital already had a minor-league affiliate of the New York Yankees, the Columbus Clippers, and Sabo says he witnessed Marge tell Steve to approach the city before the start of the designated period to negotiate with cities.

Dec. 20—Strategy was discussed about minimizing the payments distributed to the limited partners.

This came at a meeting that also included Marge's attorney, Bob Martin, and members of the Reds' external auditors at Deloitte & Touche. Sabo remembers Martin saying that if anyone asked, this meeting never happened—otherwise, that person would be "in danger."

Dec. 26—Marge called Sabo a "lousy scumball" for being with his family in Cleveland instead of in his office on Christmas Day when the pipes broke in the accounting department.

Jan. 2, 1991—Marge was eavesdropping in general manager Bob Quinn's doorway.

"The door was open," said Sabo. "She was off to the side, where he couldn't see her. There was no doubt about what she was doing."

Jan. 3—Marge decided on raises and bonuses, again without getting any input or reviews from supervisors.

For instance, she didn't give the clubhouse man a raise, saying, "Bernie Stowe—the players voted him a World Series share, that son of a bitch."

Jan. 7—Before auditors and counsel, Marge bitched about how much Major League Baseball was spending on affirmative action for "those blacks and spics."

Jan. 7—The total distribution for the partnership for fiscal year 1990 should be $27 million.

Sabo says Marge tried to pay the partnership just $5.25 million and keep the rest in reserve for the team. At the end of fiscal year 1990, the Reds had cash and cash equivalents in excess of $40 million. He did a cash-flow projection for the upcoming year and determined the Reds would have a positive cash flow in

1991 of about $4.5 million—which was abnormally low because of projected payments by the owners for their alleged collusion against free agents. With a projected $45 million to work with, Sabo concluded the $27 million payoff to the partnership would in no way jeopardize the financial stability of the Reds, considering there would still be $18 million in the company coffers. Marge's position was, once reserves are put into the Reds, they should remain there. For instance, in excess of $12 million was reserved the previous year in fear of a strike or lockout for 1990, but the money wasn't needed because a long work stoppage was avoided. Yet, Marge wanted that money kept in the team's reserves. It would later become the major issue in a lawsuit involving Marge and certain limited partners.

Jan. 16—Pam Hudson in the accounting department had a baby and decided to stay home. At first, Marge said that was great, but later said to hire an older woman in her place so Marge wouldn't have to worry about that "baby shit."

Jan. 23—The temperature was 64 degrees in the office.

Jan. 23—Marge told Joel Pieper to forge players' names on frequent-flyer vouchers so the team could get the mileage.

Jan. 24—Marge turned away scoreboard ads from Toyota and Honda, helping to result in a shortfall of income.

Jan. 25—Marge questioned having to pay $1.60 a month each for two phone lines for computers during times of the year when the computers aren't in use.

Jan. 28—Marge charged Dan Wright $660 for a $440 replica World Series trophy.

"She told him she was getting it for him at cost," said Sabo. "I saw the invoice from Balfour, and Dan gave me a copy of his letter from her."

Jan. 31—Marge called at about 9:45. It was about the 10th late-night call from her in the last several months. She likely was drunk.

April 8—Steve Schott told Sabo again that Marge had mentioned to him she was having Bob Martin look for a woman to replace Sabo.

April 19—Steve weeded out women of childbearing years to replace Kathy Shaner as payroll supervisor.

April 22—Sabo was subpoenaed.

The limited partners sued Marge, claiming she was keeping too much of the revenue for the team when she should be divvying it up among the partners. Sabo knew she was purposely holding money back from the partners, and he was worried about what to do—lie to protect his job and Marge, or tell the truth.

April 30—Marge gave Sabo a raise to $51,000, but told him to be "just a bookkeeper."

When Sabo was hired by the Reds, he wanted at least $50,000, but agreed to take $45,000 as long as it was temporary. "I agreed to take less if I could be adjusted the next year, barring no performance problems," Sabo said. For several months, Sabo kept after Marge concerning the raise she owed him, but with no luck. Suddenly, he got the raise, and Sabo believes it was basically hush money to silence his potentially damaging testimony for the limited partners' lawsuit.

May 14—Marge refused Sabo's gift idea for retiring ticket-department director Bill Stewart.

"Buried in the bowels of the files, I found out that when the Reds bought the Jumbotron scoreboard, Sony gave them $10,000 per year in free replacement parts and other catalog items so the Reds would leave the word 'Sony' on it. Marge was going to have it taken off or covered up," said Sabo. "But that credit had been lost for a couple years. Bill Stewart was retiring, and there was no way we could use all the credit we'd saved up, so I asked Marge, 'Why don't we give him a TV or camcorder?' Marge said, 'Why in the hell would I do that for Bill Stewart?'"

May 21—Scout Jack Bowen was owed $2,000.

"Scouts have to front all of their expenses," Sabo said. "The scouts were making an average of about $20,000, and Jack had fronted $2,000. He tells me he's building a house, and he needed to get his reimbursement check back so he could pay his down payment and closing costs. I told Marge, and she says, 'In that case, I won't sign it for a week.'"

Marge was notorious for sitting on bills for months or longer. And when she got around to paying them, if there was a penalty, tough. "Usually, I wouldn't pay late charges," said Sabo. "In one case, I thought it was legitimate, so I paid it." But when he submitted the check with the $3 late charge, Marge made him rip it up and write a new check without the penalty. Sabo argued on the phone about it with the creditor, then Marge called the president of the company and made threats to get her way.

June 11—Marge screamed at Sabo for not reading the utilities meter personally.

MARGE: How do you know this number's right?

SABO: I don't.

MARGE: You should read it. Most government workers are lazy and crooks.

June 18—Marge told Sabo that Schottzie is more important than any player and the entire city because of her worldwide popularity.

June 27—At extended spring training, minor-league players were given $10 per day for lodging and ended up sleeping eight to a room, some on the floor.

June 27—Bob Quinn paid his own way to the All-Star Game and had to use his vacation days.

June 28—Marge charged a $15 service charge to employees (meaning Quinn) for All-Star tickets.

July 16—Roberta Moore of the Reds' gift shop asked for two comp days after she'd worked 60 hours for a week. Marge said no. "Managers don't get comp time," she said.

July 19—Marge lost a dime in the coffee machine and wanted a worker from the vending company who was filling the machines to open it up to get her money back, but the guy said he wasn't allowed to do it. Marge threw a tantrum.

Before the vending machines were installed, the Reds' offices had a coffeepot, and Marge charged per serving, using the honor system and a cup to deposit the payments of one dime each. Sabo's department had the job of bringing in the cup of change.

"After a night game, there was $1.80 in the cup and it didn't get picked up," said Sabo. "Marge came in the next morning with the cup and slammed it down and said, 'Anyone could have taken it!'"

And if Marge wasn't supervising the coffee, there was always the refrigerator. "She thought she was the Reds, so the refrigerator was hers, too," said Sabo. "I've witnessed her opening the refrigerator and eating other people's lunches."

July 25—Backup infielder Luis Quinones's error lost a game for the Reds, and Marge rode Quinn for sending backup infielder Freddie Benevides to the minors.

"The day before, when Benevides was sent to the minors," Sabo said, "Marge had said she didn't know who Freddie Benevides was."

Aug. 23—Sabo was fired. Bob Martin and Bob Quinn were there. Martin said there was "no specific reason," but that Marge and a number of limited partners "no longer felt comfortable with you" and—unsolicited—said, "This has nothing to do with your deposition in the limited partners' suit."

Sabo didn't buy it. In his deposition, he testified that he had told Marge he didn't believe she could keep all that money from the partners. He believed the testimony was damaging to Marge's case. Baseball ended up sending an attorney to help expedite the matter, and, just before the trial started, Marge settled the case. Limited partner George Strike said Sabo's deposition "definitely" was a factor in the settlement.

"But the facts are the facts," said Strike. "He corroborated the facts, but the facts were still there. With or without his testimony, I think we would have won the suit, anyway. But he was an honest guy who told the truth."

But the truth did not ingratiate Tim Sabo to Marge Schott. Sabo insists that Marge never forgot. As nasty as she had been to him previously, it only got worse. Although she never told him he was doing a bad job, she didn't want him there. He didn't want to be there either, but neither of them would directly tell the other in so many words. Sabo hoped to land a job with the expansion Florida Marlins or Colorado Rockies, but he didn't. Before he could find another job and resign, she got to him first.

When Sabo was fired, he expected to get four weeks' severance pay. That was the agreement he had made with Steve and Marge when he was hired—if he left, he'd give four weeks' notice; if he was fired, he'd get four weeks' pay from the Reds. But it was an oral agreement, so Marge refused to pay it, denying any knowledge of such a deal. Sabo tried to fight it, but he wasn't ready to go to court over it. At least not until she held up his unemployment compensation, accusing him of having written unauthorized company checks to himself. "She hung up my unemployment compensation for almost five months by the time it was over, and she alleged I was a crook," he said. "That's when I felt I had no choice."

And so, on October 9, 1991, Timothy A. Sabo filed a wrongful-firing lawsuit against Margaret U. Schott and the Cincinnati Reds. Sabo alleged he was fired for a number of reasons, including:

• *His deposition in the legal battle between the limited partners and Marge.* In his own lawsuit, Sabo said he testified that Marge "had improperly refused to distribute to them, as limited partners of* the Reds, millions of dollars in partnership profits, and that she had otherwise managed the Reds in a manner which benefited her own interests at the expense of the interests of the partnership as a whole."

Sabo claimed that Marge gave him a raise shortly before his deposition "in a vain attempt to influence his testimony." He also claimed that after the deposition, Marge subjected him "to an almost relentless barrage of personal abuse in an unsuccessful attempt to force him to resign from his position as controller." Sabo claimed Marge regularly insulted him in front of his staff, his coworkers, and various third parties—and refused to do anything about the horrible odors in Sabo's office caused by a leak of rancid beer into his office from the stadium vending company, Sportservice.

"It would gag you," Sabo would say later. "It would give you a headache. One of my people had to go home one day, it was that bad. Marge told me it doesn't smell and to quit whining."

Marge had said the only way she would replace the carpeting would be if Sportservice paid for it, and Sabo got Sportservice to agree to do just that. "But when they agreed, she refused to let them," Sabo would say later. "Why? Just to screw with me."

•*His opposition to Marge ordering him to perform illegal acts such as reporting partnership expenses in years other than when they occurred and forging the signatures of Reds players on frequent-flyer vouchers.*

•*His opposition to Marge ordering him not to hire blacks.*

This was the allegation that would snare the most attention, especially when Marge and Sabo reacted to it in the media. Sabo told *The Cincinnati Post* that Marge had told him, "I don't want their kind here." Marge told *The Cincinnati Enquirer*, "There's nobody who respects black people, good black people, more than I do."

No matter how Sabo portrayed her, Marge made herself look worse every time she tried to defend herself. Talking about the "good black people" was demeaning, and it made Sabo's allegations seem that much more credible. She was better off letting Bob Martin speak for her. He released a statement saying that Sabo was an employee without a written contract and therefore could be fired "at will." As for the accusations of discrimination, Martin said, "Being a woman in charge of a major organization unfortunately often exposes her to unwarranted, unjustified, and unsupported charges."

The nation was already feeling the emotional charge of the Anita Hill–Clarence Thomas hearings, in which allegations of sexual harassment were leveled against the Supreme Court nominee and charges of racial discrimination were made by him. Now Cincinnati was getting its own zoom lens of race and gender issues. It could have been a powerful debate that raged around office coolers and in chili parlors all over the city. Instead, the story seemed to disappear as quickly as it arrived. Cincinnati didn't seem to care. And baseball wasn't much better. Baseball spokesman Jim Small said, "We're aware of Mr. Sabo's lawsuit," and that was about all that came out of the game's headquarters.

All of it was as mind-boggling as it was disappointing.

"What's with Cincinnati?" It became an intriguing and lingering question during the late 1980s and early 1990s. This was the town in which the Contemporary Arts Center became the first museum in America indicted under obscenity law, for displaying Robert Mapplethorpe's exhibit of photographs. This was the town that fed into Pete Rose's belief that he had done nothing wrong and worked to keep him in denial about his gambling addiction while the rest of the country was chastising him for betting on baseball. This was the town in which Bengals football coach Sam Wyche tried to keep reporters out of the locker rooms instead of telling his players to wear a robe or at least a towel. This was the town that allowed a Ku Klux Klan cross to join the Christmas tree and menorah at the downtown centerpiece known as Fountain Square. This was the town in which vice-president of the Board of Education William Seitz argued that the loud behavior of black families at a Western Hills High School graduation showed why black students were twice as likely to be suspended or expelled from the city's schools.

Such incidents diminished the glow of a city that deserved better. Yes, it is a conservative town, but it is anything but a bad town. Crime and the cost of living are comfortably low, the hills are tall and picturesque, and the people are so friendly they say, "Please" when they can't understand what you're saying. It may not be New York City when it comes to nightlife, and Cincinnati goes to bed happy every evening because of that, but it has enough small slices of the Apple when it comes to the arts and entertainment to give it just the right big-city flash. It is no wonder so many players who come to the city as temporary Reds leave the team as forever Cincinnatians.

But as wonderful a town as its citizens love to boast that it is, it's one hell of a lot more racist than they would care to admit. It's not the Old South kind of racism—the type that will burn a cross on your front lawn and make certain you know you're not welcome. It's more of a proponent of the new racism, with too many people who will shake your hand and call you friend and think of you as one of the "good blacks," all the time hoping you won't move into their neighborhoods and praying to God you aren't dating their sons and daughters. The whole town isn't like that, but enough of it is to make a difference, and the city leaders only feed into the ignorance by backing off the issue to make sure they get reelected.

Cincinnati will never be at the cutting edge of change and really doesn't want to be. Attitudes will change around the country, and Cincinnati will follow once it plays through Gotham and plays in Peoria. In New York, Marge Schott would have been a lightning rod of controversy as soon as the Sabo allegations and her response came out, and baseball would have been forced off its backstop. An investigation was certainly in order, because the last thing the national pastime needed was the perception that it tolerated racism—especially when it so embraced the role it had in the civil-rights movement by shattering the sport's color barrier with Jackie Robinson, and particularly when its commissioners publicly vowed to make their teams' front offices politically and socially correct. But as long as this issue stayed in the vacuum of Cincinnati, as long as Cincinnati didn't seem to mind Marge, and as long as the case was in court, baseball could afford to sit back and relax.

Those who knew Marge, and who knew the Reds, realized baseball wouldn't be able to relax forever—not if all the stories that had been kept private became public. If the Sabo case were to go to court, and if those who had worked with Marge and listened to her slurs were called to testify under oath, it would seemingly be over for her. Those people didn't want to come forward and speak, because they knew what she could and would do. And if they weren't sure, they could look at what was happening to Sabo. She was ripping him apart in the press, joined by her devoted fans in the city who thought she had rescued the Reds, and by her hired "gums" at WLW Radio. And she countersued Sabo, accusing him of slander and charging him with embezzling funds from the Reds. Other former employees cringed at the idea of testifying, not wanting to take on the powerful and popular Marge. Really, if they were so intent on bringing her down, why didn't they do it years ago?

Others had talked about her penny-pinching, her meddling, but the only one who ever was willing to discuss her slurs was Roger Blaemire. When he talked to Michael Paolercio of *The Cincinnati Enquirer* in 1986, the former head of the Reds' business operation also revealed the racial and ethnic epithets as well as the extent of Marge's drinking. But because Blaemire insisted on staying unnamed unless someone else would go on the record, and because anyone else Paolercio found would only agree to talk off the record, the story never ran. "I would argue until I was blue in the face that it was OK to quote her when she lies to us on the record, but it's not OK to get the truth off the record," said Paolercio. But the newspaper held to its general policy back then of not using unnamed sources.

"Marge for a long time got a free ride in this town because she came forward and more or less portrayed herself as the savior of the franchise, which is not true," said *Enquirer* sportswriter John Erardi, who has covered Marge's ownership. "She was painted as someone who was somewhat eccentric and had a dog and liked to sign autographs. At the *Enquirer*, we did a pretty good job of delving into the finances of her club, but never really looked at her personally. In retrospect, it was obviously a mistake. Roger had the goods on her a long time ago, and we didn't follow through with that. I'm sure the *Enquirer* is not the only one regretting not covering her more in depth. Any time it takes a court case to bring out what was going on there, somebody had to have dropped the ball — if they ever had it."

After Sabo's lawsuit hit the media, *The Cincinnati Post* conducted an investigation into Marge's racial and ethnic slurs. In all, eight former Reds employees who worked closely with Marge and were credible sources admitted to *The Post* that they had heard her use the epithets, some of the sources even corroborating the others' examples. This time, Blaemire was willing to go on the record, although the rest of the sources agreed to let the paper quote them only if their names were not revealed. But the *Post* opted not to run the story, deciding it needed more named sources.

Conservative decisions.

Conservative newspapers.

Conservative town.

Had the case not come to trial, the country would never have known what was going on in Cincinnati. And it would have been so easy. If Marge had just given Sabo his four weeks' severance pay and left him alone, it would have been a non-issue. For $4,000, she could have avoided hundreds of thousands of dollars in legal fees, a suspension from baseball, and the unenviable status as the nation's modern-day racist. Even after the depositions were taken, but before they became public, she could have cut her losses at maybe a quarter of a million dollars—one tenth of the $2.5 million Sabo was seeking in the lawsuit. But not Marge. To her, it was a matter of principle. She wasn't going to let some bookkeeper get the best of her.

And so the depositions became public.

And Marge's reputation began to crumble.

On Saturday, November 14, 1992, comments extracted from a handful of depositions by former Reds employees Roger Blaemire, Cal Levy, Howie Bedell, and Don Breen were printed in the local newspapers. Blaemire told his story about Marge's slur against the Simon Brothers. Bedell told his story about Moe Hill. And Breen testified that Marge didn't discriminate, she was nasty to everyone. But among all the stories of racial and ethnic slurs, the comments that hit hardest came from Levy, who told of her referring to Reds outfielders Dave Parker and Eric Davis as her "million-dollar niggers" and who claimed that Marge kept a Nazi armband in her home.

Unfortunately, the significance of the armband was twisted out of perspective and blown out of proportion, as Levy would be the first to admit. It wasn't as though Levy was suggesting Marge was secretly a member of the neo-Nazis. It was her reaction to his discovery of the item that he found so disturbing.

This all came about at a Christmas party at her house. Levy was kidding her about dinner being late, and she said, "If you're so hungry, you get the dinner bell." She told him it was in a drawer in a table in the hallway. He opened the drawer and found the swastika-emblazoned armband. He was shocked to see the symbol he found so repulsive right there, in her house. So Levy took out the armband and brought it to her.

"Just what the hell is this?" he asked her.

Marge was perplexed. To her, this was just an armband, a gift from someone, and what was the big deal? She didn't understand his reaction.

"I told her it's something I wouldn't want to see out and why—that it's offensive to the people in the Jewish community and that as a person in her position she ought to remove it," said Levy. "If it were given to her as a gift, fine. But it doesn't need to be in a place where it can be made conspicuous. This wasn't in the context of there being a sword and a holster and a pistol and a helmet—a collection of World War II memorabilia. This was an isolated situation. I was just very shocked that she wouldn't understand why certain people would be sensitive to it.

"She honestly did not get it, which is something I still believe today. She really didn't understand why it was offensive, and that's because she tends to look at things as black and white. It's like, 'No I don't want to do business with them.' Not, 'Gee, that might be a good decision three months from now.' It's 'That's how I feel now.'"

Not everyone being deposed was thrilled with the idea of testifying against Marge Schott, and it was going to be imperative that Sabo's attorney, Stephen Imm, ask specific questions and not rely on volunteered information. Breen in particular was against being there, believing that if Sabo had a problem with Marge, he should have voiced his displeasure when he was still with the Reds. Still, the allegations that did come out needed to be addressed, and Marge came back by releasing a statement:

> I usually don't like to respond to unfair and unjust allegations, but so many people who know me very well and have worked for me have encouraged me to stand up and tell the truth.
>
> I am not a racist. I have never been more hurt or disgusted in my life. I have been in business since my husband died 25 years ago and have never heard anything like this. I don't care what color, sex, or religion a person is. I judge people on the job they can do. These allegations are without any truth or foundation.

Many of the allegations would have been more difficult to submit in court if Marge hadn't accused Sabo of defamation of character in her countersuit. Now he had to defend himself and show he wasn't being malicious. Without the defamation claim, her counsel could have tried to argue that alleged slurs don't prove hiring bias. Marge asked the court for $25,000 for defamation. Also in the countersuit, Marge alleged Sabo owed her another $59,465 ($52,571 in overpayment of health-insurance premiums to retired front-office employees and $6,894 in checks he wrote to himself without her authorization) broken down more specifically this way:

•On April 30, 1991, Marge approved a raise for Sabo lifting him from $45,000 to $51,000, which Sabo says was retroactive to January 1. He calculated the difference in pay for the four months gone by ($2,000), pulled out the necessary deductions for income tax and social security, and wrote himself a check for the remainder (about $1,300). Sabo has a signed document from Marge approving the retroactive raise, but Schott claims the retroactive clause was added after she signed it.

•Sabo claims that Marge and Steve Schott promised that the Reds would pay Sabo's health-insurance premiums, but Marge fought him on that. Eventually, Sabo says, she gave him authority to reimburse himself for the money, so he wrote himself a check for it, covering more than $5,000. In her countersuit, Marge disputed authorizing that.

•When Sabo was called to give a deposition in the limited-partners' lawsuit against Marge, he worried about the repercussions from Marge if he told the truth, as opposed to the fallout from lying under oath, so he decided to consult an attorney. The bill was approximately $300, and Sabo wrote himself a check from the Reds to cover it without seeking Marge's permission. Sabo blew this one, and he knows it. Even though he believes it was a valid expense, he should have tried to get Marge's OK, but he knew it would take a miracle to get it.

"It's the one thing I regret doing," said Sabo. "I didn't want to go through the hell it would take to try to get it."

•Marge claimed that Sabo was paying the premiums of retired front-office employees when she had never authorized it. But the Reds had been paying their premiums for years. In fact, on January 9, 1985, chief financial officer Lou Porco sent out letters to the retirees saying:

We are very pleased to inform you that in addition to the benefits already offered to The Cincinnati Reds family, we have added a dental plan at no cost to you. The effective date of the plan is January 5, 1985. It is an extremely fine dental plan and completely covers twice-a-year oral examinations and cleaning, along with X-rays that accompany examinations and topical fluoride treatments. As you will see in reading your policy, our plan covers 80% of just about every other dental procedure. We would also like to inform you that in the future, effective January 5, 1985, you will no longer have to pay for your medical insurance. The Cincinnati Reds will pick up the monthly premiums for its retirees and widows. The card which is enclosed replaces the Blue Cross identification card you now carry in your wallet and insures you of first-class health and dental care.

On February 6, 1990, Sabo sent a letter to Patricia Molloy of Cohen, Todd, Kite and Stanford—a law firm that Steve Schott had told Sabo was experienced in this area—with the following introduction:

As you are aware, Mrs. Schott has asked me to look into which retirees we are paying medical insurance for and the corresponding reasons why.

[Sabo listed 16 retirees—including Bob and Janet Howsam, the former president's contract specifically calling for their premiums to be paid.]

The above 16 premiums currently cost a total of $28,458.24 annually. The Reds request you look into the ramification of the above as it relates to those we are currently paying retiree insurance for and those who might seek this in the future. Specifically, have the Reds made any offer—implied or otherwise—to its employees for such coverage? What would the possible legal ramifications be if this practice were to be discontinued? If it were to be discontinued, would you recommend the discontinuation to be retroactive or proactive? If proactive, should there be a phase-in period?

On November 19, 1991, almost three months after Sabo was fired, Lou Porco received a certified letter from Bob Martin saying the Reds had canceled his health insurance —*retroactively*.

Dear Lou,

It was recently brought to the attention of management by
Community Mutual that retired individuals of the Cincinnati Reds
and their spouses together with other individuals who are no
longer employees, were being included on the hospital and dental
coverage of the partnership. Your coverage under the Cincinnati
Reds Group Medical Insurance Plan (the "Plan") terminated on
November 1, 1991, because you are no longer an employee. Under
a federal law referred to as "COBRA," you may elect to continue
medical coverage under the Plan without interruption for up to 18
months from November 1, 1991.

This was, quite possibly, the single most cruel act of Marge
Schott's tenure as owner of the Cincinnati Reds. Here she was in
the holiday season retroactively taking away the benefits of the
front-office employees who had toiled faithfully for years before
retiring. "Merry Christmas—and bah-humbug," said Betty
Bowen, the widow of former scouting director Joe Bowen, the
day before heading to the pharmacy wondering if she'd have to
pay retail on her next prescription. We're not talking million-
dollar ballplayers here; we're talking about the Bob Cratchits of
the organization, who earned modest incomes and truly needed
a good, affordable health plan. Betty Sheldon, for instance,
retired in February 1989 as the Reds' receptionist at a salary that
topped out at $15,000.

For roughly $30,000 a year (or about 1 percent of what Eric
Davis or Tom Browning or Jose Rijo was making), Marge could
have insured all of the retirees. Instead, she not only pulled their
insurance, she didn't realize entirely what she was doing—or at
least Martin didn't grasp what he was saying. COBRA is unavail-
able to those eligible for Medicare. So the retirees were sent
scrounging for some type of supplemental insurance plan that
would cover the expenses Medicare didn't.

Now it's not exactly uncommon for companies to stop carrying retirees. But normally they do it with a grandfather clause, or
work out a co-payment deal with the retirees—or at the very least
give them sufficient notice to find a supplemental plan. But most
companies weren't making tens of millions of dollars the way the
Reds were.

"That shows you something about her personality, and that
is documented," said Porco. "That's what she thinks about
people, period."

As for the defamation of character charge, it became rather hard to believe on Monday, the day the trial started, because it also was the day Marge's own deposition was released. Nothing Sabo or any of the so-called disgruntled former employees said could be as revealing, shocking, or damaging to her case as her own words. It was a revealing look at Marge, uncut and uncensored, like no other the public or the press had seen.

The excerpts alone are astounding.

Chapter Thirteen

Marge: The Deposition

On December 6, 1991, Marge Schott gave her deposition in the office of Katz, Greenberger & Norton in Cincinnati, the law firm of Tim Sabo's attorney, Stephen Imm. Representing Marge at the deposition was her attorney, Stephen Bailey. The deposition had to be stopped and was finished on January 24, 1992, at the same location. Following are some excerpts from her deposition:

IMM:	What businesses other than the Reds do you have an ownership interest in?
MARGE:	Still have Schottco; still run a brick distributorship in St. Louis; Concrete Products, property which is leased property, where Galesberg Brick was. Oh, we have a Chevrolet store.
IMM:	Is that Marge's Chevrolet?
MARGE:	Well, we call it Marge Schott Chevrolet now, illegally.
IMM:	You say illegally because your —
MARGE:	I wasn't allowed to put the family name on the Chevrolet store. Call it Marge's Chevrolet.

***

IMM: You mentioned a concrete —

MARGE: We have a concrete block plant.

IMM: What was that called?

MARGE: Concrete Products.

IMM: Did you say, "We had that"? Do
            you no longer have it?

MARGE: No, I have the property.

IMM: You just own the land, you mean?

MARGE: Buildings, yeah.

IMM: But it's not — no business is being
            conducted there?

MARGE: No. Well, somebody is conducting a
            business there because he's renting
            it.

IMM: You just lease the business to him,
            or lease the building and land to
            him?

MARGE: Yes.

***

IMM: Is it your testimony that you have
            only given three depositions in your
            life?

MARGE: I think so, yep.

IMM: Do you know who Roger Blaemire
            is?

MARGE: Oh, yeah, he worked for the Reds.
            Was that a deposition?

BAILEY: I don't know; I wasn't involved.

MARGE: I don't know. He worked for the
            Reds as an advertising in some-
            thing.

IMM: And the Reds were involved in a
            suit with him, were they not?

MARGE: Yeah, but I don't know if that
            included a deposition or not. I just
            know it was a strung-out deal.

IMM: Did that case go to trial?

MARGE: No. Nuh-huh.

IMM: Did that case settle out of court?

MARGE: I think it did.

***

IMM: When did you first become a partner with the Cincinnati Reds?

MARGE: I was a limited partner in — I think it was in '82, when the Williamses formed the new partnership.

IMM: When did you become general partner?

MARGE: When I was stupid.

***

IMM: Would you describe your duties for me as president and chief executive officer of the Reds?

MARGE: I don't know what the duties are. I'm a hands-on operator. Most of it's aggravation. Most of my things are the business end of it. There's a business end and then there's a baseball end. It's a real life and then Disneyland.

IMM: Which is which? I'm kidding.

MARGE: Disneyland is on the field, honey.

***

IMM: Do you typically approve the hiring of new people on the business side of the Reds, or can they be hired without your approval, or do you —

MARGE: I'm pretty much on top of that. We don't have that many changes, though, really.

***

IMM: Do you know what the extent of Mr. Sabo's education was?

MARGE: No, I do not.

IMM: Do you know whether or not he had an MBA?

MARGE: Well, I'll be quite frank with you. I guess through all the years that I have been in business since Charlie died, when people come to me and say I didn't go to college, I say I don't care if you went to high school, as long as you can do the job. I'm not prejudiced by — I never have been — who's got this or who went there or anything else. It's whether somebody can do the job or not. That's the important thing to me.

IMM: Do you know whether or not he was a CPA, certified public accountant?

MARGE: I don't know. Was he studying to be a CPA, or —

IMM: I'm just asking whether you know.

MARGE: I really don't know, no. As I say, I'm not impressed by — to me, the important thing is whether some-body can do the job or not. Maybe because I didn't go to college, or stay in college, maybe that's why I'm not impressed. But I've met a lot of people who are overeducated.

***

IMM: Do you recall ever telling Tim that you wanted to limit the amount of distributions being made to the limiteds?

MARGE: Probably Tim and a lot of other
          people. As I say, my main concern
          was to keep the security in the Reds,
          which, again, probably was — is a
          stupid woman's decision. But since I
          received the majority of the money,
          that was my full objective, was
          security. I feel that way about all my
          companies.

IMM: Do you ever recall saying in Tim's
          presence, "I don't want to give those
          sons of bitches one more dime,"
          talking about the limiteds, "one
          more cent," something like that?

MARGE: I don't really recall, but it probably
          could have been said. I don't know.

IMM: Was another issue in that limited-
          partners' lawsuit whether you had
          turned down scoreboard advertis-
          ing for auto dealerships other than
          your own?

MARGE: That's a known fact, for the mere
          fact that Chevrolet is the official
          sponsor of baseball, and I am very
          much of a buy-American person — I
          will be all my life — even though
          I'm sure the Japs would give me
          Toyota, Datsun and Nissan. But we
          have stuck with the loyalty to
          Chevrolet, which I think is very
          important, since they spend a lot of
          money to sponsor all the baseball
          teams.

                    ***

IMM: You said earlier, I think, that the
          Japs would give you Toyota, Nissan
          and things like that, if you wanted

	them. Have they ever approached you about that?
MARGE:	I could have had any foreign dealership I wanted, but I buy American, personally; but I'm a buy-American person.
IMM:	How do you feel about the Japanese?
MARGE:	My last trip, I told them they were going to own us without firing a shot.
IMM:	So you have some hard feelings toward them?
MARGE:	No, I do not have hard feelings, but you have to admire the ethics that they have. A lot of the ethics they have are ethics we're losing in this country. We better get our act together.
IMM:	What ethics are those?
MARGE:	Well, you go over there, the children are all in uniforms, I didn't see any school buses, they all go on their bicycles, they don't put up with all these illegitimate children, they don't have a drug problem that I could see, and their work ethics are unbelievable.
IMM:	Have you ever thought about hiring Japanese for yourself or one of your own companies?
MARGE:	Honey, I don't care who comes in. If they can do the job, that's it.
IMM:	Do you have any Japanese working for you that you know of?
MARGE:	No, I don't. I think they all work for themselves.

***

IMM:	Is it your testimony that you wouldn't care whether or not Tim was going to be a witness in the limited-partner suit?
MARGE:	Not at all. I didn't care who they had as a witness, not at all.
IMM:	Would you care if his testimony —
MARGE:	Because my books are open, and I have nothing to hide.
IMM:	Wouldn't you care at all if Tim's testimony ended up helping the limited partners in that suit?
BAILEY:	Objection. She's answered the question. Go ahead and answer it again.
IMM:	No, she hasn't.
MARGE:	As I say, I didn't care about his testimony at all. It meant nothing to me.
IMM:	Not even if it helped the limiteds?
BAILEY:	You are badgering the witness. She's answered the question three times. You don't like the answer, young man, and therefore now you are badgering the witness.
IMM:	No, I don't like it when an attorney like you is badgering me. You think you are going to intimidate me. Forget it, because it's not going to work.
BAILEY:	You are not going to badger your witnesses.
IMM:	I'm not badgering your witness; I haven't even raised my voice with the witness, for Christ's sake.
BAILEY:	What kind of language have you used? This is a courtroom proceeding here.

IMM: I've used the word son of a bitch, and you didn't object to that.

BAILEY: That was in a question.

IMM: I'm going to ask this question once more because it hasn't been answered. Is it your testimony, Mrs. Schott, that you wouldn't have cared if Mr. Sabo's testimony helped the limited partners in that suit?

MARGE: My answer is that I couldn't care less what Tim Sabo ever had to say in his testimony, because he had nothing at all to do with the limited partnership deal.

IMM: Did you have any understanding at all of what Tim testified in his deposition?

MARGE: As I said, I didn't care what he testified in his deposition.

IMM: I'm not asking whether you cared or not; I'm asking whether you had any understanding at all of what he said in his deposition.

MARGE: I never saw his deposition.

IMM: You have answered that before. But did you have any understanding from any other source of what he said in his deposition?

MARGE: I really don't think so.

IMM: Did you ever tell anybody that you were upset about Tim's deposition testimony?

MARGE: I'm not sure. I just — as I say, I'd have to read his testimony, OK?

IMM: Well, that's not responsive to my question. Did you ever tell anybody that you were upset about Tim's deposition testimony?

MARGE: I'm not sure.

IMM: So it's possible?

MARGE: I say any time you might have an
            employee that — I just feel that the
            loyalty of an employee is to the
            employer.

IMM: And you felt that Tim might have
            been disloyal in his deposition?

MARGE: No, I didn't say that. As I say, I
            didn't care what Sabo's deposition
            was. I didn't see what his deposition
            had to do with anything. The books
            are there, the figures are there, it's
            all open.

IMM: Why did you just tell me that you
            feel an employee's loyalty is to an
            employer?

MARGE: It's just a general feeling of mine.

IMM: You didn't say that because —

MARGE: Or to the company they work for.
            And everybody knew what my
            feelings were on the partnership —
            was that to keep security for the
            Cincinnati Reds, even though a
            smarter man would say, give me all
            the money.

                        ***

IMM: You are a strong personality; would
            you agree with that? I mean, when
            you don't like somebody, you make
            it known. Is that accurate? You
            don't hide your feelings, would you
            say?

MARGE: I feel that — again, as I said, men
            would handle things a lot different
            than women handle it — but I
            always think when I feel a way

about a person, it's very obvious,
and I don't think women are the
type to suddenly, bingo, say, "You
are gone" as much as a man would.
Women do it in a cutesy-poo way.
They just make it obvious.

***

MARGE: I'd also like to make a statement. I
have been in business 23 years since
my husband died, and I've never
been through anything like that
with an employee before. It's very
cheap.

IMM: You haven't been sued by an
employee?

MARGE: Nope.

IMM: Didn't Roger Blaemire sue —

MARGE: He didn't sue me; he sued the Reds.

IMM: When you were the Reds' limited
partner.

MARGE: That's right.

***

IMM: You have given as a reason for
terminating Tim that he was doing
things other than bookkeeping.
What other things was he doing
besides bookkeeping?

MARGE: I'm really not sure.

***

IMM: Mrs. Schott, have you ever used the
word "nigger"?

MARGE: Sure. Everybody's used the word
once in their lifetime.

IMM: You have used it once in your
lifetime?

MARGE: Black —

IMM: I'm not interested in "black."

MARGE: — is a word that says — very
           seldom do I ever use the word.

IMM: The word "nigger," you mean? Not
           the word black, right? When you
           say you very seldom use the word,
           you are referring to the word
           "nigger," right?

MARGE: That's right. That's mainly a South-
           ern term.

IMM: Do you realize it's an offensive term
           to blacks?

MARGE: Yes. I think it is an offensive term to
           blacks. I don't know; I've never
           really asked them. I would think it
           would be offensive. Maybe it's not
           offensive to them; I don't know.

IMM: Have you ever referred to Martin
           Luther King Day as Nigger Day?

MARGE: I don't believe so; I wouldn't even
           know when Martin Luther King
           Day is.

IMM: Well, I'm not sure if you have to
           know when it is in order to know
           whether you have referred to it as
           Nigger Day; but it's in January.
           Does that help your recollection at
           all? Have you ever called it Nigger
           Day?

MARGE: I hope not.

IMM: Is it possible you have?

MARGE: Anything's possible.

IMM: You had a ballplayer that worked
           for you named Dave Parker — for
           you at one time?

BAILEY: "Work with" is a loose term.

IMM: You mean as applied to Mrs. Schott.

BAILEY: He's a player.

MARGE: That was a loose term, "work for us." He was down there.

IMM: He had 30 home runs one year.

MARGE: Dave Parker has been one of the very — so I have been told — complimentary players, because he's no longer with the Reds. Sometimes when people leave you, they can bash you.

IMM: You mean he's been complimentary toward the Reds?

MARGE: I have heard he's been very complimentary towards me. I have gone to weddings with him; he's a very nice person.

IMM: Did you know he at one time made a salary of over $2 million with the Reds?

MARGE: Are you kidding? That long ago? I didn't think we went that nuts that long ago. OK.

IMM: Did you ever refer to him as your $2 million nigger?

MARGE: No. I referred to Eric Davis as my $3 million baby — who called me the other day.

IMM: Did you have a Halloween party at the Reds' office this last Halloween?

MARGE: I don't think so.

IMM: Let me see if I can refresh your recollection. You got a big stuffed gorilla at this party. Do you remember that?

MARGE: I've got a stuffed gorilla that was just given to me — placed in my chair, so I could introduce him as my replacement — called Harry, from the zoo.

IMM: Who gave you that?

MARGE: A doctor dropped it off with red
          pants on and a red shirt and a red
          hat.

IMM: And that was just recently?

MARGE: Harry just came recently.

IMM: And do you recall saying when you
          got that gift that they can't accuse
          you of discrimination anymore
          because now you have got a black
          one in here?

MARGE: I don't really know. I kid a lot.

***

IMM: Do you have any prejudice against
          Jews? What are your feelings about
          Jews?

MARGE: No. They are not smarter than us,
          just sharper. In fact, my general
          manager at Chevrolet is Mel
          Lehrner; he worked for me before,
          and he's come back with me, and
          he's from a very orthodox — is that
          what they call them? — Jewish
          family.

***

IMM: Do you know who Cal Levy is?

MARGE: Uh-huh.

IMM: Who is he?

MARGE: He was in — what do you call the
          job, the one that sells promotions
          and stuff? He was in that job, the
          one Chip Baker has now.

IMM: Do you know if Mr. Levy is Jewish?

MARGE: I would say with a name Levy, he's
          Jewish.

IMM: Did you ever talk about money-
          grubbing Jews with Mr. Levy?

MARGE: I don't think so. I might have —
           who knows? — kidding.

IMM: Have you —

MARGE: Most of the terms you are bringing
           up are kind of joke terms.

IMM: Do you think "nigger" is a joke
           term?

MARGE: I think to some people it might be. I
           know it's like an offensive thing, but
           I think, just like — who was the
           governor, that old man, God love
           him, who was commissioner of
           baseball?

BAILEY: Happy Chandler.

MARGE: Happy Chandler, God love him.

IMM: What about Happy Chandler?

MARGE: Didn't he misuse a term or some-
           thing? There was no finer man than
           Happy Chandler.

IMM: Do you think Jews are more con-
           cerned with money than non-Jews?

MARGE: I don't think so. I think they maybe
           had to fight their way up maybe
           more, generations ago. Maybe had
           to use — get a lot more pushy, as I
           say, generations ago.

IMM: In your experience, have they been
           more concerned about money
           than—

MARGE: I know some very sharp Christians,
           and I know some very sharp Jews,
           and I know some very sharp blacks.

IMM: When you use the word "sharp,"
           are you referring to good with
           money?

MARGE: Just sharp. If you are sharp, you are
           usually good with money. Just a

sharp operator, just like Mel doesn't miss a trick; he's right on top of everything.

IMM: We have talked a little about Roger Blaemire before. Do you recall Mr. Blaemire trying to encourage you to do a deal with some Jewish businessmen, and you said that you didn't want to do business with those "Jew bastards"?

MARGE: No.

IMM: You don't remember that?

MARGE: I hired Blaemire because I liked his wife, who was a stewardess.

***

IMM: Do you have a swastika armband that you keep as a memorabilia of anything?

MARGE: At my home I do, in a drawer.

IMM: You do. Where did that come from?

MARGE: It came from one of the men that worked for me in the brick company in St. Louis, and he presented it to me.

IMM: When did he do that?

MARGE: Oh, God, that had to be 20-some years ago. He also gave me a — which made me feel bad — they must have cut the leg off of a deer, and you put a leather strap on it, and you could use it to hit somebody.

IMM: Do you remember the name of the guy who gave you the armband?

MARGE: I'm trying to think if it's the guy who is still down there. I'm not sure; I'm not sure whether he was in the trucking company. In the brick plant, there was also a trucking division, and I know the deer thing disappeared, but we had the armband. I think it was in a drawer in my hall or something. My mother's family were over in Germany during the Second World War, because my mother was from Germany, and all of my — her sisters had five sons in Hitler's Army.

IMM: Your sister or your mother's sister?

MARGE: My mother's sister. My mother had all girls, so her kids didn't have to fight. Her sister's kids.

IMM: When did your family emigrate from Germany to the United States?

MARGE: I guess it was my great-great grandfather Unnewehr came over here, built a house on Dayton Street, and my mother's family, the Ibold cigar people, came over. Mike Ibold is my granddad — my grandfather — and Peter Ibold migrated two brothers and opened separate companies. And my mother came over to further her studies at the College Conservatory of Music, and she was with — that was Mike Ibold and his wife were the sisters of mother's mother — and she met my daddy, and she married my daddy.

IMM: Do you know why you were given this swastika armband that we talked about?

MARGE: I don't know why. Because I'm

German. Because it's — a lot of people collect memorabilia. I guess the guy thought he was giving me something great.

IMM: Did Cal Levy ever note the presence of that armband in your house? Did you ever talk with him about that?

MARGE: I don't really know. I know if we have Christmas parties or something, maybe somebody opened the drawer and saw it, but I don't really remember showing the swastika armband. I don't even remember if it's in the drawer anymore. It was there years ago. I'll have to go check it tonight.

IMM: Do you recall Mr. Levy being offended by the armband?

MARGE: No, I don't. I don't know why he'd be offended by the armband.

IMM: Well, I mean, you understand what it represents, don't you?

MARGE: Hitler.

IMM: Yeah.

MARGE: The Nazis.

IMM: Right?

MARGE: Our family was part of the — what did they call the king, like, over in Germany, kaiser — my mother's family, but Hitler came in and took over.

IMM: You understand why a Jew like Mr. Levy would be offended by seeing the armband?

MARGE: I don't think Cal would be offended by seeing the armband, because it's just like, are all the people going to be offended — when is Pearl Harbor

	Day?
BAILEY:	Tomorrow.
MARGE:	Tomorrow.
IMM:	I don't know if they are or not.
MARGE:	If I have a Jap flag out, are we going to be offended tomorrow?
IMM:	Well, I don't know. If I was on the Arizona, I might be. Did you ever say to Mr. Levy that Hitler might have had the right idea?
MARGE:	I don't really know.
IMM:	Is it possible you said something like that to him?
MARGE:	A lot of times I make jokes, but they are usually — I wouldn't say it in front of somebody if I wasn't joking.

***

IMM:	Have you ever expressed the opinion that you prefer your female employees to be mature and beyond their child-bearing years?
MARGE:	Not really, but I have nothing against hiring older people. I know a lot of companies where you have to be a swinging teenager, maybe, to get hired — maybe that's the men — but I have no — nothing against hiring an older person, because a lot of them have good work ethics. And I have nothing against hiring young people, but I know a lot of people that when they reach, what, 40-something, it's hard for them to get a job, which is ridiculous.
IMM:	Do you get upset a little bit when one of your younger female employees gets pregnant and takes mater-

nity leave, and you have to replace her and go through all that rigamarole?

MARGE: In some departments, it doesn't make any difference. Maybe in other departments, it's an inconvenience. But I'll tell you one thing, Mister, you better not get on this subject, because I was never blessed with children — son of a bitch.

***

IMM: You don't know if she's (Cyndi Strzynski) still there?

MARGE: As I say, it's very hard when you have so many employees. That's why I'm lucky to have been a woman. I can call all the men "Hon" or "Honey."

IMM: Do you recall introducing anyone to Pat McCaffrey and Joel Pieper as saying, "Here's a mature woman who won't be having any babies," or something like that?

MARGE: If I was in a kidding mood, I might have introduced her that way. But again, I wouldn't say — you wouldn't say those type of things if you weren't kidding, but you would be insulting people.

IMM: Did you ever tell Tim Sabo that you didn't want him hiring female employees in his department who were in their child-bearing years?

MARGE: No, I didn't say he couldn't hire them.

IMM: Did you ever tell him you would prefer that he not hire them?

MARGE: I don't think I told him "I prefer." It would be tough if you had a book-keeping department that had 50 people all get pregnant at once, but I'm not against hiring people past a certain age, either. In fact, when the girl in the bookkeeping department (Kathy Shaner) had the twins, I was very happy when she came in and said, "I'm going to stay home with my children, Mrs. Schott." And I said, "I'm glad to hear that" because, personally, I like it when the wife stays home and raises the children.

***

IMM: Did you ever say to Tim that — referring to black employees — that you didn't want their kind?

MARGE: Definitely not. Best mechanic I have for 30-some years is Richard; he's a black mechanic; get a hug every time I go in. Another one of my best employees I have up in Chevrolet — he's head of a sales team — he's black. He's one of the best I've ever had; I love the man.

***

IMM: You have hired 30 employees into the front office alone in the last three years, according to documents provided to me by your counsel. Why do you have such a high rate of turnover? Do you know?

MARGE: Because baseball is a — it's an old man's club, OK? Or how do you

word that? It's a buddy-buddy club
. . . He brings his buddies in, OK,
and then you have to evaluate his
buddies and sometimes get rid of
the buddies. And then you get
another guy, and then sometimes he
brings his buddies in. But right now
I feel that I have, I guess, all my
buddies — whatever you want to
call them. It's a very different world
in baseball, OK?

***

IMM: My question is why you have had to
            replace 38 out of 40 (30 out of 48)
            front-office employees in the last
            three years.

BAILEY: Objection. That document doesn't
            indicate she's replaced 38 out of 40
            employees.

IMM: It indicates that she's hired 30
            employees in the last three years.

BAILEY: How do you know that's the
            replacement of somebody who was
            either terminated or if they left the
            business? You wouldn't know that.
            You haven't laid a foundation for it.
            That's something you have to do in
            law, Mr. Imm. If you want to ask
            her what that represents, ask her
            that.

IMM: Mr. Bailey, I'm not going to take this
            sort of abuse from you.

BAILEY: Sir, when it comes to abuse, I
            haven't even started.

IMM: You just keep going on the record;
            you just continue to abuse me on the
            record.

BAILEY: Sure.

IMM: All right, and I'll continue to try the case — all right? And I'll just let your string of abuse roll off my back.

BAILEY: The only place you are trying this case is in the newspaper and on radio and television. That's the only place you are trying this case, and that's the only place you are going to win. And don't you ever forget it.

IMM: The only place I'm trying this case is in the trial court of Judge Cartolano, and that's where I am going to try it.

BAILEY: I'm going to pack you up in a small, little package and send you back up to where you came from.

IMM: You just try it; you are in for some big surprises, Mr. Bailey, some big surprises. Why don't you just shut up and let me take this deposition?

BAILEY: Come on, we're out of here. You write —

IMM: You are going to pay for this.

BAILEY: I'm not paying for anything.

IMM: Yes, you are.

BAILEY: I'm not paying for a thing.

IMM: You are going to walk out of here — because you have been abusing me for the last three months.

BAILEY: If you are telling me to shut up — you can't tell me to shut up. I'll represent my client how I want to represent my client, OK? You ask a proper question — you ask her proper questions and lay proper foundation, and I —

IMM: I am asking her proper questions. You object to any questions you like, but I'm asking proper questions.

BAILEY: Yes, I am.

MARGE: For a young attorney, you should never be mixed up in a cheap, ridiculous thing like this.

***

IMM: Mrs. Schott, isn't it true that you have had to hire 30 new people in the last three years because of the abusive way you treat your employees?

BAILEY: Objection.

MARGE: Oh, come on, listen; I'll walk out of here, Squirt. I have been in business 23 years. I have never had a cheap thing like this, and I have had employees that are my family. I am family to my employees, Mister. Go out and talk to my other companies — family.

BAILEY: Objection. Instruct you not to answer that question. Opposing counsel is now becoming abusive and argumentative.

MARGE: This is a cheap little thing. And I worry about my families. I want to be sure that they all have babies, get married, and everything else. I'm a woman operator, which is a lot different style than a man.

BAILEY: Ask your next question, Mr. Imm.

IMM: No, I'm going to certify this question.

BAILEY: Buddy, if you feel froggy, you go right ahead and leap; certify it. Do you want us to leave now so you can get a ruling as to whether or not she has to answer that argumentative question?

IMM: Counselor, do you know what cross-examination means? It means I'm allowed to ask leading questions.

BAILEY: You are allowed to ask leading questions, but you are not allowed to be argumentative or abusive.

IMM: I'm not being argumentative. I'm asking a question.

***

IMM: When the Reds pay something, an expense of the partnership — OK, or an automobile — did you ever order Tim to report a particular expense like that in a particular fiscal year?

MARGE: Not really. We try, and like I think every other smarter businessperson does — and we're going to be more specific next year — is if you — there's something we have to do, and you have a fairly decent year, we're going to try and do it in that year because you might not be able to afford to do it the next year. That's basic business.

IMM: Did Tim ever tell you in one of these cases it might be improper to report an expense in a particular year because it didn't occur in that year?

MARGE: I'll be quite frank. I didn't pay much attention to anything he said.

IMM: You didn't pay attention to what your head bookkeeper said?

MARGE: I know accounting procedures. I have been in business for 23 years, and I think I know a little bit more than Sabo knows.

IMM: Do you have any training in accounting?

MARGE: Twenty-three years.

IMM: Do you have any formal training, something apart from running your businesses?

MARGE: You mean, have I gone to school?

IMM: Either gone to school or undergone any other form of training?

MARGE: I have been in school for 23 years.

IMM: I'm not talking about the school of life; I'm talking about other types of schools.

MARGE: What else is there? I've met a lot of educated asses that can't do anything.

***

IMM: Apart from what you have learned in your experience, your own businesses, have you had any training in accounting?

MARGE: I went to convent school; we had arithmetic.

***

IMM: People aren't allowed to use the Reds logo without the permission of the Reds, isn't that right?

MARGE: That's been the rule for years and years.

IMM: Yet you allow your dealerships to use it, right?

MARGE: The logo?

IMM: Yes. You allow them to use it free of
            charge, isn't that right?

MARGE: No, I think we use it on — I don't
            know what we used it on. I would
            say, as an owner, that would be
            logical. But I've never used the Reds
            — some of my people get upset that
            I don't take more connection with
            the Reds, with the amount I own.

IMM: Do you recall an advertisement for
            Marge's Chevrolet where you had
            Schottzie wearing a Reds cap?

MARGE: Absolutely. Schottzie wore a Reds
            cap all the time — "Doggone good
            deals." Schottzie belonged —

IMM: Did Marge's Chevrolet pay for the
            right to use the Reds logo in that
            advertisement?

MARGE: For Schottzie to wear the hat? The
            Reds did not pay for the use of
            Schottzie, OK?

IMM: That didn't answer my question.

MARGE: I think the answer is an as — OK?

BAILEY: Just answer the question, Marge.

IMM: Did Marge's Chevrolet pay the Reds
            for the use of the logo?

BAILEY: Objection. It's irrelevant and
            immaterial.

MARGE: They did not.

BAILEY: That's good.

IMM: They didn't, OK.

MARGE: You lawyers; I don't believe it.

BAILEY: When you don't have anything, you
            grab anything you can.

***

IMM: Why did you say that ("I just feel

	that the loyalty of an employee is to the employer") at that point if you didn't feel that Tim Sabo was being disloyal in his deposition?
BAILEY:	Objection. You are being argumentative with the witness.
IMM:	I'm asking a question, counselor.
BAILEY:	I'm instructing you not to answer that question.
IMM:	For God's sake.
BAILEY:	Listen, for some little punk who has never been beyond muni court, you're starting to think you are some big-time guy.
IMM:	Steve, it really gets you off to insult me, doesn't it? You really enjoy that, don't you? Why do you enjoy that so much?
BAILEY:	I just call a spade a spade.
MARGE:	I don't know why the two of you are wasting your time on this kind of junk.
IMM:	I want to know —
MARGE:	You both have bigger and better things to do.

***

IMM:	Did you ever tell Tim Sabo that all checks on the operating account were to be signed by you?
MARGE:	Probably, when it came in, because that's been a procedure since I came down there. It's been a procedure in all my companies.
IMM:	Do you specifically remember telling him that on any occasion?
MARGE:	Unless there was an emergency and I would be someplace and some-

	thing had to get paid, and then you have two signatures and you hope both people watch out for the other. I mean, that's my procedure, OK?
IMM:	Do you have a specific recollection of telling Tim that procedure?
MARGE:	Well, I'm sure he was told that when he was hired, that the checks come across to my desk. Otherwise, they would never have been on my desk, right?
IMM:	What your counterclaim alleges, Mrs. Schott, is that in the normal course of business you reviewed and signed all checks, not just most checks.
MARGE:	That's right.
IMM:	Do you remember telling Tim on a specific occasion that you wanted all checks to be signed by you?
MARGE:	I'm sure when he was hired it was said that the checks come to my desk, and I signed them.
IMM:	OK. Why do you say you are sure you said that — because you remember saying that?
MARGE:	Because it's always been a procedure down there.
IMM:	Do you remember saying that to Tim?
MARGE:	I'm sure he was told that when he came.
IMM:	Do you remember saying that to Tim?
MARGE:	Do you think I would say I'll have Schottzie come in and sign the checks?

***

IMM: This is an excerpt of what's called the Hay Management Report, and it's supposed to indicate what someone in Mr. Sabo's position —

MARGE: It's a baseball (salary) study. Yeah, I get those baseball studies all the time. For the highest, a guy's been there 100 years; or a guy who doesn't give a damn, the lowest; and the median, I've always considered the Reds being a slight bit below the median in our market.

***

IMM: Mrs. Schott, do you have any memory problems?

MARGE: No, I do not have any memory problems.

IMM: Have you ever experienced black-outs or anything like that?

MARGE: No, I have not, dear. I remember an awful lot of things, not insignificant things.

IMM: Do you have a problem of contra-dicting yourself from day-to-day, saying one thing one day and then changing your mind and ordering something else the next day?

MARGE: Not really. I'm not saying I've never changed my mind.

IMM: Well, I'm not really interested in whether you changed your mind; I'm talking about forgetfulness. Have —

MARGE: Insignificant things. There's an awful lot of things that come around me, when you are running as many corporations as I do, but the significant things — and the rules are rules with me, and I don't do any — when I put a rule in, I don't say, "Here, buddy, under the table you can do this, but the others can't do it." I've never done that in my companies, and if it's ever been done, it's been done without my authority.

IMM: Well, I'm just concentrating on what you know your memory to be at this point. Have you ever been treated for —

MARGE: Maybe at 63, you know, I might not be as sharp as a young guy like you.

IMM: You are probably more sharp. Have you ever been treated or been diagnosed as having any sort of mental memory difficulty?

MARGE: Never.

IMM: Have you ever been treated for drug abuse or alcohol abuse?

MARGE: Never.

IMM: Have you ever been in any kind of drug or alcohol rehabilitation program?

MARGE: No.

IMM: How is your health?

MARGE: It used to be great. Ninety-one wasn't too good.

IMM: Have you had to be admitted to the hospital any time in the last year or two?

MARGE: Around — was it around last year? Was it around March?

BAILEY: Before the season started.

MARGE: I was introducing my two new

Malaysian elephants at the zoo, and
I had been opening my legs, scratching, but my dad used to — so I
didn't think anything about it. We
weren't raised to be doctor people.
Somebody called from the zoo,
"Take her to the hospital, we think
she's sick." That's when they threw
me in intensive care. I had cellulitis
— colitis — I don't know what it is.
I'd never heard of it.

BAILEY: I'm going to object to her hospital
and medical condition. That has
nothing to do with the lawsuit; it's
privileged. She's answered your
question for you.

IMM: Any other hospital admissions other
than that one in the last two years?

BAILEY: Objection. You can answer, Mrs.
Schott.

MARGE: Had pneumonia. Wouldn't go in the
hospital. Got better.

IMM: Count 4 of your counterclaim, Mrs.
Schott, Paragraph 12 —

MARGE: I was born in the hospital.

***

IMM: Is it your contention, Mrs. Schott,
that Mr. Sabo should have recommended to you that these (retired)
employees have their premium
benefits cut off and make them pay
the premiums themselves?

MARGE: Well, I'm not just saying Sabo, but
whether Community Mutual maybe
should have spotted this — somebody over the years should have
spotted this, OK?

IMM: When did you first become aware—
MARGE: After Sabo left.

***

IMM: How would you feel if an employee
            like Mr. Sabo questioned your
            business practices or hiring prac-
            tices? What would be your reaction?
MARGE: I don't think I'd pay any attention
            to it. I have been in business 23
            years.

***

IMM: Do you know who Ralph Lee (a
            former Reds intern in the front
            office and an African American) is?
            Does that name mean anything to
            you?
MARGE: (Inaudible)
BAILEY: No?
MARGE: Got a mechanic at Schott Buick. I get
            a hug every time I go in there.

— Chapter Fourteen —

The Scandal That Almost Wasn't

There she was, Marge Schott under oath and in her own words, in a document that was as powerful as it was revealing as it was frightening. Here was the owner of one of the most public entities in the country and certainly the most visible institution in the city saying she didn't know if the word "nigger" was offensive . . . that Jews aren't smarter than us, just sharper . . . that "nigger" is a joke term. But the impact was cushioned if not overshadowed by the Tim Sabo trial, which began on the same Monday that Marge's deposition was released—and which ended the next day.

Hamilton County Common Pleas Court judge Fred Cartolano threw out some of the counts of Sabo's lawsuit, and Sabo's attorney withdrew the rest, figuring he'd try again in appeals court with a slightly different tack. On appeal, Sabo plans to focus solely on his belief that he was fired by the Reds in retaliation for giving truthful deposition testimony that favored the limited partners in their lawsuit against Marge. Sabo will argue that such a retaliatory firing is an exception to the general rule in Ohio that employees may be fired at the will of the employer. Otherwise, employers would have the power to discourage from speaking up or, even worse, to encourage them to commit perjury.

While the depositions from the former Reds' employees had an entire weekend to reverberate within the city, Marge's deposition barely had time to make a headline. In fact, the afternoon *Cincinnati Post* bumped its story of Marge's deposition off the front page for its final edition to make way for the breaking news about the trial's ending. In an interview with *The Cincinnati*

Enquirer, Atlanta Braves senior vice-president Hank Aaron, baseball's all-time home-run leader and one of the few black executives in the sport, called for baseball to investigate, but he was a tree falling in an uninhabited forest. The story was in danger of dying locally, and the national media barely realized what was transpiring. In New York, powerful New York, one of the newspapers even ran a brief story about the trial's end under the headline, "Schott Not Guilty Of Discrimination."

Behind the scenes, however, a small movement was beginning. Michael Rapp, the head of the local Jewish Community Relations Committee and a member of the local NAACP chapter board, called Marge on that Monday morning to arrange a meeting with her and other community leaders. She took the call herself, which surprised him and made him a little nervous. He said, "It's like calling a blind date and hoping she's not going to be there the first time." At first, Marge didn't see the purpose in having a meeting, but after a few minutes she decided to go along with him. On Friday, Marge and Rapp's group had their meeting.

This was not the first time Marge met with community leaders about racism. In 1987, affirmative action became a hot topic in baseball, with the sport celebrating the 40th anniversary of Jackie Robinson's breaking the color barrier, with Los Angeles Dodgers executive Al Campanis embarrassing himself nationally by questioning whether blacks had the "necessities" for some baseball management jobs, and with commissioner Peter Ueberroth pushing for minority front-office hires. The Reds, meanwhile, had only one minority in the front office, Hallie Kinney, a black employee in the ticket office. A number of black city leaders met with Marge to discuss the inequity and to see if the Reds would offer opportunities for minorities throughout the organization, from concessions at the ballpark to ownership of the team. There were several meetings between the city leaders and the Reds. Steve Reece, an African American businessman, says Reds general manager Bill Bergesch was especially helpful during the meetings and was slated to be the liaison to the black community. Vice-president Don Breen says he told Reece to give him a list of black front-office candidates in case there was an opening, but never heard back.

"I called him several times about it and . . . all he kept doing was asking me to hire his marketing firm to buy ads in his friend's magazine, to use the construction firm that they had recommended," Breen testified in his deposition for Sabo. "When I kept asking him what about the list of guys that you're going to give me to come down here, no list was forthcoming."

Reece says he told Breen he wasn't going to give him any list until he knew what openings there would be. That way, Reece claims, he could give the Reds a list of qualified candidates for that particular job.

In any case the group faded away, especially after Marge fired Bergesch after the 1987 season. And Marge really never did do anything about minority hiring. By the time Michael Rapp put together his group, the Reds' hiring scoreboard was exactly the same as it had been in 1987: one minority in the front office, the same one minority, Hallie Kinney.

Rapp had heard about the 1987 group and was intent on succeeding this time. He went into the meeting with Marge armed with specific goals. He said the coalition wanted Marge to (a) issue an apology; (b) look at her employment "preferences"; (c) get the Reds involved in community relations; and (d) agree to schedule future meetings with the community leaders. But before the meeting even started, Rapp got an idea of what he was facing in Marge Schott. In her office, she showed him a wind-up toy St. Bernard she had brought back from Japan—one that would walk forward and backward, lay down and get up, and do a 360-degree flip. Rapp was admittedly "in awe" of the plaything. But the feeling turned from awe to awful when Marge asked him about it.

"How do you like my Jap toy?" Marge said.

Rapp was caught completely off guard. Here he was, ready to meet with the owner of the Cincinnati Reds concerning her alleged language and actions slurring racial and ethnic groups, and she asked him about her "Jap toy." He was about to respond when someone interrupted the conversation, and the topic never came up again. But the incident certainly affected his opinion as he walked into the meeting.

"At that time, I realized that if she really understood the significance of why we were there, of the impact of her words, she wouldn't have said that—even if she believed it, she wouldn't have said that," Rapp said. "Now, in retrospect, she may just be indifferent to people's feelings."

Marge had some of her underlings at the meeting—Reds general manager Jim Bowden, Reds marketing director Chip Baker, Reds publicist Jon Braude, Reds controller Ernie Brubaker, and Marge's Chevrolet general manager Mel Lehrner. Marge was nervous, chainsmoking, talking about how she was a woman in a man's world and a minority herself. She insisted she was not a racist or a bigot and that everyone at some time had uttered some type of slur. As for the lack of minority hires, Bowden tried to explain that it took time to move up in the ranks, which sounded a bit odd coming from a 31-year-old general manager.

And then she started putting on the Marge for them—but not everybody liked it. Sheila Wilson, head of the Urban League, admonished her for continually calling people "honey." And NAACP chapter president Frank Allison took exception when Marge started passing out Girl Scout cookies. She also brought out candy. And Reds hats. And pictures. "She felt she could bamboozle most of the people who met with her," said city councilman Tyrone Yates, who claims he found it inappropriate to take her gifts. A number of others took the souvenirs, says Rapp, perhaps because they were being polite or having trouble saying no or thinking about their grandchildren.

The meeting lasted two and a half hours, with all parties laying out the issues and getting acquainted with each other. Marge agreed to put together a statement for the media, apologizing to anyone she might have inadvertently hurt with her statements. Baker, Braude, and Rapp went into Marge's office to work on her statement, and they brought it out to the group to get full approval. When the meeting ended, Marge Schott issued her first public apology.

It would be an important day for the Reds owner, but not because of the apology. On that day, halfway across the country, the Marge Schott story was finally escaping the invisible walls of Cincinnati.

Phil Mushnick, *The New York Post's* entertaining and irreverent columnist who loves to expose the hypocrisy and idiocy in sports, had been following the Sabo case more than most out-of-town journalists, writing about the former controller's initial lawsuit and allegations. On Friday, Mushnick ran a chunk of excerpts from Marge's deposition in his column. "Her defense—

stupidity—would be admissible if only she were believed to be that stupid," wrote Mushnick. "It's incumbent upon all right-headed sports fans to note some of the dialogue from the suit's deposition hearings." The story appeared under the headline "The Big Red-Faced Machine" and the subheadline "Racist, bigot or just plain dumb, Schott's an embarrassment" with a picture and cutline that read "MARGE AT LARGE: Marge Schott talks with Japanese Prime Minister Kiichi Miyazawa during visit to Tokyo. Not discussed, presumably, was whether or not the PM had any problem with being called a Jap."

Only in *The New York Post.*

Mushnick said the issue caught fire immediately in New York. "It was a big story," he said. "For the most part, it was the domain of the talk-show circuit on the radio." Then *The New York Times* jumped in. In addition to running an Associated Press story on Saturday about Marge's apology, the *Times* ran a piece of its own on Sunday summarizing the Marge Schott affair and what baseball was doing—which, at that point, was essentially nothing.

Baseball didn't need this and didn't want to have to deal with this. There was no commissioner, Fay Vincent having been forced to resign for failing to act as a marionette for the owners, so the owners were faced with having to police one of their own. The Executive Council was now running baseball, a 10-member organization consisting mainly of team owners and executives. Milwaukee Brewers owner Bud Selig headed the Executive Council, and he hoped he didn't have to deal with this. If the story had died inside the vacuum of Cincinnati, Selig would have been thrilled. At a time when baseball desperately needed a strong hand, it demonstrated weak knees.

Deputy commissioner Steve Greenberg, a holdover from the Vincent regime who lacked the power to act on his own, realized something had to be done. So on Tuesday, November 24, he sent a memo to Selig that read:

> Five years ago, Al Campanis lost his job in Baseball because he made the statement that blacks "lacked the necessities" to manage in the Major Leagues. Since 1987, Major League Baseball has made great strides in reaffirming its commitment to equal opportunity employment and affirmative action. Base-

ball has also reaffirmed its staunch opposition to racism and bigotry in any form.

Two years ago, when the Office of the Commissioner published its first *Handbook of Policies and Procedures* applicable to all employees within the Commissioner's Office, the League Offices, the PRC (Players Relations Council) and MLB Properties, we included an explicit section on "Legal and Ethical Standards." That section, a copy of which is attached for your information, makes it clear that any statement or act having the clear purpose or effect of demeaning or degrading another person on the basis of religion, race, color, or national origin is grounds for immediate dismissal.

In recent days, I have read a number of statements allegedly made by Mrs. Schott, and other statements that she admits to having made, that clearly would violate the standards of conduct imposed on Major League Baseball employees. Some people have suggested that so long as Mrs. Schott apologizes to local groups in Cincinnati for the offense that she has committed and so long as those groups accept her apology, there is no need for Major League Baseball to take any independent action. I could not disagree more.

How can we hope to hold our employees to a high standard of conduct in this important area, and then wink at, or totally ignore, offensive conduct on the part of others (i.e., owners) within Baseball? Does this not set up the most cynical sort of double standard?

On the front page of today's *New York Times*, I read a story about the rekindling of ethnic hatred and anti-Semitism in Germany, where Neo-Nazi groups have been burning apartment buildings housing various non-Arien [sic] residents and physically assaulting, even killing, members of various minority groups. Last week, the *Times* ran a series on ethnic tensions and hatreds in New York and other American cities. By remaining silent in the wake of Mrs. Schott's recent revelations, doesn't Major League Baseball send the message that we condone her ignorance and insensitivity, or at the very least don't think that it's any big deal?

I strongly urge the Executive Council to think about what it is that Baseball stands for in this regard and, at a minimum, send a strongly worded letter to Mrs. Schott—which I assume would become a public document—censuring her for her attitudes and for her admitted statements.

Greenberg was not trying to single out Selig, but he knew someone needed to pull baseball out of this voluntary paralysis, and Selig seemed the most likely candidate. "For four or five days," Greenberg said, "no one in ownership appeared to know quite how to react. And therefore, there was no reaction at all."

In fact, by the time of Greenberg's letter, the furor started by Mushnick seemed to be evaporating, and maybe Selig and baseball were on the verge of successfully ignoring the issue to death. But two days later, that all changed. Two days later, the newest revelation would force the sport and the nation to take another look at this woman—and this time not be able to turn back.

On Thursday, November 26, *The New York Times*, the nation's paper of record, ran a story quoting former Oakland Athletics front-office staff member Sharon Jones as saying she heard Marge make a racial slur during a conference call of club owners just before the winter meetings in the late 1980s. Jones, executive assistant at the time to A's executive vice-president Roy Eisenhardt, was on the conference call for the roll call until Eisenhardt could come to the phone. The other owners were already on the line, Jones said, waiting for commissioner Peter Ueberroth to join the call, when Schott began to speak:

> I wonder what the commissioner wants this time. Is it this race thing? I'm sick and tired of talking about this race thing. I once had a nigger work for me. He couldn't do the job. I had to put him in the mail room, and he couldn't even handle that. I later found out the nigger couldn't read or write.
>
> I would never hire another nigger. I'd rather have a trained monkey working for me than a nigger.

Jones said she ran into Marge at the subsequent winter meetings and brought up the remarks, and Marge responded, "OK, honey, nice meeting you."

Sharon Jones' allegation was powerful because it dispelled Marge's claim that she was the victim of disgruntled former employees—and because it implicated the other owners as being cognizant of Marge's vocabulary. Sharon Jones had nothing to do with the Reds or Marge. She worked for the A's from 1980-92, including a stint as the director of outreach activities, and had recently left the team to become executive director of college relations at Mills College in Oakland.

Marge tried to fire back at Sharon Jones with a statement of her own:

> In recent days, Sharon Jones, formerly of the Oakland A's, has reportedly accused me of having made racist remarks in a telephone conversation several years ago. Whenever the alleged conversation took place, I did not make the comments Ms. Jones has attributed to me. I would not make such comments. They are nonsense in more ways than the bigotry they express. For example, Ms. Jones reportedly alleges I made certain remarks about a black male working in the Reds mail room. In fact, the only employee we have had in the Reds mail room since I have been President and CEO has been a woman. I do not remember anyone making those comments during the conference call, nor do my secretary or other owners I have spoken with. It is important to recognize that actions speak louder than words. My actions as President & CEO of the Reds are an open book. They belie any charges of discrimination. I have nothing to hide.

Considering Marge's hiring record at the Reds, that was a dangerous statement. Plus, if Sharon Jones' recollection was accurate, Marge never said the black she hired for the mail room was with the Reds; it could have been any one of a number of different companies over the years. "I imagine she could have been referring to one of her other businesses," said Jones. "I certainly don't know what goes on in the mind of Marge Schott."

There seemed no motive for Sharon Jones to lie, especially considering this was not a new allegation—although it was the first time Jones told the story publicly in its entirety. Jones told *USA Today* the same story shortly after it happened, but she didn't name the owner and substituted the word "black" for "nigger." She wasn't sure why—maybe because she was embarrassed to use the word. It is a difficult word to say if you truly grasp the hatred in it. Reds controller Tim Sabo had the same problem even writing the word in his diary, at first jotting down "those players" and later crossing it out to put the correct reference Marge had made to "$3 million niggers."

Three days after unearthing the Sharon Jones story, the *Times* printed a lengthy feature story on Marge with more examples of insensitive comments, such as her admission that she used the term "Jap" when Bill White had spoken to her the previous week. "Bill said to me, 'Marge, will you quit that!'" Marge said, and laughed. "I said, 'Bill, I didn't know it was so bad. But I'll stop.' I didn't mean to insult the Japanese; I love them. I have great respect for the way they've come back in the world."

But Marge's most alarming comment in the piece came when she discussed how her relatives in Germany suffered in World War II. "Hitler was good in the beginning," Marge said, "but he went too far."

The evidence against Marge seemed to be growing daily. Besides Sharon Jones, some of the scheduled witnesses in the Tim Sabo case began offering their personal experiences with Marge's slurs. Keith Stichtenoth, a former ticket-office worker, came forward to say he had heard Marge say "Jew bastard" on at least a couple of occasions as though the words were common in her vocabulary. "It struck me that she used the term as if she were saying 'All-Star' or 'teenager,' as if it was one of those words that were needed to complete the noun," Stichtenoth said later.

Marge could have written off Stichtenoth as another disgruntled former employee, but that couldn't explain Max Brown—publisher of a Columbus, Ohio, weekly newspaper called *The Other Paper*—who wrote in a column that he sat with Marge during a June 8, 1989, game at Riverfront Stadium and heard her call Reds outfielder Kal Daniels "a dumb, lazy nigger." That also couldn't explain Joe Pfaffl, a local business consultant and the finance chairman of the Butler County Republican Party, who revealed he had heard Marge refer to outfielder Dave Parker as a "million-dollar nigger."

Pfaffl says what he told the media was accurate, that he was in the tunnel or gate area of an airport when he heard her use the slur. The timing of the comment was memorable because of the news of the day. "It was right after Parker was traded," said Pfaffl. "I had a newspaper with me, and I read in the paper something to the effect that she thought he was a great guy and was sad to see him go." Pfaffl, chairman of the Alcohol and Drug Addiction Services Board of Butler County, believes Marge was intoxicated when she made the comments. "She reminds me of an old drunk," he said.

Pfaffl hadn't been around her enough to say whether she was a racist, but he has been around her enough to know he preferred to be away from her. Every time he saw her, she was complaining about somebody. He saw her once at spring training, and she was carrying on about Pete Rose. He ended up on the plane from Florida with her, and Marge tried to stuff all the overhead bins in first class with containers of strawberries. The flight attendant tried to reason with her, and Marge put her hand on her hip and said, "Do you know who I am, honey?" Meanwhile, Pfaffl says, Cincinnati news anchor Jerry Springer sat in the last row with an "I wish I wasn't on this plane" look.

"She was a crabby old bitch," said Pfaffl. "For a period of three or four years, I kept running into her, and she'd say, 'Hi, honey.' I've never really had any conversations with her, per se. I really try to avoid her."

One of the strangest twists to the entire scandal would come shortly after Pfaffl's "million-dollar nigger" revelation. Reports surfaced that Joe Pfaffl had resigned, under pressure, from his position with the Republican party for coming forward with his knowledge of Marge's slurs. At the time, Pfaffl decided to avoid the media and get on with his life, but in reflecting on the incident, he says there was more to his exit than his comments. He had a personality conflict with some "zealots" in the party who didn't like his somewhat aggressive manner, and the Marge situation was an excuse by Butler County GOP chairman Carlos Todd to force him out.

Todd agrees there was more to Pfaffl's leaving—which Todd called a *dismissal*, not a *resignation*—than just Marge, and that there was a personality conflict. But Todd says he acted on his own and that removing Pfaffl was in the party's best interest because he felt Pfaffl's comments weren't. Todd claims that Pfaffl couldn't act simply as a private citizen, that his position with the party meant that what he did or said would inevitably reflect on the Republicans. Todd says he received a number of phone calls from angered party members who proclaimed that Pfaffl was wrong.

Frankly, Todd's argument is questionable. You would think the party would be proud of Pfaffl for stepping forward with any help he could lend to a court case or even a baseball scandal— that, if anything, the party would try to wrap Pfaffl in the flag and champion him as a proponent of American idealism.

"If it were me," said Todd, "I wouldn't have come forward unless I was summoned into court."

"My contention would be," said Pfaffl, "you're an American first, and you are entitled to freedom of speech morally as a human being."

After Pfaffl's accusation against Marge hit the media, there was an executive committee meeting of the local Republican party the following night, and Pfaffl claims pretty much the entire body was behind him. Todd says he got up and told the party members, "I hope you have enough confidence in me as your leader to handle the situation. Joe and I will discuss the matter and handle it privately."

They met the next day. Pfaffl says Todd wanted his resignation and he refused, enraging Todd. "He threatened me with a stapler gun, acting like he was going to hit me with it. I told him to put it down before he hurt himself," said Pfaffl. "Later, I decided for the good of the party I wasn't going to put the party through this, and I decided to step aside. I had been going to resign, anyway. I just expedited it by three months."

Todd's version? He says Pfaffl came in and said he wasn't going to resign. Pfaffl was angry at Todd, blaming him for blowing his public comments about Marge out of proportion, which Todd denied. "Out of frustration, I slammed down the stapler on the desk, and Joe acted like I was going to hit him with it," said Todd. "I said, 'As far as I'm concerned, you are no longer our finance chairman' and asked him to leave. He left and invited me to bring my stapler with me to the parking lot and told me what he would do with the stapler. Prior to that, actually, I had sent him a notice that he was relieved of his duties."

In any case, Pfaffl was gone. But the Marge Schott scandal was growing. Baseball was going to have to act, and behind the scenes it was attempting to do so. National League president Bill White and National League counsel Robert Kheel were meeting with Marge and her attorney, Bob Martin. Martin had worked with Kheel and White previously during the limited partners' lawsuit, in which Tim Sabo gave the controversial deposition. Martin hoped to resolve the matter quickly because he thought it was in Marge's best interests, and he talked about recommending a suspension in the six- to twelve-month range.

The idea that a settlement might be near met with a lot of opposition. "I told Bud that I thought that would be a giant mistake," said Greenberg. "This was not something you deal out on because you don't know the facts. The analogy would be that there are allegations of gambling and you reach an agreement with the person involved that he'll take a 30-day suspension before you ever investigate whether the allegations are true. If they are true and you find out that maybe he was gambling on games he was playing in, the 30-day suspension isn't adequate."

Indeed, how could baseball give Marge, say, a one-year suspension for what she said in her deposition and her admissions to occasionally and inadvertently using insensitive language when Tim Sabo was alleging that she had ordered him to discriminate in hiring for the Reds? Maybe there were others out there who could back him up or who had similar experiences. In fairness to all the parties, there needed to be an investigation. Even if they reached a settlement with Martin, Kheel and White planned to conduct some sort of investigation before making a recommendation to baseball's Executive Council. But would that have been enough? Really, the severity of the allegations necessitated a full-scale, formal probe. Eventually baseball did just that beginning December 1, albeit for a different reason. When Marge changed attorneys, a "formal" investigation was deemed necessary to protect the Executive Council from a legal challenge if Marge took baseball to court.

Why the change of attorneys? New Reds general manager Jim Bowden became concerned that Martin wasn't going to save the franchise for Marge. Bowden knew that Martin was talking in the one-year suspension range, but Bowden also knew that if Marge were suspended, the limited partners were ready to pounce and try to wrest the team away from her. Convinced this was too big a task for Martin, Bowden advised Marge to retain the heaviest hitter around—the same "surround yourself with the best" creed that helped make Bowden so successful so quickly—and she agreed. And when Bowden thought of the best, the first name that came to mind was the attorney who represented Oliver North in the Iran-Contra hearings, Brendan Sullivan. So Bowden called Sullivan, who recommended Robert Bennett, the Washington, D.C., attorney who was representing former Defense Secretary Caspar Weinberger in the Iran-Contra affair and former presidential adviser Clark Clifford in the Bank of Credit and Commerce International scandal.

It was a wise choice. Bennett had experience with high-profile cases and a background in affairs involving associations

Senate ethics committee in such heavily publicized cases as the Keating Five affair. Tom Schwarz, who helped Bennett represent Marge in this case, had a background in baseball legal matters. Bennett himself had never dealt with the sport, except as a fan. In his Washington, D.C., office a block and a half from the White House, Bennett had a collage of autographed postcards framed and hanging up on the back wall. When he was a kid in Brooklyn, he'd give players postcards with his return address and ask them and their "mates"—short for teammates in those days—to sign them and send them back. Among the autographs were Willie Mays, Pee Wee Reese, and Leo Durocher. The funny thing was, Durocher took the "mates" thing a little too seriously, and his is co-signed by actress Laraine Day, Durocher's wife. Bennett also has an autograph of Jackie Robinson, the pioneer whose 40th anniversary of entry into the league prompted baseball to commemorate the occasion in 1987, although Marge Schott didn't seem to get it—"Well, that's because Jackie Robinson's been a great player, I don't think so much because he was black."

It seemed a potentially awkward situation for Bennett, who also had Robinson's 1955 Brooklyn Dodgers team picture hanging in his office—defending a woman whose comments about minorities were at the very least insensitive. Carry the juxtaposition further, and you see a gift from Marge on the inside of Bennett's door, a poster depicting the Reds' owner and some of her players at Pet Night 1991 in the same office that hangs a fish on the wall bearing the expression "If I had kept my mouth shut, I wouldn't be here." But to Bennett, there was no moral dilemma with defending Marge. To him, this was not a matter of what she said, but whether she had a right to say it, his client not simply being Marge Schott, but the First Amendment and her right to free and private speech.

Bennett flew to Cincinnati on Sunday, November 29, met with Marge and Bowden, and decided to take the case. From then on, Bowden was happy. He felt Marge's interests were being protected with Bob Bennett. And they were.

Marge was taking a beating in the local and national media. If the press wasn't finding someone else who had heard Marge utter a racial or ethnic slur, columnists were lambasting her for the comments already out there. Or late-night television talkshow hosts were finally leaving Dan Quayle alone and making

Marge their favorite punch line. Meanwhile, the Rev. Jesse Jackson got involved. The nation's most recognized and publicized civil-rights leader blasted Marge for her words and saw her as a vehicle for attacking discriminatory hiring throughout baseball. Only in Cincinnati, with Marge's propaganda ministers at WLW leading the charge, was all this attention considered a witch hunt against the city's First Lady. Before Bennett was in the picture, Marge even invited Andy Furman from the station to a meeting of her confidantes to discuss Marge and the media.

Furman was sitting at his desk at about 1 o'clock one afternoon when he got a call from Marge's Chevrolet general manager Mel Lehrner asking him to come to Riverfront Stadium. Furman thought he had done something wrong, but Lehrner assured him that Marge simply wanted his input on the situation. So he immediately headed to the stadium, where he walked into a room that already included Lehrner; George Verkamp, Marge's brother-in-law and general manager at Schott Buick; Jon Braude; Jim Bowden; Dr. Beverly Carpenter, one of Marge's few close friends who have stayed that way; and Marge herself. Furman walked in and went straight into his schtick. "I don't know if I should sit next to Braude," Furman said at the meeting. "That would put two Jews in the same corner."

The barb helped cut through the tension. The clown prince of the airwaves could see Marge was down, and he felt a need to help cheer her up, kidding her about how she needed to get her hair done if she wanted to go on television. It made her laugh, and that made him feel good. But the purpose of him being there was not just as a court jester but as a media adviser, so he did a mock interview with her, telling her what to say and what not to say. Furman was asked to help decide which interviews would be most advantageous, and he was shown a long list of the people who wanted interviews, including "Good Morning America," *People* magazine, ESPN, "Today," and Jane Whitney. Furman ruled out Whitney's show, because he didn't want her in front of a live audience that could be stacked with minorities. But he felt it was important for her to do some interviews.

"You've been through this before, you've always done well with the media, you'll do fine," Furman told her. "Do one a day, then go home and rest. If you do one after another, you'll forget what you say and you could end up contradicting yourself. Do one-on-ones; that's where you shine."

They agreed ESPN would be first, and she did that. For Furman, this entrée into Marge's inner circle was a bit awkward—a member of the media advising her on how to manipulate others in the profession. He was happy that he wasn't put in that position again. But he was also happy he made Marge smile a little with his jokes, because he liked her. "I may be too close to her," he said, "but I consider myself a friend of hers."

He was a better friend than adviser, because she should never have done any interviews. That night, she ended up on WLW, as friendly an environment as possible, being interviewed by Bill Cunningham. She still blew it, saying the "good blacks" didn't like the media attention she was getting.

The media were becoming a lost war for Marge. Even her sister, Barbara Fraser, was quoted in an Atlanta newspaper story as supporting her embattled sibling but saying Marge should step down temporarily while reaction to the remarks subsided. In the article, Fraser said it was "obvious" Marge had made the comments attributed to her, that Marge "targets" color or religion if she's mad at somebody, that Marge isn't being malicious and doesn't realize the potential hurt in the words, and that Marge should take some time away from the team and "make amends."

It was a shocking story, considering Marge was close to this sister more commonly known as "Winnie," a world-class marksman and a paraplegic who occasionally made the trip from Atlanta to Cincinnati for Reds games. But Fraser later said she was as shocked as anybody about the story and insisted she was misquoted.

"I'm really upset about it all," Fraser said. "I don't think it's fair. I know my sister so well. She's not a racist. I've never heard Margie say any of those things they claim she said. Margie loves everybody. She loves the Reds, they're like her family, and she's done a great deal for the organization. She's a wonderful, kind woman and very colorful. I can't imagine what she's going through. I'm very proud of her for having the courage to fight for what she believes in."

Even after being read some of the more controversial excerpts from Marge's deposition, Fraser was unswayed in her opinions.

"I think they're badgering her over things that are insignificant," Fraser said. "I think she's being totally misunderstood. I know my sister. I know she wouldn't do anything to hurt anyone. My sister jokes around a lot. People just don't seem to see that. If there were anything misconstrued, it would be something she said in a joking manner."

If there is a living and breathing example of the good side in Marge, many point to Winnie. Marge's younger sister was a show jumper until an automobile crash left her a paraplegic right around the time Charlie died. Marge was always there, supporting Winnie and her family. And when Winnie later decided to become active again in sports, Marge was thrilled for her, even making a contribution to Winnie's rifle team. When Marge bought the Reds, she made certain to involve Winnie and share the joy with her. "Whenever anyone's in trouble, Margie's always right there to help," said Fraser. "That goes beyond family. I've seen her help lots of people in need."

With the fate of her general partnership now seemingly in jeopardy, Marge was desperately in need of stories about the good she had done to help counteract the daily revelations of her slurs.

Enter Bob Bennett. The distinguished attorney is a master at the media game. And one of the first things he told Marge was to keep quiet and let him do the talking. Charging more than $400 per hour, this was part of what he was paid to do. He made his first public appearance as her attorney at baseball's winter meetings at Louisville, where the media gathered not just for the usual fare of free-agent signings and major trades but also to see if Marge Schott would show up. Bennett encouraged Marge to go. "If you're an owner, you should act like one," Bennett told her. "Plus, if you're not there, it would be easier for them to suspend you." But baseball chose to use Louisville not to suspend her but to announce its formal investigation into Marge's conduct, with Bob Kheel as the point man in a probe that would be overseen by the politically correct subcommittee of California Angels executive vice-president Jackie Autry (a white female), Pittsburgh Pirates chairman of the board Doug Danforth (a white male), National League president Bill White (a black male), and American League president Bobby Brown (a white male). Add the head of the Executive Council, Bud Selig (a white Jewish male), and Marge was facing a regular 1990s Mod Squad—not to mention the Rainbow Coalition.

Indeed, the Rev. Jesse Jackson was in Louisville. He was unable to get an audience with the entire contingent of owners until a later meeting, but he did hold a community rally that was intended to feature a number of current and former Major League players. Not one current player showed up. Hall of Famer Frank Robinson, the assistant general manager of the Baltimore Orioles, stood beside Jackson, as did a couple of players who wished they were still active, Leon Durham and Dave Parker. The lack of current players only added credence to the notion that today's players are too busy counting up their money to worry about anyone or anything else. Whether they wanted to appear with Jesse Jackson or not, here was an opportunity for them to take a stand against Marge Schott's comments specifically or racism in baseball generally and send a dynamic message to the sport and to the fans—and especially to the kids.

Imagine the impact of 25 of the top black ballplayers uniting at Louisville, standing side by side to denounce the dehumanizing words of the Cincinnati Reds owner and calling for swift and severe action by baseball—particularly if they threatened to boycott games against the Reds or at least vowed never to sign with Cincinnati. It didn't have to be just black players, it could have been the top 25 players of any race, creed, or color, because you don't have to be black or Jewish or Japanese to be offended by Marge's comments. At the very least, there should have been more comments similar to what Reds shortstop Barry Larkin said, that if the allegations against Marge were true he'd have a tough time playing for her, or what 1992 Reds Most Valuable Player Bip Roberts said, that if Marge was allowed to continue as owner that would be a factor in whether he left Cincinnati for free agency after the 1993 season.

Instead, most of the top baseball players said nothing. Or worse. Reds reliever Dwayne Henry, an African American who didn't live in Cincinnati, said he was not familiar with the details of the case and had no opinion, except to say, "As long as she treats me all right, I'm fine." Fortunately, not everyone felt the same way. It's easy to say that the players were in the awkward situation of having to criticize their own bosses—but these are employees who do that all the time. They terminally rip management if they feel they aren't getting enough playing time or money, insisting they're not respected, knowing full well that the owners won't retaliate. What would an owner have done if his black superstar spoke out against Marge Schott? Absolutely nothing, or that owner would have had hell to pay from the media, Jesse Jackson, and every black group in America—if not the owner's conscience. If the players want respect, they have to speak out against something other than feeling slighted for getting only $3 million a year instead of $4 million—this was a chance to earn respect not simply as players but as people.

Barry Bonds was in Louisville hoping to announce a landmark contract with San Francisco that would pay him $43 million over six years, and with the nation's sports reporters ready to chronicle his every word, the soon-to-be richest player in baseball history spoke not one word about Marge Schott.

"I talked to Barry Bonds about it in Louisville," said Parker. "He damn near sprinted past me, and I pulled him aside and talked to him about it. He said, 'If you need me, I'm there.' Then he disappeared."

It bothered Parker. It bothered him that Barry Bonds and the rest of the black stars of today would turn their backs on their forefathers of the game, the players who had endured the segregated hotels and drinking fountains and restaurants and who had fought through the slurs and threats and sneers to establish an equal playing field. "The black players of today are the recipients of the benefits of all their struggles," said Parker. "This was a disgrace to them. I knew what Frank Robinson and Willie Mays and Hank Aaron and Jackie Robinson had left before me, but what legacy will these guys today leave? Just because they make millions of dollars is no reason to sell your pride and your soul."

Don Newcombe agreed. The former Brooklyn Dodgers pitcher remembered the day when the Rev. Martin Luther King, Jr., came to his house for dinner and told Newcombe the impact that black players such as himself and teammates Roy Campanella and Jackie Robinson had on the civil-rights movement. King wondered how he would have been accepted by society before Robinson's entrance into the national pastime. Newcombe never forgot that dinner, particularly because one month later, Martin Luther King, Jr., was assassinated. And here, a quarter-century later, Newcombe was sickened by the hateful words of the

Cincinnati Reds owner—"I'm sure glad for Mrs. Schott that Jackie Robinson is dead now. That man is turning over in his grave"—and by the reaction of today's black players. The Barry Bondses and Bobby Bonillas and Rickey Hendersons didn't seem to appreciate what the Jackie Robinsons and Roy Campanellas and Don Newcombes went through to make all these riches possible. Newcombe recalled a trip to Cincinnati, when the Dodgers were staying in a downtown hotel that insisted Robinson, Campanella, and Newcombe eat in their rooms and not in the restaurant. Worse yet, Robinson received a letter saying, "If you three niggers show up, we're going to shoot you." So half a dozen security members accompanied the Dodgers on their trip to the ballpark, and the three Dodgers retaliated the best way they could in those days. Playing, excelling, and winning. Their silence back then made it possible for more outspoken resistance now.

And what about Parker? He didn't break the color barrier, but while with the Pittsburgh Pirates he became the first player to crack the million-dollar barrier, and that opened him up to a tremendous amount of flak. Imagine what it was like to be the first player—and a black player at that—to command a seven-figure salary. When he wasn't fighting off the names, he was dodging batteries flying at him in the outfield. But Parker understood what it took for him to get there. "The struggles that the Hank Aarons and Willie Mayses and Jackie Robinsons went through made it possible for me to be the first million-dollar player," he said.

At first, Parker was stunned to hear of the allegations against Schott. The woman who was supposedly calling him a "million-dollar nigger" behind the scenes had always seemed so good to him. Eric Davis didn't know what to believe, either. The two were friends, Parker the veteran who had acted as sort of a guru to Davis when the two were teammates with the Reds. When the story broke about the allegations against Marge, they weren't sure what to believe. They talked to each other on the phone, and they started to wonder if the negative things that happened to them with the Reds stemmed from Marge Schott's hidden feelings about her "million-dollar niggers." Davis, who had been giving Marge the benefit of the doubt over the airplane snafu when he left Oakland, now asked himself if Marge was not only behind it but if her racial views were the cause of it. And what about the two of them being traded? Parker and Davis asked themselves if Marge's views on blacks had anything to do with that.

"For the production I gave her, I should have been her seven or eight million-dollar nigger," said Parker. "She spent all this time putting up a major front, laughing and talking and faking embraces, it couldn't have been genuine with her. She probably went somewhere after we hugged and washed her arms in Clorox."

If Parker and Davis had any inclination to believe Marge, that ended quickly when parts of Marge's deposition were read to them individually over the telephone. They were floored. Davis, who had been trying to hold off judgment, was speechless for a few seconds, then said, "That's deep. It leaves me at a loss for words. If that's the case, then something definitely should be done. Sometimes, actions speak louder than words. In this case, words speak louder than actions." And it told Parker that his fears were correct. He believed everything that was said about Marge Schott and was determined to fight. And he showed up at Jackson's side at Louisville, hoping to make a difference.

Jackson's involvement drew a mixed reaction. On the one hand, he had more influence and impact than any leader for any minority group in the country. Once he stepped into the fray, the rights and issues involving blacks would be protected if not improved. On the other hand, he was criticized as being an opportunist and a hypocrite, for he was the same man who had spoken with such ethnic insensitivity some years earlier when he referred to New York as "Hymietown." Maybe he was the last person to be judging Marge Schott; or maybe his own experience made him the best.

"The issue is deeper than a slur," Jackson said. "This is a pattern of institutional behavior that is fundamentally against United States law. We're not talking about a gaffe, we're talking about a pattern of behavior. We're talking about zero presidents and general managers and scouting directors. We're talking about a policy of locking people out by race. This is much beyond Marge Schott and Al Campanis."

Jackson got his chance to address the owners at their next meeting. But Marge? Where was Marge? In Louisville, actually.

Bowden called her from the winter meetings and encouraged her to come to Louisville and defend herself. She snuck into town to be a part of the meetings and to hold a press conference, at which she read a statement that Bennett had prepared. It was an apology, and it was no coincidence her mouth tripped over the word "apologize"—a word she has difficulty saying or believing. But Bennett knew that the sport and the public needed to hear a contrite and apologetic Marge Schott. And Bennett didn't stop there. He became her mouthpiece, regularly answering or returning the phone calls of reporters covering the case, pleading her First Amendment rights and revealing the status of the proceedings.

Bennett was effectively spinning the stories toward his client, and the local newspapers teemed with his comments almost daily. Meanwhile, baseball attempted to conduct its investigation as privately as possible, the Pirates' Doug Danforth the only member of the subcommittee willing to speak openly about the progress of the probe. Nationally, Bennett could have dominated the public-relations war if it hadn't been for Sharon Jones, who was regularly blasting both parties—Marge, for her slurs, and baseball, for its lack of an independent investigation. She claimed that baseball's attempt at a fair probe was "like investigating your mother."

But Bob Kheel pressed on, quietly doing his job. Frankly, if everyone in baseball had kept completely quiet, that would have been fine with Kheel. The point man in the investigation, Kheel wanted to avoid any leaks that could be construed as the Executive Council's prejudging the case. This not only would protect baseball if the case ended up in court, but also in the public's perception. The investigating subcommittee wanted to avoid the criticism that had been directed at then-commissioner Bart Giamatti and his independent investigator, John Dowd, during the Pete Rose gambling scandal. Giamatti was blasted for prejudging Rose when he sent a letter to the judge in the Ron Peters case saying that Rose's bookmaker offered "significant and truthful cooperation" in baseball's investigation of Rose. Even Giamatti admitted he should have been more careful, noting that the letter was actually written by Dowd and signed by Giamatti. Dowd also was chastised for drawing a conclusion in his report on Rose to Giamatti instead of letting the commissioner weigh the evidence and decide.

Ironically, baseball was heavily criticized in the Marge scandal for not hiring an outside investigator such as Dowd, who also investigated New York Yankees owner George Steinbrenner for paying known gambler Howard Spira to try to get dirt on Yankees outfielder Dave Winfield. More than anything, this was a public-relations blunder, because even an "independent" investigator would have been retained by baseball and would have reported to the Executive Council. But we're talking perception here, and the Executive Council already was taking a drubbing. And rightfully so. Here was baseball's owner-laden Executive Council already facing questions of whether it could properly rule on another owner, and the last thing it needed was to be perceived as hiring someone who might shade the truth, if not cover it up. The owners had just fired commissioner Fay Vincent because he was acting too independently of them, and their credibility to act in the best interests of the game as opposed to their own interests was in doubt—especially with a high-powered lawyer named Bob Bennett threatening to expose some of their darker secrets or at least send them into court over this matter. In Congressional hearings into whether baseball should retain its antitrust exemption, Ohio Senator Howard Metzenbaum even challenged Bud Selig as to whether there was any way baseball could deal fairly with Marge Schott without an independent-minded commissioner in there.

The public and the press knew little of Bob Kheel, who was quite the counterpart for Bob Bennett stylistically. Bennett is a very public and powerful force who will take his case not only to the masses but directly to parties who can help him. Bennett doesn't just walk into a room, he'll work it, a master spin doctor who designs his points specially for the person he addresses at the moment. Kheel, on the other hand, can slip into a room or out of a conversation unnoticed. Where the outspoken Bennett might give you a lot of reasons to think his client is in the right, the soft-spoken Kheel will give you very little, period.

They were two successful lawyers with two different styles, and they would be the key players in constructing and disproving the case against Margaret Unnewehr Schott.

— Chapter Fifteen —

Marge's Heavy Hitter

I f anyone questioned why Marge Schott chose Bob Bennett to represent her, that was squelched before her verdict was ever reached, when he helped earn U.S. Defense Secretary Caspar Weinberger a presidential pardon for his role in the Iran-Contra affair. Still, Bennett felt strapped from the beginning of this case by Bob Martin's early negotiations with Bob Kheel and Bill White, in which a one-year suspension was discussed. Bennett felt it would be difficult now to go back and say Marge would not accept a suspension, but he argued the point, anyway. He wanted this to be a First Amendment issue, posturing publicly about Marge's right to free speech while working privately to establish her actions as affirmatively as possible in the area of race relations.

Suddenly, Marge's hiring practices progressed from the Mesozoic Era into the 1990s. She promoted Doc Rodgers, a black, from minor-league pitching coach to assistant/baseball operations. She added Ferguson Jenkins, Tommie Reynolds, and Grant Jackson, three African Americans, to minor-league coaching and managing positions. She established an equal employment opportunity program for the Reds. She donated a $100,000 scholarship fund to the Cincinnati Academy of Physical Education, a predominantly black high school. All of this was a transparent attempt to help Marge withstand the crisis, because this certainly was not her style. From July 1985 until about the end of 1991, the Reds had 97 openings for positions excluding minor-league players major-league players, and coaching staff. Only two were filled by African Americans. One was field superintendent Tony Swain, who was made full time instead of part time, and the other was Rodgers, whom Quinn had approved on his own to be a minor-league coach. Although Rodgers would later tell then-farm director Jim Bowden that he wanted to move into the front office some day, he realized that day came early as an attempt to ease the pressure on Marge.

"You'd have to be naive if you say it's not," said Rodgers upon his hiring. "The reality is, they picked a qualified person."

The reality also is, this was not Marge Schott's doing but Bob Bennett's. He choreographed all of these moves, believing they would help Marge in her fight with baseball. He and his legal team also realized they were the right things to do. Nobody was going to believe Marge Schott had suddenly awakened like Scrooge on Christmas morning to see the wrongs she had done— that wasn't the point. Bennett was trying to show that even if you couldn't change Marge, you could at least change her actions, and that baseball and the community would be better off with her in the game than out of it. Who knew if the next owner of the Cincinnati Reds would be so willing to set a trend in minority opportunities?

Then again, who knew if Marge would revert to her old ways once the pressure was off?

Meanwhile, Kheel and the Executive Council subcommittee were investigating leads into Marge's slurs. The media did a lot of the groundwork for them, and baseball's gumshoes acquired the depositions from Sabo's lawsuit, including the one by Sabo himself that was never made available to the public. Some of the witnesses, Kheel and Co. interviewed themselves, some in more depth than others, some not at all. Sabo, Blaemire, and Stichtenoth, for example, lauded the thoroughness of the process. Sabo underwent three one-hour interview sessions over the phone, two to go over what he knew and one to make certain baseball was correctly depicting what he had stated in the first two interviews. Howie Bedell, on the other hand, was never contacted. And Cal Levy's interview lasted a mere 15 minutes, which consisted of reviewing his deposition for Sabo and asking if he had remembered anything else since then.

Of all the people interviewed, baseball appeared most concerned with Sharon Jones. She was becoming more and more outspoken about baseball's investigation and its handling of the Marge Schott affair, from the lack of an independent probe to the possible cover-up of Marge's conference-call comment. Kheel *and* Bill White *and* Jackie Autry went to interview her in person about her allegations, and Jones showed up with an attorney. Afterward, Jones said she still was not impressed and told the media that baseball was now conducting two separate investigations—one into Marge Schott's racial slurs and another into whether there was a cover-up of Jones' alleged conference call. The fact was, nobody else knew anything about a second investigation. When told as much, Jones conceded that maybe she was mistaken and had jumped to an improper conclusion.

It wasn't the only time Jones did that. When baseball found no record of a conference call during the two-month period in which Jones alleged it took place, she at first insisted that Jackie Autry had told her there were conference calls during one of the months. Later, before that was printed, Jones softened her stance and said, upon reflection, maybe that wasn't quite right. Now perhaps this hurts her credibility by making these mistakes or perhaps this helps her credibility by proving she'll admit she's wrong. The truth is, there was something about Sharon Jones when you'd hear her talk about this matter, a sincerity, a conviction, that made her believable. No matter how many people questioned the circumstances or contradicted her story, she stuck to her contention as she has since the alleged incident first happened. Nobody doubted the integrity of Sharon Jones, who was head of the Athletics' outreach program before leaving the team.

Baseball's investigation covered people who weren't so willing to talk to the media but cooperated with the sport. General managers Murray Cook and Bill Bergesch talked to baseball, although Bergesch said that if baseball wasn't serious about taking action against Marge then he wanted no part of it. He was assured this was no smokescreen. George Brinkman also participated, albeit quietly, because he steadfastly refused interview requests. But he told baseball his story in a sworn declaration.

Brinkman said he had been an insurance-claims adjuster for GAB Business Services for more than 25 years. In the early morning of September 3, 1981, a fire broke out on the second floor of Marge's home. She reported the fire to her insurance agent, who reported it to her insurance companies, who assigned investigation and assessment of the loss to GAB. Brinkman estimated the damage at about $56,000 and attributed it to "careless smoking." And when he met with Marge, she asked if he knew any contractors she could hire to repair the damage. He said he knew several.

"I was shocked when Mrs. Schott then asked about the contractors, 'Do any of them have any coloreds working for them?' or 'Do any of them have any niggers working for them?' I am uncertain now whether Mrs. Schott used the term 'coloreds' or the term 'niggers,' but it was definitely one or the other," stated Brinkman. "I interpreted Mrs. Schott's question to mean that she would not hire any of these contractors if they had black employees. I told her that I didn't know all of the contractors' employees. Later in my meeting with Mrs. Schott, I asked her whom she had hired in the past to do decorating work in her home. Mrs. Schott said that she had hired Dick Greiwe, a local interior decorator. I told her that I was familiar with Dick Greiwe. Mrs. Schott then made another shocking statement, 'You know how hard it is to find a good decorator who isn't either a Jew or a queer.'"

Again, this was not another "disgruntled former employee." Neither were the two unnamed witnesses that baseball found—one a policeman, and neither of whom had met Marge previously—who told baseball they heard Marge use the word "nigger" while she sat in her box at Riverfront Stadium during Reds games. What did they have to gain by coming forward? Certainly, if they had talked to some of the higher-profile people involved in the case, they might have been driven away instead. Joe Pfaffl's exit from his Republican Party position was the most publicized fallout, but others were facing their own problems as a result of speaking up, and not just the onslaught of phone calls from the insatiable media.

"I wasn't sure what to expect, but I've been involved in these kind of situations before, so it wasn't totally unexpected," said Cal Levy, who had been through public turmoil before, as promoter of the 1979 Who concert in Cincinnati, where 11 fans died. "But my kids got heat at school—'Why is your dad lying about Mrs. Schott?'"

Roger Blaemire says people would call him on the phone and tell him he was a "nigger lover" and say, "If you know what's good for you, you'd get out of town." Sharon Jones received some hate mail from the Cincinnati-Dayton area that was so derisive the FBI was contacted.

Dave Parker, who was born and raised and still lives in Cincinnati, says his daughter came home and said he was the topic of conversation at her school. At home, Parker was getting hate letters every day; one included an article about Parker along with a drawing of a swastika.

Now that the issue was public, a friend of Parker's told him about another incident he had been hiding from the former outfielder. While in Chicago for the All-Star Game in 1990, Parker ran into Marge at a party the night before the game. Marge and Parker hugged, but after Parker walked away to see someone else, Parker's friend stayed near Marge. One of the other people with Marge asked who Parker was, and Marge replied, "One of my nigger friends." At the time, Parker's friend didn't want to tell him and cause a scene. But Parker wishes he had. Then Parker would have known what he was facing years earlier than he did—and he no doubt wouldn't have contacted the Reds about being their hitting instructor prior to the scandal. Parker says the Reds were looking for someone with more experience and turned him down, which turned out to be wise, because Parker would have left the job once the revelations about Marge's slurs became public. After the scandal broke, Parker was unable to get a playing job in baseball for a second straight year, and he wonders whether his outspokenness concerning Marge had something to do with it.

"People look at me like I'm a Martian for saying these things," said Parker. "But if it gets bad for me, I'll move."

Tim Sabo did leave town. He couldn't get a job in Cincinnati, and it probably didn't help that the popular owner of the Reds was regularly slamming him in the newspapers and had accused him of stealing money from the team. So Sabo moved back with his family in Madison, Ohio, and helped out his parents' struggling nursery business at no pay while he continued to search for employment. The ordeal has been hard on him, not just ridding him of his admitted bent toward cockiness but attacking his confidence, leaving him moody, quiet. Meanwhile, his wife Linda developed Bell's Palsy and Graves' disease, and though there's no way to unequivocally connect those to the tension caused by fighting Marge Schott, doctors confirmed the Sabos' fear that nerves may have contributed to weakening her system. Sometimes Tim Sabo wondered if it was all worth it.

"Marge," he said, "did all that to my family."

At least a few of the limited partners felt bad for Sabo, considering he had tried to help them in their legal dispute with Marge. But they were in an awkward position, as he was suing not just Marge but also the team, meaning they were involved, too. By unseating her, they could help Sabo and help themselves, but that was an all-but-impossible task with Bob Bennett around.

Bennett received baseball's report on Marge on December 22, and baseball wanted a response by January 6. Bennett told Kheel that was absurd. He originally wanted until the week of January 25 but eventually said he would settle for January 25 itself. When baseball came back and announced publicly that the response would be due on January 20 and that it would interview Marge on January 22 at the Dallas-Fort Worth Airport Hyatt in Grapevine, Texas, Bennett took the offensive. He told the media that baseball had promised Marge due process, and this showed it was going back on its word—that it would have been fair for him to ask for three months, and all he wanted was one. After all, he had to endure the holidays in conducting his own inquiry into the case and answering the charges, and he was hampered by the time he'd spent on the Weinberger case.

"If it's an all-out battle they require, and they're not giving us a reasonable amount of time, that's their decision and not ours," Bennett said.

Bennett also ridiculed baseball's report on Marge as being "raw data" filled with innuendo. The part about raw data was essentially correct. While baseball did not want to draw any conclusions, it believed the report offered relevant information and testimony. Baseball could have spent years investigating and probably still not have contacted everyone who had heard Marge say something insensitive. But once it believed an obvious pattern had been established, there was no need to continue. Bennett backtracked with some of those witnesses, sending one of his associates to conduct a far more probing interview with Levy than baseball had conducted. And on January 20, Marge and Bennett turned in their response to baseball's allegations— more than 200 pages of evidence, testimony, and argument prepared by Bennett and a half-dozen others at his law firm. The council had two days to decipher all of it, which Bennett said was a ridiculously short period of time. But on January 22, the council convened again in Grapevine, which was becoming familiar territory.

Two weeks earlier, the council and the owners had a special session there to discuss issues they had put on hold at the winter meetings because of the fatal heart attack suffered in Louisville by Florida Marlins president Carl Barger. Marge said she wouldn't attend that meeting, but snuck into town, anyway, which meant she could hear the Rev. Jesse Jackson address the owners about what they should do concerning her.

A few days before Jackson met with the owners, he met with Bennett and his legal partner Carl Rauh, who is the son of attorney Joseph Rauh, Jr., the former civil-rights leader and a friend of Bennett's. Bennett told Jackson that it wasn't in anyone's interest to make Marge a scapegoat and that Marge wanted to help solve the problems of racism in baseball. Bennett found Jackson to be in general agreement and pretty responsive. In fact, when Jackson met with the owners in Grapevine he told them that Marge should not be made a scapegoat—but should not be ignored, either. Jackson told the owners that Marge should be fined, sent to diversity training, and removed at least temporarily from the game for her racial and ethnic slurs. But he also wanted to see institutional changes throughout the game, pointing out the gross lack of minorities in major front-office positions. Jackson said he and his new Rainbow Commission for Fairness in Athletics were going to monitor the hiring patterns and opportunities for every city with a major-league professional sports franchise and would boycott any team that wasn't making strides. Much of what Jackson said made sense, but when Jackson repeated his proposal to the media, he was loose with his facts.

"We do not understand the lack of use of a major pool of African American and Hispanic former player talent that is available to it," said Jackson. "How can Willie Mays, Reggie Jackson, Bob Gibson, Lou Brock, Bobby Tolan, Joe Morgan, Ferguson Jenkins, and many others not have a place in baseball beyond their playing days?"

Although his point was well taken, the fact was that Ferguson Jenkins was employed in baseball—by none other than the Reds.

And Morgan had been pursued as a manager in the past but said no, and was doing well in business and in baseball broadcasting. As for a boycott, Jackson overestimated the social awareness of the typical sports fan, who uses athletics as an escape from issues and not as a forum. During the height of the Marge Schott controversy, the Reds sold all their roughly 14,500 available Opening Day tickets in a record 65 minutes. Besides, baseball's penetration into the black community is poor, and only a fraction of the spectators at the stadium are African American. Although Jackson didn't want Marge to be the issue, she was destined to be the lightning rod. Baseball could have given lip service to minority hiring without affecting Opening Day attendance; but if the Executive Council let Marge Schott go unpunished, there was some question about whether this would incite a riot. Perhaps it was an outlandish thought, but nobody wanted to find out. The country was still reeling from the race riots in Los Angeles following the acquittal of the police officers who were video-taped beating Rodney King.

Ironically, at the end of Jackson's meeting with the owners, the Reverend and Marge Schott got together and hugged. But that was the extent of the discussion concerning Marge Schott at that meeting. Once again, Jackson had planned to meet with current and former players, this time from all sports, in conjunction with the owners' meeting. Once again, he was basically stiffed. This time, the only ones to show up were former Red Bobby Tolan and former Dallas Cowboys Drew Pearson and Pettis Norman.

For Marge, the meeting that would matter most would be the next one in Grapevine, on January 22, when the Executive Council would have her response and be able to question her directly. After months of answering accusations and being constantly on the defensive, this was Bob Bennett's day to plead his case to the court of baseball and to argue his point to the people. Bennett released to the media huge excerpts from his response to baseball, including a six-page statement by Marge to the Executive Council:

> I appreciate the opportunity to come here today to address the allegations against me. The past months have been very difficult. Many things have been said about me that simply are

not true. However, as I already have acknowledged, I have occasionally made insensitive remarks in private conversations that I now realize have hurt others. I sincerely apologize for those remarks.

I want to emphasize that I never intended to offend anyone. Like many people my age, I was raised at a time when racial and ethnic remarks were commonplace. Growing up, I heard these words and phrases at home and at school. As an adult, I heard them at work—in the brickyards and in the car dealerships. In Major League Baseball, I heard similar language. Perhaps subconsciously, I may even have thought that these words made me sound "tough," "aggressive," or "masculine" to my male competitors in the business world.

But my purpose is not to offer excuses for why I made these comments. My purpose is to acknowledge my mistakes and to apologize for my insensitivity. Although I did not intend to offend anyone, it is now quite obvious that I have done so. I sincerely apologize for having used offensive language and for the hurt that I have caused. I am firmly committed not to use such language in the future.

I want to be part of the solution, not part of the problem. In that spirit, I have instituted an Equal Employment Opportunity Program at the Reds. This program addresses minority hiring problems. Furthermore, I have established a Human Resources Advisory Group, comprised of local African American community leaders, to advise the Reds on community relations and human resources issues. I also have established a scholarship to assist financially needy students at the Cincinnati Academy for Physical Education—a school whose students are predominantly African American. I have scheduled meetings with the NAACP, the National Urban League, and several prominent Jewish organizations to determine what else can be done.

When I purchased the controlling interest shares of the Cincinnati Reds in 1984, it was a decision made with my heart and not my head. I did it because I did not want the oldest franchise in baseball to leave the hometown that I love. I soon realized that, from a financial standpoint, it was not one of my better decisions. The organization was in serious financial distress. The Reds were losing vast sums of money, and attendance was dropping dramatically. I acted quickly to bring in new personnel who would be willing to do things my way. I acknowledge that I was both demanding and impatient. My tough style of management improved the Reds' financial condition, but it also sowed the seeds of this current controversy.

Many of my accusers are disgruntled former employees. For example, I fired Timothy Sabo because of his performance. While I was still providing him with paychecks, he was keeping a secret diary of things he hoped to use in a vengeful lawsuit against me. After bitter litigation, the court dismissed two of his claims and he voluntarily withdrew the others. His allegations are entirely untrue. As for Sharon Jones, I want to stress that I did not make the comments that she has alleged. I have never and would never say anything like that.

In addition to Mr. Sabo and Ms. Jones, some others have made unsubstantiated allegations against me in the media and others have been quick to judge me based on these allegations. For example, Senator Howard Metzenbaum declared me to be "unAmerican" for keeping a swastika arm band in a drawer in my home. Unfortunately, Senator Metzenbaum did not bother to discover that this was memorabilia from World War II that I received as a gift from an employee named Jay Carrigan, a veteran who earned two Purple Hearts and was left disabled as a result of his fight against Nazism. I was proud to accept this gift from a man who risked his life for his country. I resent the suggestion that my acceptance of this gift means that I support Nazism. This is outrageous.

As a woman in this male-dominated "fraternity," I have never been fully accepted as an equal. Now, once again, I feel as though I am being discriminated against. My attorneys advise me that the Commissioner's Office has never disciplined any owner, player, or manager for the type of speech alleged here. Moreover, in those few instances where the Commissioner has punished someone for any kind of speech, the maximum penalty was a $5,000 fine. Thus, the suggestion of some critics that I be suspended, that my management authority be removed, or that I not be permitted full access to Riverfront Stadium is grossly disproportionate and unjust.

Calvin Griffith, the former owner of the Minnesota Twins, made terribly ugly racist remarks, far in excess of anything I said, in a public speech in 1978. In fact, he indicated that a crucial baseball decision—his decision to move his team from Washington to Minnesota—was racially motivated. However, nobody in baseball suspended Mr. Griffith or restricted his management authority. Indeed, he was not even reprimanded. When I read in the papers that a few are suggesting that I be suspended or barred from Riverfront Stadium, I cannot help but think that I am again being singled out because I am not "one of the boys."

I believe that I am good for the Reds, good for Cincinnati, and good for baseball. Many people agree with me. I have received hundreds and hundreds of letters written by people from all across the country who like what I have done with the Reds. They like the fact that we have the lowest ticket prices in the game. They like the fact that we still sell hot dogs for one dollar. They like the fact that I am one of the few owners in Major League Baseball who really spends time talking to fans at the ballpark.

Those fans, particularly the children, are my greatest joy as an owner. I try to make every decision with them in mind. Going to the stadium and visiting with the fans is like visiting with my family. I love the Reds, I love the fans, and I love Cincinnati. I would never deliberately hurt them, and I will work to make them as proud of me as I am of them.

Marge also addressed the Executive Council personally, but not at the start of the meeting. Bennett arrived with partner Tom Schwarz and associate Michael Levy and made a 40-minute oral presentation about why baseball shouldn't go forward with any action against Marge. Marge came in and read a statement, then Kheel questioned her. Meanwhile, the media were out in the hallway digesting the portions of the report Bennett had released, which tried to pick apart the accusations and the accusers.

His attack on Sabo was scathing. Bennett revived the allegations that Sabo had written unauthorized checks to himself and depicted the former controller as a "bitter, desperate man who spent months plotting to sue Mrs. Schott. He even tried to set her up by interfering in a hiring decision in a blatant effort to encourage discriminatory hiring and then blame it on Mrs. Schott." This supposed setup was alleged in a sworn declaration by Reds controller Ernie Brubaker, who was the Reds' internal auditor before replacing Sabo.

"As a result of Mr. Sabo's dismissal, an opening was created in the accounting department," stated Brubaker. "In September 1991, I took some things to Mr. Sabo's house, and he mentioned this opening. He asked me to hire a woman of non-childbearing age, explaining that such an action would help him in his lawsuit. I replied that I would make no such promise, as the position would be filled based on merit."

Sabo says not only is that a lie, Ernie Brubaker came to Sabo's house within a week after Sabo had been fired and told him that

Marge wanted to hire a woman for Brubaker's old job. In fact, Sabo says he brought up this incident long before Brubaker's deposition, pointing to a memo dated August 29, 1991, and written by Sabo's attorney, Stephen Imm, that says, "MUS (Marge) told Ernie Brubaker to hire a woman to replace TAS (Sabo) in EB's (Brubaker) former job." If it is fair to doubt the testimony of the so-called disgruntled former employees, then it is imperative that the testimony of a current employee be viewed with a certain cynicism. Marge intimidates her employees into lying for her publicly and covering up for her, for fear of dismissal. Many of those who now speak openly and candidly about Marge were equally as supportive and defensive of her when they still worked for her.

Still, this was all Bennett and Marge needed to call into question Sabo's testimony and credibility and keep the focus on Marge's slurs and away from her hiring practices. Sabo might not have received the headline splash of Sharon Jones, but his allegation that Marge ordered him not to hire blacks had the most damage potential. Prove that, and Marge was out of baseball—if not in court. With Brubaker and Reds payroll supervisor Gail Robbins also swearing that Sabo plotted the demise of Marge Schott by gathering information in his diary about her—not to mention Bennett's charge that Sabo doctored his notes by scratching out "those players" and writing in "3M niggers" in one diary entry—Bennett clearly acomplished his goal.

Marge's hiring practices were given only minimal attention in baseball's report, anyway. Indeed, this was about Marge's slurs, with Sabo's contention about her hiring saved perhaps for his own continued litigation against her. As for Sharon Jones, Bennett pointed out that nobody had come forward to corroborate her allegation about Marge's slur during the conference call, and he claimed she had contradicted herself by first saying Marge used the term "black" and later saying "nigger" and by changing the year from 1988 to June or July of 1987. Bennett discounted the allegations of Bill Bergesch, Roger Blaemire, and Keith Stichtenoth as "hearsay" from "disgruntled former employees." In the name of fairness and due process, he said baseball owed Marge a full hearing so that she could confront her accusers and he could cross-examine them to establish their credibility.

Bennett argued that baseball had no legal authority to restrict Marge's "management authority or ownership rights—including her right of access to Riverfront Stadium." This was his big push to flex his legal biceps to convince baseball it had no power to suspend Marge Schott. He pointed to Rule 21 of the Major League Agreement, which gives the commissioner—or the Executive Council when the game is between commissioners—disciplinary power over "acts, transactions, practices, or conduct" not considered in the "best interests of baseball." Nothing specifically is said about speech. "It is clear from a long line of Supreme Court cases," Bennett wrote, "that 'speech' is very different from 'conduct.'" He also claimed that free speech was protected by the Ohio Constitution, even in the case of a voluntary association such as baseball.

But baseball had been fining players and managers for years for comments it felt were detrimental to the game. As Bennett saw it, baseball got away with this because nobody ever challenged it in court. Besides, he claimed it would be "unfair and indeed discriminatory" if Marge were suspended for her comments when Calvin Griffith had made a public speech stating he moved the Washington Senators to Minnesota because "you only had 15,000 blacks here" and "because you've got good, hard-working white people." Bennett claimed that Griffith wasn't even reprimanded, although former commissioner Bowie Kuhn claimed in his book *Hardball* that he did reprimand Griffith.

"The most severe sanction of which we are aware that a commissioner has ever imposed for *any* type of offensive or embarrassing remarks was a $5,000 fine," Bennett wrote. "In the face of charges against Major League Baseball as a whole, to hold the only woman owner in Major League Baseball to a different standard than others have been held to in their private conversations and then impose an unprecedented sanction would be patently unjust and against the law."

Although Bennett made some good points, there also was a lot of smoke. Using Calvin Griffith was a good example, but if baseball had to live by all the verdicts it rendered or didn't render from past generations, it would still allow owners to exclude blacks from the playing field; the game has evolved through the years and the commissioners.

There were some pretty forceful declarations on behalf of Mrs. Schott. Besides those of Robbins and Brubaker to discredit Sabo, George Verkamp (Marge's brother-in-law and general manager at Schott Buick) tried to discredit George Brinkman by saying he was present during Marge's conversations with Brinkman and that he heard none of the alleged slurs. Alfred Hoffman, Jr., CEO of a real-estate development company in Plant City, stated in his declaration that Marge had lent her "name and support" to local charity events for underprivileged children in the Florida city and he had never heard her slur blacks or Jews. Bennett included a letter Hoffman had sent to two newspapers and to Selig, on Marge's behalf, that backed Bennett's claim that players used slurs—if she were punished, they should be, too.

"I have to say that the only derogatory language I heard her use in private was only against *individuals* in baseball, not against a race," Hoffman wrote. "More specifically, her sharp tongue and quick wit was actually directed to white men in baseball *more* than to certain black ballplayers. I have also been in the private company of some of the same individuals who were in conflict with her, and more than once I heard the words 'bitch' and 'cunt' used to describe her—by a black ballplayer as *well* as whites. If baseball is to purge itself of prejudiced people, it shouldn't focus only on Marge Schott or white versus black, or Jew versus Gentile. Let's throw in the gender issue, too. So I say, 'Let *he* who is without guilt cast the first stone.'"

Hoffman said we shouldn't lose track of what was good about Marge Schott, such as her work with kids and the emphasis she placed on the fans by keeping ticket prices down, signing autographs, and talking to them at the games. "And who else has better represented women in a traditionally man's field than Marge Schott in baseball? The only other women in team sports seem to be the women who are chasing players, who are eager to seed them in return for fun, AIDS, or paternity suits."

Among those offering declarations on Marge's behalf were Reds player Bip Roberts, Reds general manager Jim Bowden, and Reds manager Tony Perez. Some of the people giving declarations, including Roberts, claimed they heard Marge use insensitive terms toward ethnic groups. Roberts also said Marge treated all people equally and shouldn't be punished when others guilty of similar actions aren't. "I have heard numerous people of various ethnic and racial groups use derogatory language about others," said Roberts. "In baseball, subtle racism—and sometimes not-so-subtle racism—exists. For that reason, I do not believe that it is fair for Mrs. Schott to be singled out for punishment."

Perhaps as telling as anything in the declarations was what wasn't in them. Cal Levy, for example, was interviewed for more than an hour by one of Bennett's associates, yet there was nothing from him. And Joyce Pfarr, Marge's chief administrative assistant at the Reds, gave a declaration but didn't address Marge's slurs as a number of others had. The closest she came was to skim the issue.

"I have personally witnessed countless occasions on which Mrs. Schott has treated African Americans with affection," stated Pfarr. "Furthermore, at virtually every Reds home game she spends hours talking with fans and signing autographs. She treats every fan with respect and affection, without regard to race or religion. All that matters to Mrs. Schott is that they are Reds fans. In the eight years I have worked for Mrs. Schott, I have never seen Mrs. Schott discriminate in employment, including her hiring, firing, and promotion decisions, on the basis of race or religion. Nor have I ever heard Mrs. Schott tell anyone in the Reds organization that they should not hire anyone of a particular race or religion."

By this point, however, both sides agreed Marge Schott had used slurs, although they disagreed on the frequency. Now baseball had to decide on a suitable penalty, while Marge continued her cries of discrimination against a woman in a man's world. Nobody questioned that she was a minority among the owners of Major League Baseball; far more debatable was how often that worked against her.

"She often used to complain about that," said Peter Ueberroth, adding he felt she was doing that somewhat in humor. "I didn't see any of that. I think, in most cases, she could hold her own."

"She said that in almost every conversation one had with her—how the Old Boys didn't accept her and how she didn't feel like she was part of the group,'" said Steve Greenberg. "I don't think anything that has happened to the Cincinnati Reds or to Marge Schott has had anything to do with her sex. I imagine that it's somewhat awkward being one of the only women in that setting. On the other hand, Jackie Autry seems to handle it with a certain amount of equanimity. On one level, Marge handled it very well; on another level, she complained a great deal about being discriminated against, and I always wondered whether that complaint wasn't, in fact, one of her best weapons. It did tend to catch people somewhat off-guard and put them on the defensive. By her demeanor, one never sensed she was intimidated."

Greenberg remembers that she used her favorite refrain when she wanted to send the Reds to Gifu, Cincinnati's sister city in Japan for an exhibition game. Greenberg explained to her that she couldn't unilaterally send the team to Japan because the Reds and the other 25 clubs had granted Major League Baseball International Partners all of the major leagues' international rights. This was an organized and systematic way to keep teams from haphazardly making deals to play all over the world and a mild form of revenue-sharing among all of the clubs. But Marge didn't understand that and had forgotten signing such an agreement. Instead of dealing with MLB International, she decided to try working through Greenberg; and when that didn't work, she tried working through Fay Vincent, who concurred with his deputy commissioner. Marge was not happy and fell back on her favorite excuse.

"Marge certainly was one who would look for extraneous reasons that things weren't going her way," said Greenberg. "I think this was another case where she felt the Old Boys were beating up on her."

Then there was the time CBS wanted to change the starting time for a Saturday Reds game by a few hours, which CBS contractually had the right to do. The network called baseball's broadcast department to get the change. When Marge found out about it, she became angry, saying that fans drove in from hundreds of miles away to see these games, and how was she going to be able to get word to all of them in time? No, Marge said, she wasn't going to allow it. Greenberg knew Marge meant well and had the fans' best interests in mind, but it was a moot point because CBS was entitled to do it. She had no choice but to follow. It took Greenberg two or three phone calls to Marge before she finally accepted the situation. Those were the types of situations in which Greenberg would normally spend more time with Marge than with most owners and in which he would inevitably be hit with her "woman in a man's world" refrain.

"There was hardly a conversation in which that didn't come up," said Greenberg. "I came to view it almost as a knee-jerk reaction, as part of her vernacular. There are some people you talk to where you can't have a conversation without them asking how the weather is where you are. It was one of those things."

Greenberg would guess that there probably were some times when being a woman and being as outspoken as she was probably didn't sit too well with the other owners. But he figured that with roughly two dozen white males in the 50-75 age bracket, there were bound to be views at both ends of the spectrum. Still, Greenberg never saw any evidence of sexism. "Listen," he said, "you don't have to use sex as an excuse to put Marge in a different category. She does have certain eccentricities that transcend her sex."

On the other hand, Greenberg applauds her unique style of interacting with the fans in the stands. And Marge always listed Ueberroth among her biggest supporters, often quoting him during his reign as lauding her for doing a good job and helping to make the Reds financially vibrant. "I don't know that I told her she was doing a good job," said Ueberroth. "But I try not to be negative."

Ueberroth does give her credit for winning a world championship. He says she's not as bad as the media portrayed her—that she's been painted as more of a caricature of herself than the Marge Schott he knew. He realized she wasn't perfect, but also not the pariah she was made out to be. "I think she's basically a well-meaning person with a good heart who was often poorly advised," he said, "and *evidently* has old-fashioned and incorrect ideas about a lot of different people in society."

He was talking about the slurs, the racial and ethnic terms that Ueberroth insists he did not know of when he was commissioner and so never discussed with her. In line with that, he says he knows nothing about Sharon Jones' alleged conference call, that nobody ever addressed that with him. Ueberroth refuses to discuss the issue of Marge's drinking, but former Reds general manager Murray Cook says Ueberroth once told him and a group of others that he had addressed the issue with Marge. Fay Vincent says he never talked to Marge about slurs during his tenure, nor about her alcohol consumption — although he did mention her drinking in a national-television interview with Bob Costas. "I would say to you that, without limiting it strictly to

Marge Schott, we have owners who have severe alcohol problems that cause aberrant behavior," the former commissioner
told Costas. Greenberg says he and National League president
Bill White would talk to Vincent about the problems of dealing
with the general issue of owners and alcohol. When do you step
in? Whose jurisdiction is it? What can you do? With Marge
specifically and her drinking, it was decided that the league
should handle it. "There was an attempt within the National
League to broach the subject," Greenberg said, "with no success."

The commissioner's office heard of other incidents with
Marge. Her frugality, for one: The infamous leftover doughnuts
sale to her employees made it all the way to New York. And the
problems between her and her limited partners were pretty
common knowledge, prompting the commissioner's office to
step in from time to time; but limited partners from other teams
would complain about their general partner, too. The
commissioner's office did intervene when Marge tried to keep
Reds visiting clubhouse man Roger Wilson from taking a job at
about double the salary with Pittsburgh, but the commissioner's
office felt powerless to act against Marge's embarrassing record
of minority hiring.

Marge's new influx of African American employees and
minority programs proved to be one positive by-product of her
scandal, and some of the Cincinnati community leaders were
eager to take at least partial credit for that. It was wishful if not
self-serving thinking, but an open dialogue certainly meant the
possibility of future advances in community relations. For the
time being, however, Bennett saw the coalition as a vehicle to
neutralize some of the criticism against Marge and to show her
willingness to work with city leaders to make positive changes—
and to let baseball see that the city leaders didn't require Marge
to be lynched. The coalition was generally trying to stay out of the
conflict between baseball and Marge, looking to transcend the
current owner of the Reds and set up programs with the team that
would carry on even if Marge didn't.

Bennett sat in for Marge in the second and third meetings
with the coalition, in the second one basically getting caught up
on the issues presented to Marge at the first meeting. The third
meeting was held three days after Marge's powwow with the

Executive Council, and Bennett tried to use the confab to elicit support for his claim that suspending Marge would be a mistake—that in Marge Schott the group had an owner open to their concerns and that it was in their "mutual self-interest" that she remain as general partner. In fact, he said that if the case ended up in court, the coalition would become meaningless because Bennett would have to spend all his time working on her lawsuit and would have no time to deal with the local leaders.

Bennett's biggest obstacle in the coalition was Cincinnati city council member Tyrone Yates, whom Marge kept referring to as *Tony* Yates, the former University of Cincinnati basketball coach. Tyrone Yates is an African American who grew increasingly critical of both Schott and Bennett. After the first meeting of the community leaders—before Bennett—Yates was all but making excuses for Marge, as he was quoted in *The Cincinnati Enquirer* saying, "You have to understand Mrs. Schott. She'll say anything to anyone anytime. She's colorful, and she's valued for that. We just want to make sure it's not racial." Yates later said he was only trying to provide some balance to the issue—that he realized the remarks were typical of people from her generation and he didn't want to see her banished from the game for what seemed to be isolated incidents, that she had apologized for her past insensitivities and now seemed intent on showing some progress on minority issues in the future. If nothing else, Yates was guilty of reacting too quickly without knowing the facts. When Sharon Jones' allegations and other evidence of Marge's slurs came out, Yates' support of Marge eroded, and his tone toward her changed so much that there almost wasn't a second meeting.

While so many others in power were ducking the issue, Yates was blasting Marge regularly and getting an abundance of ink and air time every time he did. Bennett decided to cancel the second meeting of the coalition at least partly because of Yates' comments, and Joyce Pfarr of the Reds called Rapp to convey the message. Rapp called Bennett and convinced him to reconsider, and he did. But Yates wasn't just alienating Bennett; other members of the coalition were wearying of him, as well, and some would have rather excluded him. But Bennett preferred to have Yates as part of the coalition, and when the council member threatened to walk out during the two meetings Bennett attended if his views weren't wanted, Bennett encouraged Yates to stay. Bennett preferred to work with Yates so it would appear that even the most critical voices against Marge were being heard and considered. Bennett knew Yates had every right to speak out as he did, but was concerned that Yates had his own political agenda — to act tough so he'd look good to his constituents — that superseded and disrupted the goals of the group. Yates, on the other hand, found Bennett to be transparently attempting to con him into reversing his position or trick the group into turning against Yates and toward Marge. Failing that, Yates says, Bennett knew the group's credibility would be hurt if Yates were excommunicated.

"It's very much like the old adage Lyndon Johnson used to quote," said Yates. "It's much better to have me on the inside of the tent urinating out than on the outside of the tent urinating in."

Yates insists he stood up to Marge not for political reasons but because somebody had to, that if he had to play the bad-cop role it was all right with him because his concerns were legitimate and his opinions sincere. No matter what the motivation, and no matter how inappropriate his initial excuses for Marge seemed, Yates' voice became a necessary and welcome counterbalance in a city that seemed to champion the embattled Reds owner. None of the other politicians was willing to attack this most public of figures who was beginning to look more and more like the town racist. Even Mayor Dwight Tillery, an African American himself, clung to the background. Although Yates was labeled an opportunist, he claims he was only emulating such heroes as Martin Luther King, Jr., and John and Robert Kennedy—standing up for what was right, even if it meant facing abuse in the community and the potential to meet the same fate as his role models.

The councilman received several hundred phone calls and another hundred pieces of mail from as far away as Butte, Montana, most of it negative and calling him everything from an "ape" to a "nigger." He received about five serious death threats (people claiming they would shoot a bullet through his head or get him some other way), and in anticipation of Marge's suspension and as protection for his staff, Yates requested and received police protection at his office for three days. The only time he was nervous came when WLW's Bill Cunningham encouraged his listeners to throw Yates out of office on his "black ass" if Yates continued to press for tough sanctions against Marge. To Cunningham, this was just his typical act and not meant to be harmful—he even apologized later. Only it wasn't funny, and it was potentially dangerous considering the hard feelings Yates was inspiring. Fortunately, nothing happened besides a flurry of phone calls to Yates' office and some anxious moments thanks to one irresponsible radio personality.

Still, Yates didn't back down in his call for Marge to be suspended for three years. More surprising was his refusal to give in on another issue involving the coalition that should have been a point of embarrassment—the exclusion of a group representing Japanese Americans. After all, there were three groups Marge had regularly slurred—the blacks, the Jews, and the Japanese—but only black and Jewish groups were represented in the coalition. When the Japanese American Citizens League (JACL) asked Michael Rapp to be included after the group's first meeting, he recommended it to the rest of the coalition and was voted down. The reasoning was that since the Japanese group hadn't been part of the first meeting, it couldn't join now—that the integrity of the coalition had to be maintained, and that if every group that had now shown interest in joining were admitted the coalition would be too big to function. Patricia Ikeda Carper, who was president-elect of the JACL's Cincinnati chapter, said Rapp was shocked after the coalition unanimously voted him down, and that Rapp told her the rest of the group wanted to know why the JACL hadn't tried to get involved earlier. Actually, it did, only privately.

Bill Yoshino, Midwest director of the JACL, wrote a letter to Marge when her references to "Japs" first became public, asking her for an apology and explaining to her that it was a slur. Marge called Yoshino, apologized if she had offended him, and assured him she was not a racist. She told him that she had made several trips to Japan and admired the Japanese, and he explained to her that she needed to understand the distinction between *Japanese* and Japanese-*Americans*—that people sometimes took out their grudges on Japanese-Americans for the trade problems and other disputes with the Japanese. But Marge didn't get it. Yoshino spent a good 15 or 20 minutes trying to make her understand, and she responded with such comments as, "I respect the prime minister of Japan." Finally, Yoshino gave up. He decided it would be best to explore another avenue, which was when the idea of joining the Cincinnati coalition came up, only to be shot down. Yates chastised the Japanese group for trying to handle the situation quietly instead of publicly. "Freedom," Yates said, "is not something you fight for quietly."

In the third meeting between the coalition and the Reds, the second involving Bennett, the city council member from Cincinnati and the attorney from Washington, D.C., clashed again. During the meeting, Bennett said that most people used a racial or ethnic slur at some point during their lives and then focused on his adversary, saying, "I would even wonder if Mr. Yates used the word 'honky.'" Yates waited a few seconds and realized he had to answer or his silence could be mistaken for agreement. He responded, "I could withstand the test of never having called a person such a term." And Yates credits Bennett for apologizing.

Yates took his own shots at Bennett after the meeting, revealing the details of Bennett's strategy toward baseball, which the attorney had shared with the community leaders. Bennett told the coalition what he had already told baseball—that a suspension of Marge could land baseball in court. Bennett also said he knew baseball wanted to take some type of action against Marge, so he was willing to accept a fine and proposed that Marge head a committee to address minority issues industrywide.

Bennett wasn't surprised that Yates leaked all of this information to the media. In fact, he anticipated the possibility and says, "I said nothing in the room on the assumption it wouldn't get out."

With Tyrone Yates around, privacy was impossible. So was the notion of getting unanimous support from the coalition for Bennett's assertion that Marge should not be suspended from baseball. Although some of the members did say she shouldn't be suspended, they also said they did not want to interfere with baseball's decision on whether to penalize her or not. That was a decision that would be handed down at the next meeting of the Executive Council, in Chicago, when Bennett would try to weave a little more Weinberger magic.

— Chapter Sixteen —

Banished—Sort of

Baseball was keeping pretty quiet about when the final word would be handed down on Marge Schott. Doug Danforth of the subcommittee assured everyone that it would happen before baseball spring training, which began February 19. The last thing baseball needed was to have this dragging on into spring training, when the game was supposed to be the focus.

Finally, as Sunday night, January 31, turned into Monday morning, newspaper reports surfaced quoting an unidentified owner as saying that the Executive Council would meet on Wednesday, February 3, in Chicago to announce that it was suspending Marge Schott for one year. Bob Bennett found out about it through a call from a Cincinnati-area newspaper at about 1 a.m. He talked to Bob Kheel at a more reasonable hour to find out what was going on. If baseball had already made up its mind, Bennett would do what he had to do—take it to court. Kheel assured Bennett that no decision had been made, but that the council was indeed going to meet on Wednesday in Chicago. Bennett wanted the meeting changed so as not to give the story any credibility, but that was already set. Bennett also was assured that the Executive Council was willing to work with him on a settlement. So off they went to Chicago.

There had been some discussion about possible sanctions against Marge before Chicago, but it was mostly an exchange of information. The talks intensified Tuesday night at the O'Hare airport hotel, when Bennett and colleagues Tom Schwarz and Michael Levy met with Kheel and Bob Dupuy, a legal advisor for Bud Selig and baseball. They talked for a couple of hours about the issues important to both sides. Kheel and Dupuy wanted to confer privately, so Bennett's team went to dinner before talks resumed from 11:30 p.m. to 12:15 a.m. Both sides agreed it was worth continuing the negotiations, so they reconvened in the morning.

That's when Bennett was told the matter would be decided that day.

No matter what.

Dupuy declared that if an agreement was not reached, baseball was going to issue a decision and resolve the matter, anyway. Bennett said that if baseball had already made up its mind, why waste time? He was prepared to take legal action and even had brought the 53-page lawsuit he was ready to file. Kheel and Dupuy assured him that no decision had been made and that continued negotiation made sense. So the three attorneys spent the day trying to work out an agreement that would be suitable to Marge and to the Executive Council and appropriate for the severity of her racial and ethnic slurs. Bennett told the group of lawyers that he knew why baseball decided to stay away from Marge's hiring practices—because the other owners didn't want their own practices questioned. And if the case went to court, Bennett was ready to pry into the hiring practices—and the comments—of other owners, something he had avoided in his written response to baseball's report on Marge. Baseball didn't want to go to court with Bennett, but also didn't want to bend on suspending Marge as part of her sanctions. The rest of her penalty wasn't much of an issue. Bennett had no problem accepting multicultural training for Marge and was more than willing to accept the $25,000 maximum fine for an individual—because Marge was prepared to accept the $250,000 maximum fine for a club. Baseball believed that Marge was acting as an individual and should be responsible for paying the fine herself; had the club been fined, the partnership would have had to pay.

The suspension was going to take some dealing. Knowing that baseball was intractable on the issue of there being some type of a ban, Bennett set out to limit the suspension and take the substance out of it. He eased his insistence that there be no ban at all and offered that Marge would sit out for one month, then went up to two. Baseball started at one year and eventually came down to essentially eight months with four months off for good behavior. Agreed. But two provisions were paramount to Bennett:

1) *Marge's status as general partner must be protected.* This was the main concern of Bennett and Marge because they knew some of her limited partners were ready to try to take the team away from her in court if she were stripped of her responsibilities as general partner. In fact, that very morning, Bennett read in the newspaper of the limited partners' plans to do just that. That's why it also was important that Marge be allowed to pick the person who would run the club in her absence, someone she could trust and not a limited partner. Baseball understood and was willing to comply. Once baseball decided one year was appropriate, it didn't want to do anything to precipitate legal action by the partners. Baseball also had no problem with her naming new general manager Jim Bowden to run the day-to-day operations of the team during her absence. Had the suspension been longer, baseball might have questioned Bowden's selection, but not for an eight-month period — and especially not for this one. Baseball and Bennett agreed to a March 1 start for the suspension so Marge could get her affairs in order; by then, all the major financial decisions would have been made for the 1993 season.

2. *Marge must be allowed to continue attending games.* This was an important issue to Marge, whose identity had become so linked to the Reds over the past eight seasons.

Kheel left the room to talk to the Executive Council, came back, and said he had good news and bad news. The good news was that Marge could go to all of the games. The bad news was that the Executive Council was going to issue a "decision" on the affair to the media. Bennett told Kheel that wasn't fair—that it was inconsistent with, and violated the spirit of, their negotiation, the whole purpose of which was to *avoid* a decision being issued. Baseball had wanted Bennett not to comment publicly on the negotiations and sanctions if they could work out a deal for Marge. Now Bennett said that was impossible—that if baseball issued a written statement of its views, he'd respond. Bennett also asked that baseball's "decision" be changed to an "opinion." When Bud Selig came into Kheel's suite and was told Bennett's reaction, Selig turned to Bennett and said, "You're hairsplitting with me." Bennett replied, "The two lawyers never agreed to anything like this." It was a minor point, and Selig gave in.

With Selig in the room, Bennett made another attempt to save his client from punishment by baseball. "Why don't you go out there and say, 'We believe in the First Amendment, and though we may deplore the comments attributed to Marge Schott, let's take some more positive steps than trying to punish someone for her private free speech. Let's form a committee to oversee minority issues industrywide and put her in charge. It's in the best interests of baseball to keep her as owner of the Cincinnati Reds.'" But it was too late for any of that now.

With all of the principals of the agreement reached, Bennett was handed the "opinion" signed by all the members of the Executive Council, a number of whom had already left. Bennett acted upset, saying it looked like baseball was trying to do an end run around him. Still, Bennett agreed to the major points that had been negotiated and been put on paper, but said he was not going to sign anything prepared just minutes before a press conference. He wanted more time. Selig tried to hurry him up, seeming concerned that the media had been waiting for hours and had seen some of the owners already leave. Bennett said he didn't like being rushed, that this was too important, and he hadn't even talked to Marge yet to see what she thought of the agreement. Bennett told Selig he would be willing to write out the essential points agreed upon by both sides during the negotiations, and he jotted down about half a dozen points on a yellow piece of paper. For instance, even though Marge wasn't allowed to communicate with her club about its normal financial or business dealings, Bennett wanted to make certain she could talk to her employees on a social basis—say, if she wanted to have Jim Bowden over to her house for dinner or a party. Bennett also wanted the wording changed concerning Marge's time off for good behavior. He wanted it made clear that she *would* be reinstated after eight months if she complied with the sanctions, not that she would be *eligible to apply* for reinstatement after eight months.

Bennett handed Selig the paper, and Selig left the room with Kheel and Dupuy. They returned a half-hour later and agreed to all of Bennett's provisions. Selig went to the meeting room of the Executive Council, and Bennett waited outside. When Selig came out, Bennett asked, "Where is he going?" and was told, "To the press conference." Bennett followed him and asked Selig about the yellow paper with the provisions on it.

"Are you going to read it?" Bennett asked.

"Here, you read it," Selig said.

And Selig gave Bennett the paper and headed for the media, who had been waiting eight hours. There was no gag order on Bennett, so when Selig stepped in front of the media, Bennett's response would be predicated on Selig's approach.

At the press conference, Selig read the statement prepared by the Executive Council as baseball employees passed out the more detailed "opinion" of the Executive Council. Selig's statement offers a little background, then gets to the essence of the matter:

> The final report of the subcommittee contains substantial and convincing evidence that, while serving as the principal owner of the Reds baseball club, Mrs. Schott commonly used language that is racially and ethnically insensitive, offensive, and intolerable. . . . We do want to say that Mrs. Schott's remarks reflect the most base and demeaning type of racial and ethnic stereotyping—indicating an insensitivity that cannot be accepted or tolerated by anyone in baseball.
>
> It should be noted that Mrs. Schott, in her submission to the subcommittee of the Executive Council, has apologized and has recognized that this type of language is insensitive and offensive and that Mrs. Schott has been meeting with diverse members of the Cincinnati community on these issues. We are also mindful that Mrs. Schott and the Cincinnati Reds ball club have done substantial community service for the City of Cincinnati. Nevertheless, we find, based on considerable evidence, that Mrs. Schott's practice of using language that is racially and ethnically offensive has brought substantial disrepute and embarrassment to the game—and it is not in the best interest of baseball. There should be no question that the type of language commonly used by Mrs. Schott is offensive and unacceptable. There is simply no place for this in Major League Baseball.
>
> Accordingly, and pursuant to the authority granted the Executive Council under the Major League Agreement and Major League Rules, we unanimously impose the following sanctions on Mrs. Schott:
>
> 1. Commencing on March 1, 1993, and for a period of one year, Mrs. Schott shall be suspended from baseball. In the event

Mrs. Schott complies with the terms of this decision and the order of implementation, she will be entitled to reinstatement on November 1, 1993, after which date, if reinstatement is granted, until February 28, 1994, she will be on probation.

2. Mrs. Schott is fined $25,000, the maximum fine permitted of an individual under the Major League Agreement.

3. During 1993, Mrs. Schott is directed to attend and complete multicultural training programs.

4. Mrs. Schott is reprimanded and censured in the strongest terms for her use of racially and ethnically insensitive language and sternly warned not to engage in such conduct in the future.

It might not have been as strong or as long a penalty as some had pushed for, especially when the scandal first broke, but at least baseball had succeeded in suspending her without having to go to court. Selig said he could not announce any details of the suspension right then, but that it would be consistent with past suspensions. Selig also insisted that baseball did not kowtow in the fear of a lawsuit or to any outside parties—that this was a decision made by the Executive Council and imposed upon Mrs. Schott, who had agreed to accept it.

And then came Bob Bennett.

Had Selig simply told the press conference that this was the agreement reached by both sides, Bennett wouldn't have said anything. Instead, Bennett immediately took a shot at Selig.

"We worked well past midnight in negotiating this *nonnegotiated* and *imposed* agreement," Bennett announced, dripping sarcasm.

Perhaps it was a matter of semantics. Baseball looked at the decision of the Executive Council as *imposed*, with the details and the language of the suspension being *negotiated*. Certainly, Selig's language made the Executive Council sound tough—much tougher than it really was—but it was not worth the risk of angering Bennett. He proceeded to announce the details that proved the suspension was more style than substance:

• General manager Jim Bowden would run the day-to-day operations of the team while Marge was exiled from the Reds' offices.

• Marge still could attend games at Riverfront Stadium but must watch from her executive suite instead of her familiar seat alongside the dugout, and she would not be allowed on the field.

- Nothing in the sanctions would affect Marge's standing as the general partner of the Cincinnati Reds.

Bennett said that he and Marge thought baseball was wrong to suspend her and that she would win a lawsuit if one were filed, but she decided in the interests of herself, her team, and baseball not to do it. And why would she? Baseball got its suspension, but Marge got almost everything else. She kept her team, had her own man running it, got the proper time to put all of the major financial affairs in order, and still could go to the games. In fact, when the final agreement was worked out, Marge was allowed to move from the executive suite beginning May 1 to any area of the stadium where the public was permitted (but not the clubhouse, offices, field-level owners' box or its vicinity, press box, or spring-training facility). She also was allowed to handle "material and extraordinary financial or business affairs," such as TV and radio contract negotiations, advertising and concessions talks, governmental negotiations or agreements, banking and investment decisions, and nonplayer deals in excess of $500,000.

Baseball thought this was a fair and just punishment for the crime and for the criminal. For another owner, the sanctions would seem minimal if not trivial—at least much more minimal and trivial. But for Marge Schott, taking away her ability to schmooze with the players, to sign the checks, to be *Marge*, did carry some impact. The Executive Council had gone back and forth about what was fair, 10 members varying in opinion from strict to lenient. They wanted to send a strong message that her behavior was intolerable, but they didn't want to destroy the stability of the club and, honestly, they were afraid for her health. They worried about the effect of separating her for a long period of time from a team that was such an integral part of her life.

"There was a lot of pretty intelligent discussion about the First Amendment," said deputy commissioner Steve Greenberg. "I think that what was lost on some people is that the First Amendment had absolutely no application in this process because the First Amendment only protects against governmental restriction of speech. There was no governmental action here. This was a private association taking action.

"Basically, the concerns were what you'd expect them to be— concerns for Marge on a human level, concerns about a woman who loves her team and has relatively few things in her life which appear to give her great pleasure. On a personal level, how is Marge Schott going to function for a period of a year or whatever with the loss of this great source of joy? I think it's great that people talked about that. I'm not cold-hearted. I think that was quite properly a subject of discussion. On the other hand, that's only one factor, the compassion factor. Ultimately, one has to step back and look at baseball's interest, which is, after all, what this process is all about—make a judgment in terms of what the conduct was and what it wasn't, analyze the conflicting testimony and evidence and balance things. I think that's what the council attempted to do—balance the compassion on the one hand for a woman who is on one level almost pathetic and the loss of her enjoyment of the club against the injury to baseball and the message to the public that needed to be sent in terms of baseball's standards and what it will tolerate and what it won't tolerate."

Greenberg, who had been so concerned with baseball's handling of this situation at the beginning, who showed such concern for the overall direction of baseball that he left office in 1993, said he didn't have any problem with baseball's verdict.

"In the final analysis, although it was a little slow in the beginning, Bud Selig clearly came around to what I think was the appropriate position with respect to this issue—he clearly was the driving force behind the level of discipline that we have imposed," Greenberg said. "And he ultimately dismissed the threat of a lawsuit as a factor that should be taken into consideration. I think that, ultimately, Bud did a decent job coalescing the council behind an acceptable level of discipline. Anytime you have a committee dealing with an issue like this, by definition, you're going to get a watered-down result, especially a committee of 10 people, because you want to have a unanimous result. By definition, there will be those who will be more dovish on the issue. If you hear those people out and try to coalesce them into a unanimous decision, you're going to get a watered-down result. I think that's what happened here. And it goes to the problem, if you will, of having a sport—let alone baseball—operate without a commissioner. There is no doubt in my mind that the Schott affair would have been handled somewhat differently, certainly more expeditiously and, I think, with a more positive spin for baseball had Fay Vincent or any commissioner handled it."

Peter Ueberroth agrees. He believes the discipline handed down to Marge Schott was proper and just—with one exception.

"It took much, much, much too long and therefore was blatantly unfair to her," Ueberroth said. "She sat out there and was a sitting duck for the media for month after month after month on something that should have been no more than a week long."

Ueberroth says that if he had been commissioner and had heard Marge was using racial slurs, he would have heard it only once because then he would have effectively stopped it. "It would have entailed some discussions and a quiet, in-person hearing to review the facts," he said, "and then action." Ueberroth says his action wouldn't have been too different from the one that was taken in the end. He says there would have been some differences, but he wasn't privy to all of the facts in the case and doesn't want to second-guess the decision that was made.

However, under Ueberroth's strategy, a one-week process would have precluded a full-fledged investigation.

"Of what?" Ueberroth said.

Of Tim Sabo's allegations that Marge ordered him not to hire blacks. In the end, baseball was forced to leave that one alone, and even Sabo could understand its reasoning. He stood by what he said, as emphatically as ever, but conceded that Bennett's ability to find witnesses to counter his claims left baseball having to deal with what was out there and unopposed—Marge's racial and ethnic slurs. The Executive Council neither backed nor refuted Sabo's allegations, concluding, "There is conflicting evidence about the circumstances of hiring decisions, and the Executive Council notes that the Cincinnati Reds have recently increased the number of minority management employees and now currently employ an Hispanic manager [Tony Perez] and two minority employees in its front office. The Executive Council is also aware of Mrs. Schott's meetings with diverse members of the Cincinnati community on these issues and urges that they continue. In light of these actions, the Executive Council is limiting its decision to the issue of the use of ethnically and racially insensitive remarks."

As for Marge's other chief accuser, Sharon Jones, baseball complimented her while at the same time contradicting her—in other words, baseball played diplomat. "In the case of Ms.

Sharon Jones, the Executive Council acknowledges her sincerity and earnestness. While the Council has found no records of any ownership conference calls during June/July 1987, the period during which Ms. Jones states that a telephone conversation took place, the Executive Council notes that two senior officials of the Oakland Athletics vividly recall Ms. Jones being concerned in the summer of 1987 about the contents of a one-on-one conversation with Mrs. Schott." Jones was hardly placated. She blistered the Executive Council for covering up for the owners and said it was not a one-on-one conversation because there would have been no reason for her and Marge to have one.

"What are they pumping into the stadium elevators other than music?" Jones said. "I think they should put a sign at all the stadiums that says, 'Racist-Free Zone.'"

As for Jesse Jackson, he released a statement immediately after the verdict that supported Major League Baseball's decision. "Twenty-seven other white owners of Major League Baseball teams have agreed that Marge Schott's words and behavior were so embarrassing, so unacceptable, and such a threat to the interests of baseball that they had to do something," said Jackson. "Today they took responsible steps to reprimand and rehabilitate her." But five days later, Jackson ripped baseball's verdict as bending to the threat of a lawsuit.

"It's clear that the attorney Bennett was able to intimidate the owners and demand that they not create a standard for her that they couldn't live by," he said. "He was going to expose all the parties on Sharon Jones' telephone call, I'm convinced of that. He was going to question their authority to question her speech against their speech patterns. And if it comes to that, the whole ownership facade could have unraveled. She was sustained, not suspended. Her air-conditioned box is not a hotbox—she's overseeing all things. She has shifted seats in the stadium and not around the boardroom table. Nothing has fundamentally changed, because the owners don't have the moral authority to issue a tough remedy."

The about-face made sense if Jackson hadn't known the details of the suspension when he made his initial statement, but he said that's not the case. He found no inconsistency here, saying that the initial statement was made knowing that nothing could be done about baseball's decision at the time. Still, Jackson was consistent in arguing that Marge Schott should not be used as a martyr or a scapegoat, and he continued fighting to promote minority opportunities in baseball. He organized an Opening Day demonstration outside Oriole Park at Camden Yards in Baltimore to protest the sport's lack of direction and commitment to affirmative action. With Marge gone, however, so was much of the interest in the issue. Jackson was lightning without a lightning rod.

But Marge was doing her part to keep the controversy alive. A week after she received her penalty, she was at it again, saying things she shouldn't say.

Only this time, America was there to see it.

Chapter Seventeen

From Primetime to Perez

Bob Bennett advised Marge Schott not to appear on ABC-TV's "Primetime Live" with Diane Sawyer. But she wouldn't listen. She allowed the reporter and the camera into her home for what could have been the best thing she'd ever done. She could have elicited the sympathy and support of a nation if she had shown that she was truly sorry and asked forgiveness for her slurs, if she'd said she had been through a living hell and wanted to thank the people who were behind her, if she'd insisted she had learned from her mistakes and vowed to be a leader in the fight for minority opportunities.

Instead, she showed the nation who she really was.

It was a sobering interview for anyone who thought Marge was the victim of a "witch hunt," as she put it. After issuing all of those supposedly sincere apologies for her insensitive language, she suddenly was defiant and all but claiming innocence. She said she couldn't remember saying these slurs against Jewish people, and she said everyone has used the word "nigger."

"I'm sure you have, Diane, too, right?" said Marge.

"No."

"Never?"

"No."

Marge also said of the swastika, "It's not a symbol of evil to me. I hate to think that somebody died wearing it." And Marge claimed it's no tougher to be black in America than white, downplaying the existence of racism in the world by saying, "I think sometimes it's created by the press, that it really isn't there." The only sad side came when a teary-eyed Marge said she was hurt that none of the other owners had called her since the suspension was announced to tell her to hang in there—but the sadness came from Marge's failing to see why they wouldn't be supportive of her. Or even what she had done wrong.

She just didn't get it. It was a theme that became painfully obvious to anyone who watched the scandal unfold, and this was a chance for the country to see for itself. Throughout Cincinnati the next day, the media were filled with callers and commentators advising Marge to just keep her mouth shut, saying she should never have agreed to the Diane Sawyer interview. But if Marge had declined, America would have missed the truth and perhaps the point—that the world wasn't out to get her, but that she just didn't get the world. To those who didn't know her, who wanted to believe her and believe in her, it must have been uncomfortable. You couldn't watch that one 20-minute segment and assume that Marge was a victim. Instead, you wanted to shake her and wake her up from her decades of social hibernation.

She might never change.

She might never understand the commotion.

Or the suspension.

"It hurt her a lot," said her friend, Mary Clair Torbeck. "Once she apologized, once she agreed to hire more minorities, it should have ended. She felt, 'OK, I've done it, I'm sorry, why can't we end it right there? What more do they want, and what more can I do?'"

Marge's beliefs are as deep as her denial. She is oblivious to what she has done, to the hurt she has inflicted and to the hate she spreads. She is a bigot—of course she is. A bigot doesn't have to walk around in a sheet and doesn't have to call every African American a "nigger" to be a bigot, just as an alcoholic doesn't have to walk around with a flask and be drunk all the time to be an alcoholic. Just because she hugs and even dotes on some of "the good blacks" who work for her doesn't make her free-thinking and open-minded—it just shows that she is more progressive than some of those who shared her plantation-owner mentality during the era of slavery. Indeed, in another century, Marge Schott might have been lauded for her actions and her attitudes, donating money to such charities as the National

Conference of Christians and Jews and the United Negro College Fund, even hiring Cuban-born Tony Perez to manage her team for 1993. But in the late 20th Century, for someone to be throwing around such terms as "nigger" and "Jew bastard" as freely and easily as she does is indefensible, and for her to be doing it while making hiring decisions as the very public owner of the very public Cincinnati Reds is appalling.

"A lot of people have asked me my impressions of whether she wasn't let off with a ridiculously light sentence, and I think you have to have a broader perspective," said Branch Rickey III, the grandson of the man who integrated baseball. "Marge Schott will go to her grave labeled broadly throughout the United States as a racist. And many people seem to regard her as a buffoon. That's a terrible thing to have attached to your name and reputation."

But she doesn't realize that. She may have convinced herself that she was persecuted by the Old Boys, just as she has talked herself into believing all of the other lies about saving the team for Cincinnati and bringing Pete Rose back to town. She can't see clearly, and the alcohol has certainly dimmed her vision. She won't trust people, particularly men, and she won't let anyone too close to her, even though many have tried. She could be absolutely beloved if she'd give people a chance. For all the money she has, she won't let herself enjoy it, and she pushes her misery onto everyone else, especially her employees. If she ever turned them loose and let them do their jobs, she could make them happy and make even more money than she has. The Cincinnati Reds have made an estimated $75 million to $100 million during her eight years and could have made far more if she had just backed off, but she could never do that with "the help." She won't let go. She won't surrender that control.

And because of that she is, quite simply, her own worst enemy.

Being suspended from baseball isn't going to stop that, isn't going to make her look at herself instead of blaming others, isn't going to change her. When the Reds convened for spring training in 1993, she wasn't wanted down in Plant City, but she didn't see that. She didn't understand how awkward it was for the players to be around her, particularly the African American players and specifically Barry Larkin. The team's best player and a hometown product had listened through the off-season to the reports that Marge had referred to his friend Eric Davis and his mentor Dave Parker as "million-dollar niggers," and the diplomatic shortstop had tried to lay as low as he could, saying only that if the allegations were true he would have a tough time playing for her. But then he started hearing from outside sources that she also had called him a "nigger"—and that unnerved him. Suddenly his words in the press became sharper about the owner, prompting Larkin to receive some ugly mail in his own hometown.

"Marge has had a personal relationship with me and my family, and it's been great," Larkin said at the start of spring training. "She had us over to her house when I signed my [$5 million-a-year] contract. And I think she respects me because of the way I go about my business. But now I have to take a step back and say, 'When I'm there with my wife and family, she's going to treat me the way I think I should be treated. But when I leave, am I going to be called a million-dollar nigger?' From some of the prominent friends I have in the Cincinnati area, I've heard that's the case."

Dave Parker understood what he was going through.

But he couldn't understand why he waited so long to face it.

"I love Barry," said Parker. "He's like my son. But he should have addressed this issue when it first happened. For him to be worrying about whether she called him specifically a 'nigger' is pathetic. She called me one and Eric one. That should have offended anyone who's black."

Although Marge's sanctions were rendered before spring training began, Larkin's continuing comments proved that the matter was hardly resolved when the players reported to camp. New general manager Jim Bowden wisely decided to hold a clubhouse meeting to let the players air their views on Marge, so that the team could then move on to the business of baseball. The meeting was beneficial, but the message of Bowden was surprising.

"He went in there backstabbing Marge," said outfielder Tracy Jones, trying for a second stint with the Reds that spring. "For instance, in talking about her racial remarks, he said, 'She's never said it to me, but I'm sure she's said them.' He was trying to act like one of the guys, sucking up to the players and slamming Marge. We'd never heard anything like that. Players were still talking about that two weeks later. One star player came up to me and said if Marge heard that, he'd be fired. I like Marge. For someone to be talking about his owner like that is unfair. He screwed up. He's very arrogant. If Marge was a fly on the wall, he'd be gone in a minute."

Tony Perez corroborates that Bowden made the comment about Marge's slurs in that meeting, but he disagrees with Jones' opinion about it. In fact, he thought Bowden handled it well. "I don't think he was backstabbing her," said Perez. "He tried to make it clear he was with the players. I don't think he did anything wrong. We cleared the air."

Bowden discussed other issues at the meeting, including the impending labor negotiations between the players and the owners. He said he believed the owners should open the books to the players to show how much the teams are really making and help settle the dispute. Jones said, "I thought to myself, you know what, a general manager shouldn't say things like that. He doesn't understand he was only going to keep 25 guys, so 35 were going to be pissed off at him. Someone could really get back at him and tell what he's doing."

Jones would be the first to admit this is sour grapes on his part. After just four at-bats in the spring—and three hits—Bowden demoted him to the minor leagues. Jones was in shock when Bowden first told him. But after thinking it over, Jones came back and confronted Bowden about it, questioning him for bringing more than 60 players into camp, including a number of journeymen like himself vying for the same backup positions, and not telling him he'd be facing such a cut-throat atmosphere. When Bowden told him that was the style that made him successful, Jones said, "Successful? You haven't been at this job one fucking year!" To which Bowden replied, "You're released."

But at least there were no punches thrown. Bowden had already been through that before spring training, when he and Reds publicist Jon Braude got into it. Consider that the normally meek and amiable Braude was one of the few front-office survivors of Marge's entire tenure, because he knew how to avoid trouble. But this problem began when Bowden became enraged that Greg Hoard of Channel 5 had run an ESPN report by Peter Gammons saying Perez was about to be named manager by the 50-some-thousand-dollar-a-year general manager. Understand,

Channel 5 has faced the awkward position of being the Reds' TV station during Marge's tenure, meaning an ever-present anxiety of Marge leaving for another channel. When Tony Kiernan was the general manager, says Hoard, "Any time anything happened with Marge, we were told to be there. We even had to send a reporter to an elephant wedding. And when I reported that Eric Davis was rumored to be traded for Ellis Burks, Kiernan told me, 'You don't realize what you've done. These negotiations are very delicate.'" But now Kiernan was gone and the stranglehold seemed eased, and this was Bowden and not Marge. Still, Bowden tried his own brand of intimidation.

He called Hoard at home at 8:30 the next morning and was "just livid. He said he made four times that much" in salary. Bowden also had called Gammons to protest ESPN's report, and Gammons agreed to broadcast that Bowden disputed his reported salary. Hoard said Channel 5 received no correction at the time of its report. Bowden tried to retaliate by not allowing Channel 5 to televise live from the press conference that day for Perez. Bowden met with resistance from Channel 5—and from Braude, who told Bowden the Reds had no authority to do that. They argued, but eventually Bowden gave in. Later, the two started arguing again, and Bowden began chewing out Braude, who couldn't take it anymore. Braude, who had never hit anyone in his life, smacked Bowden upside the head, and Bowden came back and pushed Braude, ripping his shirt. End of fight.

Jim Bowden rose fast in the organization, but his intensity made him a candidate to either burn out or burn enough bridges to plummet just as quickly. Under Marge, no general manager was bound to last very long, anyway, so he had to enjoy the early honeymoon period. All of the GMs experienced it—Bill Bergesch, Murray Cook, even Bob Quinn. Bowden took full advantage of his, upping the payroll that Marge so consistently lamented to more than $42 million for 1993, the second highest in baseball. His acquisitions of such high-priced players as free-agent pitcher John Smiley and outfielders Kevin Mitchell and Roberto Kelly enlivened the team and interest and proved once again to the city that it had an owner willing to pay for a competitive club. For so many baseball fans, good teams and low ticket prices helped them to forgive or ignore many a sin.

"We've had very healthy arguments about certain issues," Bowden said during spring training. "I believe that the ticket prices should be raised, from a business standpoint. She insists they're gonna be the lowest in the National League. She insists on the $1 hot dog and that the concession people must keep the money down. Obviously, I like more revenues, because with higher revenues it would be easier to have expenditures for the ballplayers, which is consistent with my job. We've had very strong arguments, and when it's all done, whether she agrees with me or disagrees, I think she appreciates the fact that I'm honest and up-front with her."

But neither Bowden nor Larkin nor anybody else was going to talk Marge out of coming to spring training before her suspension commenced. And she did, acting as though there was nothing wrong, hugging the players—even Larkin—while continuing to assert that she was the victim of a witch hunt. And then she was gone, allowing the players to go about the business of baseball, preparing for the first Opening Day when Marge Schott would not be parading on the field—and neither would her dog. Indeed, baseball decided to ban Schottzie (02), too, prompting Bob Bennett to write this response to Bob Kheel:

> I am in receipt of your letter of February 26, 1993, in which you indicate that "it would be inappropriate" to allow Mrs. Schott's dog and the Cincinnati Reds' Club Mascot, Schottzie 02, on the field during the 1993 season. As a dog-lover, I am dismayed and disappointed at baseball's inhumane and insensitive treatment of this fine animal, who is a totally indiscriminate lover of mankind.
>
> Your letter identifies no provision of the Major League Agreement or Rules that gives the Executive Council the power to exclude a Mascot from the field of play on the basis of alleged insensitive remarks by his owner or trainer. Certainly, nothing in the Agreement and Implementing Resolution signed earlier this month by Mr. Selig and Mrs. Schott, which governs the terms of Mrs. Schott's suspension, purports to affect Schottzie 02 in any way.
>
> Moreover, to the best of my knowledge, Schottzie 02 himself has never used racially or ethnically offensive language. If you are aware of any accusers, please bring them to my attention as soon as possible. I would, however, caution the Council to be wary of any claims made by cats. They are notorious

prevaricators, and many of them have exhibited deep envy of Schottzie 02's stature. If the Council's concern is offensive conduct rather than offensive speech, rest assured that at all times Schottzie 02 will be restrained by a leash in the hands of a responsible dogmeister and he will not be given free run of the field.

On a more serious note, Schottzie 02 is the Reds' Official Team Mascot. His predecessor, Schottzie, was officially honored with a photograph and caption in the Reds' 1992 Yearbook, and similar treatment of Schottzie 02 likely will occur in the 1993 Yearbook. Banishing Schottzie 02 from the field of play does not punish Mrs. Schott, who has been punished quite enough already; it punishes the fans of Cincinnati—and especially the children—who look forward to seeing Schottzie 02 at the games. If the fans in Montreal can have their Youppi, the fans in Philadelphia can have their Phanatic, and the fans in Miami can have their as-yet-unnamed fuzzy fish, then the fans in Cincinnati should not be deprived of their lovable Schottzie 02.

Moreover, any restraint on Schottzie 02's presence at Riverfront Stadium as the Official Team Mascot of the Reds would constitute an unconscionable restraint of trade. By what right should other baseball owners—the Reds' competitors— be allowed to interfere in one of the Reds' most important and successful marketing tools? Surely the Council does not seek to eliminate from Riverfront Stadium anything that might remind the fans that Mrs. Schott—who is still the General Partner and can attend all the games—owns the Club. Will you next try to prohibit the Club from wearing the new uniforms she helped design? Plainly, there is nothing inherently offensive about Schottzie 02, who carries with him none of the negative aspects of Chief Noc-a-homa or the tomahawk chop. Nor is he even remotely as troublesome as the old Oakland Athletics' mule, Charlie O., who rumor has it repeatedly made quite an ass of himself.

Schottzie 02 is not a symbol. He is a dog. To turn him into a pariah for matters that occurred outside of both his ken and his kennel would be grossly unfair. Is the Council trying to take all the fun out of baseball in Cincinnati? I am sure that Seattle's Moose, St. Louis' Fred Bird, and Pittsburgh's Parrot would agree with me that team mascots are an important part of baseball's success. For the fans' sake, let Schottzie 02 on the field and let's play ball.

But come Opening Day, the dog and the dog owner were not allowed on the field. Marge was at Riverfront Stadium in her own personal doghouse, the executive suite, where she decided who would enter and who wouldn't. Limited partner and long-time adversary Carl Kroch tried to enter and was denied access, even though it was the owners' box. "It does not belong to Marge Schott, but they had a guard outside of it with a list, and I wasn't on the list," he said. In Marge's familiar front-row box seat, there sat a black ribbon and a bouquet of flowers, and Marge's face was everywhere, thanks to a local radio station that passed out hundreds of fans with her smiling visage on one side. One patron displayed a banner before the game reading, "Marge of Arc," but the sign police removed that vestige of free speech early in the game. And Marge being Marge, she tried to circumvent baseball's banishment by videotaping a 15-second message—before her suspension, the Reds claimed—that was shown on the scoreboard at Riverfront on Opening Day, Marge proclaiming to the fans, "I love you, I miss you," as the crowd cheered.

Marge stayed in her executive suite until more than an hour after the game ended, finally leaving amid a circle of security types. As she headed into the elevator, Marge Schott was asked for her final thoughts.

"Woof, woof," she said.

Major League Baseball would have a few more words on Marge's Opening Day antics, however. The Executive Council wasn't pleased by her nose-thumbing toward its penalty with the videotaped message to the fans, but the Reds assured baseball's ruling body that it wouldn't happen again, and the matter was settled. That one, at least.

Come May, Marge was allowed to leave the private box and go back into the stands, although not in her trademark front-row seat alongside the back of the dugout. Instead, she moved two aisles to the right so that she was in the first row behind the dugout—as if daring baseball to do something to her, to stop her from making her suspension agreement look even more like a joke.

Yet, being off the field and out of the offices was getting to her. In early May, she told Marty York of *The Toronto Globe and Mail*, "The skin on both my legs has opened up, and they're fully wrapped. I get blue patches on my arms, too. I've seen four doctors, and they think it's nerve-related." She said she missed being around the team and figured the team missed her, too. They missed her pep talks, she said. They missed her dog, she said—adding that when it was a puppy and "pooped" on the field, it got a louder ovation than Pete Rose ever did. The team had lost nine of its first 11 games and was still struggling at 9-16, and Marge said, "They've embarrassed me a great deal"—quite a statement from an owner just banned from the game for her racial and ethnic slurs. She wondered whether it was worth it, whether she should come back when she was eligible for reinstatement, but she said the fans would miss her.

Marge Schott wasn't going to leave. It would take a civic uprising of proportions perhaps even beyond what her general manager faced three weeks later, when he suddenly fired Tony Perez.

Forty-four games into his rookie season, one of the most beloved figures to ever wear the wishbone C was dumped ever so cruelly. Perez arrived home late from a 1-6 West Coast trip that left his team 20-24, a particularly disappointing stretch considering the Reds had just run off a 7-0 homestand before the excursion. At 8:30 a.m., with Perez still sleeping, the phone rang in Perez's apartment. Tony's wife, Pituka, answered the phone. It was Jim Bowden, and she gave the phone to Perez.

"I've got bad news for you," said Bowden.

A groggy Perez thought there must be a problem with a player.

He was wrong.

"We just fired you," said Bowden.

"What?"

"We just fired you."

"What for?"

"We think the players aren't playing for you, and the team isn't going well. We're having a press conference at 9:30. You'd better take your phone off the hook because you're going to get swamped with phone calls."

"OK."

And Perez hung up the phone, still half-asleep. He knew what he'd heard, but it all happened so fast that it didn't sink in right away. The city felt the same way when Bowden announced the decision at a press conference. But for both manager and masses, the shock quickly turned to anger, and Bowden turned into arguably the most hated man in town since Dick Wagner fired Big Red Machine manager Sparky Anderson 15 years earlier. And even Wagner had the decency to fly to California to fire Anderson in person, Perez pointed out. The lingering question was "How much did Marge Schott have to do with this?"

Marge called Perez that first day. "She said she was sorry about it, and she had nothing to do with it," said Perez. "At the time, I believed her. But I didn't know she had met with Jim Bowden two days before."

Indeed, the two had met on Saturday. Bowden received permission from major league baseball to discuss the proposed national television contract and realignment of teams, subjects that are allowable under her suspension agreement. Both Bowden and Marge claimed the Perez situation wasn't discussed, but the timing of the meeting and the history and credibility of the Reds owner made that hard to believe. "I have my doubts," said Perez. It was not Marge's style to allow someone below her to make such an important decision without at least consulting her, and it was not like Bowden to make a move without seeking or receiving permission from Marge. "Knowing Jim as well as I know him," said former Reds co-worker Brad Del Barba, "I find it hard to believe he did it on his own."

In fact, Perez felt used. He believes his hiring was a ploy to help the image of Marge, the appointment coming October 30, 1992, about two weeks before the scandal first broke. Perez was one of seven candidates interviewed for the job, along with Davey Johnson, Bobby Valentine, Marc Bombard, Dave Miley, Ron Oester, and Ken Griffey, Sr. The Griffey interview appeared a crock. Griffey was the only African American candidate, yet his interview took place about two hours before Perez was offered the job.

"I believe the purpose for Ken Senior's interview was for window dressing," said Griffey's agent, Brian Goldberg. "I believe that it was done for PR reasons more than a legitimate shot to be the manager—the PR being that Kenny was the only black candidate for the managerial job when Marge was in the midst of her image problem regarding minorities."

Perez was misled about his meeting that would follow the Griffey interview. Perez was told it would be his second interview for the job when it turned out to be nothing of the kind. "They put a contract in front of me and said, 'Sign it,'" said Perez. "I think I made a mistake signing a one-year contract. They told me the press conference was going to be the next day, and the only thing I thought about was getting my wife out of Puerto Rico, not about getting a two- or three-year contract. I never asked for more than one year when I was a coach. I felt confident I could do the job. I never knew I'd only have 44 games to prove myself."

Perez shouldn't have taken the job as it was offered. He should have insisted that he have an agent take over the negotiations, then gone after a multiyear contract; and he should have demanded more of a say in his coaching staff. Instead, the Reds all but set him up to fail. Everywhere he looked, there were potential rivals. Two of the managerial candidates he beat out became coaches (Miley and Oester), one the Triple-A manager (Bombard), one a major-league consultant (Johnson), and one the advance scout/player personnel adviser (Valentine)—and that wasn't counting former major-league manager Jack McKeon, who became another major-league consultant. Actually, Perez wanted the final candidate (Griffey) to be a coach, too—and the Reds were all for that, even asking Griffey if he was interested in a coaching spot during his interview. But Griffey decided to return to Seattle to become a coach with the Mariners.

"Kenny wanted nothing more than to be a coach on Tony's staff," said Goldberg. "However, good business sense and family reasons dictated it was best for Kenny to take the job in Seattle. The Reds offered Kenny a one-year contract at $45,000 per year, as opposed to the Mariners, who offered him two years at $75,000 per year. In addition, the Mariners allowed Kenny to be the hitting coach from the dugout while the Reds would have wanted him to be the hitting coach and double-up as the first-base coach. Beyond those considerations, staying with the Mariners allowed him to be close to Ken Jr., and keep tabs on his son Craig, who is on Seattle's high-A team."

Not to imply that the other coaches would be disloyal and look to unseat Perez, but the entire situation dictated that Perez find as many people he could trust and lean upon as possible. So he turned to Dave Bristol, his former major- and minor-league manager in the Reds' system. Perez wanted Bristol to be his coach and hitting instructor, but Bowden told him no, that Miley would be the bench coach and Bristol would go to third base while doubling as batting coach.

Put all of this together, and it was not exactly the way a new manager wanted to get started. "What it reminds you of is a bowling alley, only he's all the pins," said Detroit Tigers manager Sparky Anderson. "When you throw the ball down, you can't miss him."

Despite the Reds' struggles, Bowden never told Perez he was doing a bad job. In fact, during the team's seven-game winning streak that raised the overall record to 19-18, Bowden told Perez, "What are you trying to do, be the Manager of the Year?" And during the ensuing West Coast slide, Bowden told Perez, "Hang in there, you're doing a great job." Bowden said he didn't feel it would help to *discourage* rather than *encourage* his manager—but then how was Perez supposed to know there was a problem? Perez said Bowden had suggested a few changes, such as putting second baseman Bip Roberts in left field and giving Juan Samuel some playing time at second—but Perez said Roberts was promised he was going to be the second baseman and not moved all around, as he had been the previous year. And Bowden never told Perez that Samuel had been promised 300-400 at-bats to sign with Cincinnati. Besides, Bowden had signed Gary Varsho and Cecil Espy from Pittsburgh and kept defensive specialist-turned-nightmare Cesar Hernandez for outfield help, and Perez figured he should utilize them. "Am I going to be blamed for using the players we signed over the winter?" he said.

To make matters worse, Perez didn't get the advance scouting reports on time for both stops on the West Coast trip. "It was frustrating," said Perez. "It's something you need to see, what other teams are doing."

It wasn't as though there was a conspiracy going on to make Tony Perez fail—it was more like there was no understanding of his situation and no effort to help him. If Bowden and Marge were hell-bent on winning, they never should have hired a man with no experience managing in the major or minor leagues. A first-year manager needed some time to get the feel for the job, same as a first-year general manager. If Bowden were judged on 44 games, he should have fired himself, too; after all, he provided Perez with this team of struggling players, including free-agent pitcher John Smiley, who was 1-6 after 44 games. Sure, when Bowden replaced Perez with Davey Johnson, he was getting a more polished and proven manager—but if that was what he wanted, he should have hired Johnson in the first place.

Then again, Davey Johnson wasn't a minority.

Perez appeared to be nothing more than an interim manager. If the team flourished under him quickly, great; if not, he was gone. From a business standpoint, there was a certain cold logic there, but it discounted people. Marge never understood the people factor, and Bowden underestimated it. Bowden brought more than 60 players into spring training and didn't grasp that a reserve outfield candidate (Tracy Jones) he signed early when there appeared a legitimate shot for a job would be offended when a number of others were signed—and that there might be repercussions. If you were a borderline player, would you sign early for Bowden in future years? And Bowden should have anticipated the backlash from the players and the public from firing a popular manager after just 44 games—especially by phone. Especially when Perez lived in an apartment about a five-minute walk from Riverfront Stadium. Even Bowden later admitted that he should have done it in person, explaining that he was fired by the Yankees by phone and he'd seen the same thing done when he was with the Pirates. But the Pirates later claimed that they did nothing of the kind.

For Perez, the show of support was overwhelming. Besides the fans and the media, he received phone calls of encouragement from the likes of Ken Griffey, Sr., Pete Rose, Sparky Anderson, Joe Morgan, Lou Piniella, Dick Wagner, and Johnny Bench. But the most impressive display of loyalty came from Oester, who resigned as coach when he learned that Perez was fired.

"My hero," said Bench, "is Ron Oester."

"I think Ron Oester showed a lot of class," said Morgan. "Anybody could see it wasn't fair what was done to Tony, it wasn't right."

Morgan contended that you had to be kidding yourself to believe Marge Schott wasn't consulted, and he agreed with Perez that the man called "Doggie" was hired to help Marge Schott's image. Perez deserved better.

"To be perfectly honest with you," said Morgan, "class is not something you equate with the Reds, anyway."

If Jim Bowden was lying to protect Marge Schott and deflect the criticism onto himself, he was simply doing what so many others have had to do over the years. And though Marge has cried wolf so often that her credibility in such matters has been strained—especially considering she met with Bowden two days before the decision—the general manager was the one getting the majority of the flak. Even if Bowden *had* consulted with Marge over the firing, it turned out that Marge didn't have to worry about breaking the terms of her suspension agreement. National League president Bill White said that she had the authority to be in on the decision.

Every day, it seemed, Marge's suspension from baseball looked more and more hollow, as she continued to dare the sport to do something to her. During one of Davey Johnson's first games as manager, Marge sent a win-one-for-me note to him in the dugout via the batboy. The National League reminded Marge of the sanctions against her, but what good would that do? She conducts herself the way she chooses, and warnings won't stop her. Not her insensitive comments. Not her drinking. Not her mistreatment. Not her lies. The question shouldn't be if Marge had anything to do with the firing of Tony Perez, but how anybody could still believe her when she claimed innocence.

Marge Schott has embarrassed herself, her city, her team, and her sport—but she can't see it, so she can't change it. She won't sell the team as long as she believes the fans are behind her, and she won't stop pushing baseball until it takes some meaningful action against her—and follows up on it.

Meanwhile, the chaos will continue.